‖ Irreconcilable
Differences? ‖

Irreconcilable Differences?

The Waning of the American Jewish Love Affair with Israel

Steven T. Rosenthal

Brandeis University Press

Published by University Press of New England

Hanover and London

Brandeis University Press

Published by University Press of New England, Hanover, NH 03755

Printed in the United States of America   5 4 3 2 1

Library of Congress Cataloging-in-Publication Data

Rosenthal, Steven T.
  Irreconcilable differences?: the waning of the American Jewish love affair
with Israel / Steven T. Rosenthal.
     p.cm.—(Brandeis series in American Jewish history, culture, and life)
Includes bibliographical references (p.) and index.
  ISBN 0-87451-897-0
1. Jews—United States—Attitudes toward Israel. 2. Jews—United States—
Identity. 3. Jews—United States—Politics and government—20th century. 4.
Zionism—United States. 5. Israel and the diaspora. I. Title. II. Series
  E184.355.R67 2001
  973'.04924—dc21   00-011567

Brandeis Series in American Jewish History, Culture, and Life

Jonathan D. Sarna, Editor

Sylvia Barack Fishman, Associate Editor

To Mary and Claudia,
the lights of my life

Contents

Acknowledgments

This book and its author greatly benefited from the material, intellectual, and emotional contributions of many people. I would like to thank the Maurice Greenberg Center for Judaic Studies of the University of Hartford and Arts and Sciences dean Edward T. Gray Jr. for making possible a sabbatical that enabled me to complete the manuscript.

Jonathan Rieder, Warren Goldstein, Peter Breit, and Jonathan Kantor read the manuscript at various stages of preparation, and their often detailed critiques vastly improved its style and content. The comments of Jonathan Sarna, the series editor, were also extremely incisive and helpful. The reference staff of the Scarsdale Public Library responded to my inordinate demands for periodicals with great professionalism and efficiency. At Yale, Gerald Acquarulo time and again was instrumental in finding books "lost" in the controlled chaos of the Sterling Memorial Library stacks.

The contributions of Phyllis Deutsch transcend the tasks of editor. Her encouragement, structural suggestions, and immense good sense were instrumental in shaping the book. All writers should be fortunate enough to have such an editor. Susan Gottlieb prepared the manuscript with great technical skill and, more important, with a fine sense of humor and immense tolerance. It was a pleasure to work with her.

Besides being an inspiration for all I do, I could always count on my daughter Claudia to come to my rescue when I became lost in cyberspace. She also took the photograph on the jacket of this book.

This book would not have been possible without the love and support of my wife, Mary. For two decades, while successfully pursuing an extremely demanding career, her laser-sharp intellect has provided me with a full-time colleague upon whom I constantly try out ideas and phraseology. She has contributed to this book in innumerable large and small ways.

S. T. R.

Introduction

"Never in the past was the great Jewish community of the United States so united around Israel, standing together."[1] On June 18, 1982, Prime Minister Menachem Begin addressed those words to a gala dinner at the Waldorf Astoria Hotel in New York City. Attended by Jewish notables, representatives of major Jewish organizations, and wealthy donors, the dinner's purpose was to provide financial support for Israel's invasion of Lebanon, which had begun twelve days earlier. The fact that the affair raised a record $27 million was impressive but not unexpected. American Jews had long been extremely responsive to Israel's needs, especially in times of crisis. Equally predictable, not one of the assembled guests gave the slightest public expression to American Jews' growing anxiety about Israel's decision to extend the invasion beyond her self-imposed twenty-five-mile limit. Critical silence concerning Israel's policies had become as much a characteristic of American Jews as their generosity. The unification of American Jews around Israel, the creation of hugely successful mechanisms for financial and political support, and the nearly absolute prohibition of public Jewish criticism of Israel were among the most noteworthy achievements of organized American Jewry during the 1960s and 1970s. Whatever the issue, Israel could count on the enthusiastic, unified support of American Jews almost without exception.

Fifteen years later, in November 1997, Prime Minister Benjamin Netanyahu visited the United States. At his principal speech in Indianapolis many in the audience protested, by wearing buttons that read "Don't write off four million Jews,"[2] Israel's failure to fully recognize the religious legitimacy of America's Conservative and Reform movements. Others passed out leaflets admonishing the assembly not to applaud too loudly lest the prime minister confuse respect for his office with support for his religious and political policies. In contrast to the usual rapturous reception given by American Jews to an Israeli prime minister, Netanyahu was accorded a polite but distinctly chilly hearing. Especially noteworthy was that he was speaking to the General Assembly of the Council of Jewish Federations, an organization distinguished both by its pivotal role in the Jewish community and by its long tradition of largely unquestioning support for the Jewish state. Indeed, local federations had done much over the years to enforce the ban on public Jewish criticism of Israel. But to Netanyahu's consternation, sharp disagreements over religious legitimacy, the Palestinians' political aspirations, and the peace process had reached the center of the Jewish Establishment—which now felt little inhibition in airing its dissatisfactions publicly.

The division at the center reflects the centrifugal forces that have divided the rest of American Jewry from one another and from the State of Israel. Jewish unity has fragmented, the vaunted Israel lobby has often been paralyzed for lack of community consensus, and the disciplined public statements regarding Israel have given way to very public disagreements over politics and religion. Remarkably, some American Jewish organizations don't even hesitate to lobby Congress *against* Israeli policies. Conflict between American Jews and Israelis over the "Who is a Jew" question has reached such levels of public rancor that principals and commentators speak of irretrievable breaches and of declarations of war. While such threats may be more rhetorical than real, there is no doubt that we are witnessing the emergence of a new relationship between American Jews and Israel.

This book examines the nature and development of American Jews' relations with Israel since its birth in 1948. It emphasizes the rise of community consensus and its subsequent dissolution in the face of a series of critical confrontations between American Jews and the Jewish state. The invasion of Lebanon, the Pollard spy case, the Palestinian Intifada, and the "Who is a Jew" controversy have transformed the American Jewish relationship with Israel. Any attempt to understand this transformation must also examine the larger story upon which it is based—the evolution of Jewish identity in both America and Israel.

* * *

The relationship between American Jews and Israel has long been notable for its ironies and contradictions. In the pre-state era, even though Zionism was personally irrelevant to most American Jews, their extraordinary fundraising efforts and political support made possible the very birth of the Jewish state. Once Israel was established and particularly after the 1967 war, no citizens of one country have ever been so committed to the success of another as American Jews have been to Israel. Yet the vast majority of American Jews have remained astonishingly ignorant about the object of their devotion. Despite their support of and obsession with Israel, the Jewish state has had relatively little effect on the religious and cultural life of American Jews. The key to these apparent contradictions lies in the fact that from the 1890s to the present, American Jews' response to Zionism and Israel has been circumscribed by American priorities and needs. From their early indifference to Zionism, through a quarter century of unequivocal support for Israel, to the breakdown of consensus in the 1970s and 1980s and the present fragmentation, American Jews have related to Israel primarily through their identity as Americans.

It was in part because Israel met the domestic needs of the majority of American Jews that the community was able to unite so strongly around the Jewish state. In the post–World War II era, American Jews moved into the mainstream of American life. As they assimilated their way toward the creation of what Charles Silberman has called "the first free Diaspora society," overt religious observance declined, and Judaism became increasingly nostalgic and sentimental. To equate Israel with Jewishness was for many a comforting way to avoid the encumbrances of religion by focusing one's Jewish identity on a secular state eight thousand miles from home. Israel's image as a secular, progressive, pragmatic, and democratic state accorded with American Jews' self-conceptions and provided a convenient way to present their identity to the larger society. The new Jewishness, which arose in suburban America, built itself primarily around participation in local Israel-centered organizations or activities, which became for many the principal component of Jewish life.

* * *

The Six-Day War of 1967 transformed Israel into an object of secular veneration. More than any other single event, it forged the American Jewish unanimity on Israel. The slowly developing crisis of May and June, which, in the language of some, seemed to presage another Holocaust, elicited an unprecedented level of concern and support from American Jews. Immeasurable relief and pride in the magnitude of

Israel's unexpected victory led to an outpouring of emotion that stunned even Israel's most fervent supporters. In addition, when certain portions of American Jewry who felt attacked by elements of the Left saw the same forces castigate Israel as conquerors, their sense of parallel beleaguerment further strengthened identification with the Jewish state. Since the emergence of Black pride had made overt ethnicity acceptable, American Jews felt increasingly free to express their attachment to Israel in ethnic as well as religious terms. Given Israel's new status as a target of the Left, the American Jewish community devoted much of its efforts to political lobbying, which was so effective that by 1970 support of Israel had become a foundation of American foreign policy.

Feelings of pride and vulnerability determined the American Jewish relationship to Israel for the next fifteen years. Scholars spoke of "Israelolatry."[3] The Jewish state had become "the new civil religion of American Jews."[4] In this devotion the role of prophet was filled not by the remote and forbidding Theodore Herzl but by the charismatic and sensationally photogenic David Ben Gurion. The role of high priest was played by United Nations representative (and sometimes foreign minister) Abba Eban, loved by American Jews for his urbane sophistication, for his beautifully crafted speeches defending Israel, and for his Cambridge-accented bons mots. The romantic warrior figure of General Moshe Dayan, who more than any Israeli captured the imagination of American Jewry as the exemplar of the "new Jew," provided an avenging angel. These larger-than-life personalities, collectively embodying Israeli virtues of vision, intelligence, and courageous action did battle against the forces of darkness symbolized by Egypt's Gamal Abdel Nasser whose threats might not always be credible but could invariably be counted on to be suitably apocalyptic.

In such circumstances a body of dogma arose that was accepted by both Israeli and American Jews. The first was expressed by the Hebrew phrase *Ein Breira* (There is no alternative). Given the eternal vow of the Arab "confrontation states" to destroy the "Zionist entity," Israel had no option but to pursue the hardest line of political and military policies. The other was expressed by *Ma Yomru ha Goyim?* (What will the Gentiles say?). Because of the pervasiveness of world anti-Semitism and Israel's political and military vulnerability, any public criticism of Israel by the Diaspora, it was feared, would play into the hands of those who wished to destroy her. Even private criticism was discouraged, since

American Jews generally felt that only Israelis could assess their own situation and that it was immoral for those who lived in peace and security to discuss policies that might put Israeli lives at risk. At the local level, enforcement of this orthodoxy often fell to the federations, which did their job so effectively that by the late 1960s criticizing Israel was seen as a worse sin than marrying out of the faith.

* * *

For over a decade, American Jews were able to maintain their comfortable and closed system of black-and-white morality. The 1973 war and the success of the oil embargo seemed to have made the Arab states even more uncompromising. The infamous United Nations resolution of 1975, characterizing Zionism as racism, highlighted the persistence of anti-Semitism and of world hostility to Israel. If the word *Palestinian* was mentioned at all, it was usually in connection with the appalling terrorism that made Israeli hard-line policies and world Jewish unity all the more imperative.

Beginning in the late 1970s, however, fundamental changes in both Israel and the Middle East began to undermine the old certainties. In May 1977 the Labor Party, which had ruled Israel since its inception, was unexpectedly defeated by the Likud coalition of Menachem Begin. The vision, tactics, and ideals of the new prime minister and his party starkly contrasted with the liberal and pragmatic secularism of the Laborites, who had detested Begin during his three decades of political opposition. A disciple of the rightist Vladimir Jabotinsky, personally Orthodox, and allied with the religious parties, Begin's program and priorities differed greatly from the American Jewish mainstream. His small stature, thick glasses, and thicker Polish accent were a far cry from the urbane, sophisticated, tough Israeli "new Jew" with whom the Americans so happily identified. It was both an indication of the power of Israel-centered American Jewish organizations and the good faith of their constituencies that, initially at least, American Jews lined up solidly behind the new prime minister. But in the long run the rise of Likud, with its alternative vision and policies, meant that for American Jews there was no longer one Israel from which to take direction.

Anwar Sadat's peace initiative was of even greater importance in ultimately undermining American Jewish unity. It fulfilled the overworked term *revolution;* a sudden, unexpected sea change in the diplomatic and psychological structure of the Middle East. It provided

Israel, for the first time in almost thirty years of existence, major alternatives in foreign policy. In the short run it provoked conflict within Israel and with American Jews over how to best respond to the initiative, particularly over the desirability of Israeli settlements on the West Bank. More crucially, it set into motion events and developments that both increased Israeli security and presented its government with a whole range of controversial choices. The former made conflict within Israel more acceptable; the latter provided a seemingly endless basis for it.

Presented with a politically divided Israel and with new and portentous policy choices, American Jewish unity on Israel began to break down. A series of crises, both foreign and domestic, within and outside the Jewish community, pushed American Jews toward a less idealized view of Israel and encouraged their growing sense of independence. The first of these was Israel's invasion of Lebanon in 1982. As Israel's first "optional war" it was fought not only to free Northern Galilee from PLO shelling but for the political objective of suppressing Palestinian nationalism. Within Israel the invasion elicited unprecedented domestic protest, particularly after the army disregarded the government's self-imposed twenty-five-mile limit and headed toward Beirut. In what might be seen as the last hurrah of the old patterns, most American Jews initially swallowed their own misgivings and strongly supported the action. But the Sabra and Chatilla massacres, committed by Lebanese forces while Israel controlled the region, led to a level of shock and protest that was an actual if pale reflection of the level of anguish in Israel itself. Appalled by Israel's association with the massacre, many American Jews for the first time began to consider that the potential benefit of public protest might actually outweigh its long accepted negative consequences. For others the massacre called into question the cherished notion that Israel was qualitatively different from other states. At the very least the subsequent Israeli inquiries into the massacres forced American Jews to see that Israeli leaders could be just as prone to stupidity, arrogance, and mendacity as those of other states.

The Pollard spy case was even more divisive. While Lebanon was an Israeli concern, the arrest of an American Jew on charges of spying for Israel went to the heart of the American Jewish–Israeli relationship. By exposing American Jews to charges of dual loyalty and by putting Israel's "special relationship" with the United States at risk, Israel's leaders were seen by American Jews as having been arrogant, stupid, or both. In the United States they took the lead in protesting Israel's actions and in demanding that those responsible be punished. The Israelis, who saw their running of an American Jewish spy as promoting their paramount concern of national survival, considered the American Jewish protests to be naive, self-serving, and even cowardly. The exposure of this gulf between the two peoples produced a rancorous public airing of mutual resentments that had been carefully kept in check for almost four decades. Most significantly, mainstream American Jewish organizations took the lead in criticizing Israel and in defending American Jewry from Israeli attacks. Their new independence and diminished view of Israel's leaders would soon impel them to take their own Middle Eastern initiatives, even on security issues.

The Palestinian Intifada, which began in 1987, converted American Jewish disagreement with Israeli policy into a mass phenomenon. American Jews were so deeply affected by television images of Israeli soldiers clubbing young rioters that they did not rush to Israel's defense when its methods of suppressing the rebellion were universally attacked. Instead, unprecedented numbers joined the critical chorus, leading to what would become a permanent cleavage in the American Jewish community. Many American Jewish supporters of Israeli policy considered the American Jewish critics to be politically naive traitors whose actions might fatally weaken the Jewish state. Critics replied that Israeli policies were so dangerous that failure to criticize might have the same result. For the first time a substantial portion of the American Jewish community had begun to attack not specific Israeli actions but the whole thrust of Israeli foreign policy. By 1990 about three quarters of American Jews declared themselves to be in favor of talks with the Palestine Liberation Organization (PLO).

By raising the possibility of a peace treaty with the Palestinians, the election of Yitzhak Rabin in August 1992 reinforced the fragmentation in both Israel and the United States. In America the religiously Orthodox and the politically conservative, who had long equated public Jewish criticism of Israel with treason, now excoriated the Rabin government as too willing to trade land for peace. As conflict within Israel over a possible settlement reached a level of bitterness that encouraged Rabin's assassination, Israeli politicians, especially from the Right, moved to co-opt American Jews into the rough-and-tumble of Israeli politics. Many came to America to raise funds and build new constituencies, which, after all, were only a fax transmission away. American

Jewish reaction to the Oslo Peace Treaty in October 1993 again highlighted the growing fragmentation among American Jews. While most gave the treaty at least lukewarm support, the Right adamantly opposed it and even lobbied Congress against the Labor government policies. The assassination of Rabin and the election of Benjamin Netanyahu replaced rightist outrage at the "selling out" of Israel with liberal outrage at Netanyahu for "destroying the peace process." In any case the image of American Jewry "united around Israel standing together" became only a fond memory.

The most protracted and bitter crisis, the "Who is a Jew" controversy, embodies many of the societal tensions released by Israel's new position of relative security. The philosophical contradictions of Israel's foundation, its imperfect parliamentary system, the growing power of the Orthodox, and the decline of traditional Zionism, as well as the growing assertiveness of American Jewry, produced a political cataclysm, the substance of which is overwhelmed by its symbolism. The ostensible issue—whether Israel will continue to recognize as Jews those converted outside the state by Conservative or Reform rabbis—affects no more than a handful of American Jews per year. But American Jews rightly recognize the controversy as having greater import for both themselves and Israel. They see the Orthodox rejection of their converts as delegitimizing over 80 percent of the community, reducing them to "second-class Jews." Psychologically, this strikes at the heart of their connection with Israel, which is so vital to their sense of Jewish identity.

The loud condemnation of the Israeli Orthodox by many American Jews, the drop in charitable contributions, and the endless stream of Conservative and Reform leaders journeying to Israel to express their objections, indicated the depth and breadth of American Jewish rage. The controversy also highlights the ever growing connections between the American and Israeli ultra-Orthodox and the distancing of both from the American Jewish mainstream. For many years one of the principal advocates of nonrecognition of Conservative and Reform conversions was the Brooklyn-based Lubavicher Rebbe, Menachem Schneerson. It is hardly coincidental that at the height of the crisis the Union of Orthodox Rabbis of the United States and Canada, a minor but vocal rabbinical group, issued an inflammatory statement declaring that Conservative or Reform Judaism is not Judaism at all. For their part many mainstream American Jews no longer view the Israeli ultra-Orthodox as benign surrogates for their own religious impulses but as dangerous fanatics threatening both Mideast peace and Israeli society. The outcome and implications of the controversy are of utmost importance for Israel's future. Beneath the religious rhetoric the real issue is what kind of Israel will emerge, one increasingly dominated by a triumphantly uncompromising Orthodoxy or a democracy embodying the values of pluralism and pragmatic compromise. The external implications of the crisis are equally important, since its outcome will do much to determine Israel's future relationship not only with American Jewry but with America itself.

Ironically, the current tumult masks the most crucial transformation in the American Jewish–Israeli relationship, a decline in the importance of Israel to American Jews. While the volume and variety of public dissent has increased among the committed, overall fewer American Jews may be listening or caring. This is in part the inevitable result of the passage of time. Those who experienced the Holocaust and the birth of Israel are dying, and emotions, even of unimaginable horror and boundless ecstasy, lose potency over generations. Israel's heroic age has similarly passed. The desert *has* bloomed, millions of immigrants have been absorbed, the country has defended itself against great odds, and it has produced a high culture with democratic values. Fractious normalcy has replaced the emotional high points of the founding of the state, the Six-Day War, and the Entebbe raid. A contemporary video clip of young Israeli soldiers manning a check point in East Jerusalem simply lacks the emotional resonance of the image of their fathers praying at the newly liberated Western Wall.

* * *

Other bases of the bond between American Jews and Israel also are weakening. The secular, humanistic Zionism with which American Jews have so identified has become passe—Israeli commentators now speak of a post–Zionist Age—and the religious nationalism that threatens to replace it inspires few American Jews but the ultra-Orthodox. Israel's economic development has made American Jewish contributions far less crucial, and the decline in political consensus has often prevented the unified lobbying that has historically been the other major task of American Jews. Given the failure of Israeli and mainstream American Jewry to produce meaningful cultural bonds, there is less and less to connect the two peoples.

Indeed, American Jews have begun to focus on their own internal problems. Less than half of American Jews belong to a synagogue, many spend less than three days a year there, and an intermarriage rate of close to 50 percent has raised questions about the future of the Jewish community. Among many Jewish professionals there has been a belated recognition that a half century of obsession with Israel has encouraged the neglect of the educational and spiritual infrastructure necessary to assure American Jewish continuity. Any number of studies, commissions, and task forces have identified a crisis in Jewish education resulting from underqualified teachers, ossified curricula, and an inability to reach the younger generation. As one educator noted, "America is where the battlefield is, not the Mideast."[5]

* * *

This is something of a false dichotomy. There is little to suggest that had Israel not come into existence, American Jewry would somehow have done better at arresting its spiritual decline. On the contrary, even the vicarious identity that Israel provides is, for many Americans, the major focus and expression of their Jewishness. At worst, Israel has for two generations furnished a rear guard defense against the assimilationist forces that have affected almost all immigrant groups. Short of a spiritual revival within the Jewish mainstream, Israel still remains the best hope of maintaining a mass American Jewish identity. If, however, the gradual distancing of the mass of American Jews from Israel continues, it may lead to a final irony—that for all American Jews' sincere concern and obsession, their relationship with Israel might be simply a way station on the road to assimilation.

|| Irreconcilable
Differences? ||

| | 1 | |

Zionist Ideology, American Reality

American Jews have long been Israel's most ardent foreign supporters. When the UN General Assembly's cynically infamous vote of November 1975 condemned Zionism as racism, vast numbers of Jewish Americans publicly deplored this institutional hypocrisy and demonstrated their solidarity with Zionism and Israel. Hundreds of protest meetings, vigorous statements from almost all Jewish organizations, and innumerable letters to the editor testified to the truth of the slogan emblazoned on the button that many American Jews then took to wearing: "We Are One."

By 1975, American Jews' identification with Israel and their loyalty to the Jewish state had become so strong that such emotions appeared unremarkable and routine. American Jews had embraced Israel as the culmination of Jewish history, as the highest expression of Jewish virtue, and as an indispensable component of modern Jewish identity. They saw their roles as providing automatic financial and political support for whatever goals or policies the Jewish state chose to pursue. Critics of Israel were simply read out of the organized Jewish community.

The creation of the American Jewish consensus on Israel, as well as its subsequent breakdown can be understood only within the context of the general relationship among American Jewry, Zionism, and the Jewish state. The historical experience of American Jews contrasted sharply with that of European Zionists, resulting in great differences between the two groups in worldview and priorities. A brief examination of the evolution of Zionism and American Jewry provides critical insight into the development of their relationship.

American Jews' near total support for Israel masked a century of ideological struggle between Zionists and their religious and secular opponents both in Europe and in the United States. It also concealed the vast gulf in worldview between classical Zionism and American

Jews. The Zionist notion that the "Jewish Problem" of persistent anti-Semitism could be solved only through the development of a Jewish state conflicted with the deeply held beliefs of both traditional and modern Jewry. Zionism placed its trust neither in God—as did Orthodox Jews, who were content to await the Messiah—nor in the prospect of a better, more accepting world, as did the assimilated Jews of the West. Instead, Zionists emphasized Jews' own capacity to mold history. The development of a Jewish state would be both manifestation and cause of the spiritual regeneration of the Jewish people. It would revolutionize the relationship between Jews and non-Jews. The Jews, Zionists believed, would cease to be a passive people resigned to an exile borne as an indication of God's love. Nor would they be a frantic, insecure people trying, forever unsuccessfully, to be accepted as individuals by the rest of the world. Rather, Zionists put forth the astounding notion that if Jews would look to earth rather than heaven, to nationalist politics rather than individual assimilation, they could collectively take their rightful place as a people, nation, and state.

* * *

In Western Europe the gradual waning of liberalism by the mid-nineteenth century and the growth of nationalistic anti-Semitism impelled Moses Hess, a well-known German socialist theoretician who had previously abandoned Judaism, to discount the possibility of further progress. In *Rome and Jerusalem*, published in 1862, Hess contended that individual assimilation was impossible.[1] The only way in which Jews would be accepted and respected was by assimilating collectively in the form of a nation. Just as the Italians had achieved a national and political liberation, so too must the Jews take their rightful place in the developing world of national cultures. Hess's dream of a national movement of return to Zion attracted few adherents. Most Western European Jews were busily engaged in taking advantage of their newly acquired rights of citizenship and, despite some ominous signs, were still willing to place their trust in liberalism. In the East the problem was the opposite. Though the victims of great oppression, the Jews of Poland and Russia were too tied to traditional religious conceptions to respond to any program of self-help at variance with passively waiting for the Messiah.

* * *

Gradual changes in European conditions forced the Jews of both Eastern and Western Europe to look more favorably upon Hess's prescriptions.

The new series of pogroms that began in 1881 disabused many Russian Jews of their faith in liberalism. A large number of the disillusioned replaced their hope of acceptance with a program of Jewish nationalism and mass colonization of Palestine. Chief among these was Leo Pinsker, whose pamphlet *Self-Emancipation* presented "the earliest sustained formulation of political Zionism"[2] and a modern theory of anti-Semitism that became a cornerstone of Zionist ideology. A one-time enthusiastic assimilationist and a leading member of the Society for the Dissemination of Culture among the Jews of Russia, Pinsker was shaken by the pogrom. In recoil, he fashioned a highly original theory of the origins and nature of anti-Semitism. Hatred of Jews, Pinsker maintained, was not a mere carryover from the Middle Ages doomed to disappear as society progressed. On the contrary, it was an incurable psychological disease rooted in the unique social, political, and economic position of Jews. Everywhere aliens, the Jews were a "ghostlike" people, whose unnatural status inspired in Gentiles fear and revulsion. For this reason even immigration to other countries that might initially welcome their presence was but a temporary solution. Once the majority felt threatened by Jewish economic competition, anti-Semitism would recur. Pinsker's most powerful barbs were reserved for those Jews who still believed in the progress of mankind:

For the sake of the comfortable position we are granted for the fleshpots which we may enjoy in peace, we persuade ourselves and others that we are no longer Jews, but full-blooded citizens. O idle delusion! Though you prove yourselves patriots a thousand times, you will still be reminded at every opportunity of your Semitic descent. This fateful *momento hori* will not prevent you, however, from accepting the extended hospitality, until some fine morning you find yourself crossing the border and you are reminded by the mob that you are, after all, nothing but vagrants and parasites, without the protection of the law.[3]

The only possible solution to the problem of anti-Semitism was the creation of a Jewish state, of a people living upon its own soil, of a people who could bring about their own self-emancipation: "We must prove that the misfortunes of the Jews are due, above all, to their lack of desire for national independence; and that this desire must be aroused and maintained in them if they do not wish to exist forever in a disgraceful state—in a word we must prove that *they must become a nation.*"[4] The creation of a Jewish state not only would protect those who resided there but would lessen, though not eradicate, anti-Semitism by making the Jewish status more comprehensible to the world at large.

Pinsker's views were dismissed in the West and enthusiastically received by only a small number in Eastern Europe. They nevertheless set the tone for most subsequent Zionist analysis.

While *Self-Emancipation* had little impact in Western Europe, the growth of racially based anti-Semitism provided the objective support for Pinsker's analysis. The fifteen years between Pinsker's pamphlet and Herzl's publication of *The Jewish State* in 1896 saw the Jews of Western Europe placed in an increasingly defensive position. Movements to limit Jewish participation in government in Germany, increased social discrimination, and the Dreyfus trial in France revealed the precariousness of Jewish security. It was from this context that Theodore Herzl, the true founder of the Zionist movement, emerged. Born in Bohemia and almost totally assimilated, Herzl had become converted to Zionism by a traumatic event. As Paris correspondent for Vienna's most prestigious newspaper, Herzl was present at the ceremonial degrading of Alfred Dreyfus, a Jewish captain on the French general staff, whose conviction on trumped-up spy charges provided the focus for a struggle between French liberals and advocates of the prerevolutionary political order. To Herzl the miscarriage of justice was less shocking than the crowds who clamored for death to Jews. As Herzl emotionally wrote, "In republican, modern, civilized France, a hundred years after the Declaration of the Rights of Man . . . the edict of the Great Revolution has been revoked."[5]

Herzl quickly reached a conclusion that the Jews must reestablish themselves as a nation. In 1896 he published *The Jewish State*, in which his analysis of the Jewish problem was strikingly similar to that of his predecessors. Herzl's view of the impossibility of assimilation was particularly akin to Pinsker's:

We have sincerely tried everywhere to merge with the national communities in which live, seeking only to preserve the faith of our fathers. It is not permitted. In vain we are loyal patriots, sometimes superloyal, in vain do we make the same sacrifices of life and property as our fellow citizens, in vain do we strive to enhance the fame of our native lands in the arts and science, or her wealth by trade and commerce. In our native lands where we have lived for centuries we are still decried as aliens, often by men whose ancestors had not yet come at a time when Jewish sighs had long been heard in the country. The majority decide who the "alien" is, this and all else between peoples is a matter of power.[6]

Herzl's solution sprang naturally from his continuing faith in the other great Enlightenment virtue, rationality. Anti-Semitism could be put to rational use by convincing the nations of Europe that it was in their self interest to solve their Jewish problems by providing the Jews with a territory on which to establish a state of their own.[7] "Let supremacy be granted us over a portion of the globe adequate to meet our rightful natural requirements, we will attend to the rest."[8] The resulting state would not be merely a refuge but the focus of a new society that would again make the Jews an inspiration to the world. The last pages of *The Jewish State* express the sense of utopian exultation that formed a large part of Herzl's appeal: "We shall live at last as free men on our own soil, and in our own houses peacefully die. The world will be liberated by our freedom, enriched by our wealth, and magnified by our greatness. And whatever we attempt there for our own benefit will redound mightily and beneficially to the good of all mankind."[9]

Herzl's originality lay in his conversion of "the Jewish problem" into a political question. In contrast to the limited and ad hoc colonization of Palestine that was then occurring, Herzl envisaged the eventual total ingathering of the Jewish people. But such colonization, he insisted, had to be preceded by guarantees of political support from the great powers of Europe.

The notoriety resulting from the publication of *The Jewish State* gained Herzl access to the most important Jewish philanthropists, Baron Maurice de Hirsh and Baron Edmund de Rothschild. He had hoped to gain their political and financial support; but, afraid Jewish nationalism might subject the Jews of Western Europe to charges of dual loyalty, they refused to give colonization any moral or material backing. Herzl's response was to attempt to revolutionize Jewish life from below and appeal directly to the Jewish masses—especially those of Eastern Europe, who had greeted his program with great enthusiasm. Over the sometimes frantic objections of Western assimilationists, he organized a Zionist Congress to legitimize and carry out his program for establishing a Jewish state.

Meeting in Basel, Switzerland, in 1897, the First Zionist Congress drew two hundred delegates from all over the world, from across the spectrum of Jewry. The first sentence of the Congress's statement of purpose proclaimed: "Zionism seeks to secure for the Jewish people a publicly recognized, legally secured home in Palestine."[10] To enlist the support of both Jews and the world at large, the Congress created the World Zionist Organization. Herzl, elected as its first president, could now speak as the representative of a formal organization that had received a substantial mandate from world Jewry. After the Congress, Zionist societies sprang up all over the world. These were particularly successful in attracting the Eastern European Jewish masses, who declared their formal adherence to the movement by paying the modern equivalent of a biblical shekel.

Zionism quickly encountered the fierce opposition of groups as diverse as the Orthodox, the assimilationists, and the socialists, all of whom rejected the idea of a national return to the Promised Land. The Zionists replied that traditional Jewish life in the Diaspora (exile) was unproductive, abnormal, and inferior. Yet Zionism's appeal to the Orthodox could only be on the basis of religion, since Herzl's rapturous reception by Eastern European Jews was based on the belief that he was a kind of modern Messiah who would lead his people to the Promised Land. In this sense Zionism presented itself as the fulfillment of Jewish history. But despite its messianic component, Zionism remained a great departure from traditional Judaism. It perceived most of Jewish history, from the dispersion to modern times, as irrelevant, ignoble, and an unworthy expression of the Jewish spirit, resulting from the abnormal condition of exile. Yet it was just this period that had produced the Talmud, much of religious ritual, and most of the institutions of Jewish life. By deemphasizing these foundations of normative Judaism and substituting nationalist activism for what it considered the passivity of the Diaspora, Zionism sought to revolutionize Jewish life.

* * *

Despite Zionists' efforts most West European Jews remained tied to assimilationism and pointed to the real gains in legal and economic status they had achieved. Zionism, building upon its conception of the unworthiness of Diaspora life, now began to emphasize the effects of exile on the internal world of the "liberated" Jew. This theme was sounded by Herzl's colleague, Max Nordau, at the First Zionist Congress:

The emancipated Jew is insecure in his relations with his fellow man, timid with strangers, and suspicious, even of the secret feelings of his friends. His best powers are dissipated in suppressing and destroying or at least in the difficult task of concealing his true character. . . . He has become a cripple within, and a counterfeit person without, So that like everything unreal, he is ridiculous and hateful to all men of high standards.[11]

The only way for a Jew to escape this psychic hell was to embrace Zionism, which promised "an assured place in society, a community which accepts him, the possibility of employing all his powers for the development of his real self instead of abusing them for the suppression and falsification of his personality."[12]

* * *

Herzl's later followers went even further in their rejection of Diaspora Judaism and its values. As Zionism came into increasing contact with Eastern European socialism, it was influenced by the latter's social criticism of the ghetto and its total rejection of religion. Partly to outbid the socialists, particularly after a new period of pogroms in Eastern Europe, Zionist criticism of Jewish life became more and more strident. Zionist "negation of the diaspora" reached a high point in the writing of Jacob Klatzkin, a Jewish National Fund official and editor of the official journal of the World Zionist Organization, *Die Welt*. In Klatzkin the image of the Jew as a rootless cosmopolitan (as first used by Nordau) reached its highest development:

Galut [exile] can only drag out the disgrace of our people and sustain the existence of a people disfigured in both body and soul—in a word, of a horror. . . . Such a life, even if it continues to exist, will represent no more than a rootless and restless wandering between two worlds. It will cause rent and broken human beings to persist—individuals diseased by ambivalence, consumed by contradictions, and spent by restless inner conflict.[13]

Thus, the *Galut* was simply unworthy of survival and any efforts to keep it alive could be only temporarily successful. But the Jews of the exile had a function: to serve as a source of supply for the renaissance of the homeland. "Without *this raison d'etre*, without the goal of a homeland, the Galut is nothing more than a life of deterioration and degeneration, a disgrace to the nation and a disgrace to the individual, a life of pointless struggle and futile suffering, of ambivalence, confusion and eternal impotence. It is not worth keeping alive."[14]

A minority group within the Zionist movement, the cultural Zionists led by the Hebrew essayist Ahad Ha'am, had a higher opinion of the potentialities of the Diaspora. Unlike Herzl, whose point of departure was the ineradicability of anti-Semitism, Ahad Ha'am was more concerned with the internal crisis of Judaism. However great the physical threat to Jews, Ahad Ha'am felt that assimilation was an even greater threat to Jews' moral and spiritual uniqueness. Rather than building a political refuge from anti-Semitism, Ahad Ha'am saw Zionism's primary task as the creation of a national cultural center that would revive the Jewish spirit. Since he felt that a total ingathering of Jews was neither desirable nor possible, "from this center the spirit of Judaism will radiate to the great circumference, to all communities of the Diaspora, to inspire them with a new life and to preserve the overall unity of our people."[15] Rather than doing everything to convince the Diaspora Jews to settle in Palestine, cultural Zionists feared that the exclusive concentration upon politics at the expense of Jewish culture and education would create a state of Jews that was not a Jewish state.

But cultural Zionism's more accepting view of the Diaspora remained a minority position. The political Zionists achieved a great victory when Great Britain, seeking Jewish support during World War I and looking to a new postwar Middle East, issued the Balfour Declaration of 1917, declaring Great Britain's readiness to support the establishment of a "Jewish Homeland." Britain's assumption of the mandate for Palestine after World War I made mass colonization possible. In their zeal to attract immigrants and to provide motivation for the building of the new land, Zionists naturally exalted the new life and denigrated the old. The "negation of the Diaspora" remained a prevalent theme within Zionist thought. Ever desperate to attract settlers by pointing out the shortcomings of traditional Jewish life, Zionist propaganda reached such a state of virulence that in the 1930s a debate took place within the movement concerning the propriety of what was termed "Jewish anti-Semitism out of love." This Jewish anti-Semitism was expressed in endless condemnations of the external and internal lives of Diaspora Jews, in the exaggerated exaltation of physical labor in Palestine as a cure for Jewish problems, and in slogans such as "revival of the land, revival of the parasitic people."

* * *

The Zionist notion that anti-Semitisim was ineradicable and that Jewish life in the Diaspora was doomed could not have been more inimical to the worldview and daily concerns of American Jews. In fact the American Jewish experience posed great theoretical and practical problems for Zionist ideology and recruitment. On a theoretical level, Jewish life in America seemed to undermine Zionist analyses concerning the inevitability and prevalence of anti-Semitism. For millions of Jews who felt that *their* Promised Land lay somewhere between the Battery and the Bronx, political Zionism was irrelevant at best. In 1885, American Reform Judaism declared that Jews "were no longer a nation but a religious community" and did not expect "a return to Palestine."[16] Zionism raised the specter of dual loyalties and appeared to threaten the Jews' position in their homeland. As a result, during the first years of the twentieth century the American Zionist movement developed very slowly. The impetus to its growth was not domestic anti-Semitism but American Jews' identification with the plight of their Eastern European brethren. The anti-Semitism that fueled American Zionism was mostly secondhand, and American Jews joined the fledgling Zionist movement as a possible solution to the persecutions in Poland and Russia. Since the security and opportunity of America was in such contrast to the European environment, the Zionism produced by American Jews was greatly different in ideology, goals, and methods from that forged on the anvil of czarist persecution. While this caused numerous conflicts, only by adapting to American conditions did Zionism make any inroads among American Jews at all.

Just as the "Jewish problem" in Europe was the product of general European history, the uniquely favorable position of Jews in America was similarly bound to the development of the larger society. Although many Americans still harbored the traditional anti-Jewish attitudes of Christian Europe, the demographic, political, social, and intellectual characteristics of the United States had discouraged religious anti-Semitism and created a society whose ethos worked against the institutionalization of racial anti-Semitism. Many of the conditions that had led to the growth of anti-Jewish feeling in Europe were absent in America or mitigated by other circumstances. As a new society whose political system was a conscious product of Enlightenment thought, America was devoid of those medieval institutions and structures that in Europe had produced or perpetuated anti-Semitism. There was no established church to foster universal detestation of the Jew, no medieval corporations or communities to separate Jew from Gentile, and relatively few economic and social restrictions. In the absence of a formal tradition of anti-Semitism the American Revolution's commitment to liberalism provided no special benefits for Jews. Jewish enfranchisement took place as a part of the process that conferred citizenship upon all Americans. As a result, the emancipation of Jews could not become a symbol of the new liberal social order as it had in Europe. In any case, liberalism itself, far from being a subject of debate, was enshrined as the basis of the American political system. Even the most conservative American could not help but invoke the Revolution with its emphasis upon individual freedom.

The social and demographic characteristics of America also discouraged systematic anti-Semitism. Ethnic and religious diversity, the separation of church and state, the need for immigrants to develop the land, and the egalitarianism of a frontier society, all confirmed and strengthened American commitment to the liberalism of the American Revolution. Anti-Jewish feeling had little intellectual or social basis in American society, and the first century of the Republic was relatively free of official anti-Semitism. The most famous exception is General Grant's "Order Number Eleven" by which the Civil War commander in 1862 expelled all Jews from the war zone. After being informed by the American Jewish community, President Lincoln canceled the order immediately.[17] Yet the infamous status in American Jewish history of this, comparatively mild and isolated case of official anti-Semitism demonstrates, as nothing else, the security of American Jews during the early years of the Republic. Anti-Jewish attitudes persisted, however, in church doctrine, in popular culture, and in individual prejudice.[18] In the 1880s there was a growth of popular anti-Semitism, fueled by Jews' economic success, by antiurban sentiment, by pseudoscientific racism, and by resentment of the new commercial society in which Jews enthusiastically took part. But even then anti-Semitism was predominantly restricted to social ostracism of Jews and did not seriously threaten either their material or their personal security.[19]

If the quality and content of Jewish-Christian relations in the United States was unusual, the relationship of Jews to one another was unique. Since there was no official Jewish community empowered and supported by the government, American Jews were free of any coercive religious or social control by their coreligionists. Since one related to society as an individual and not through a corporate religious body, a person was free to choose his religious belief. For the Jewish immigrant especially, the informal religious sanctions of family and village quickly broke down under the stresses and opportunities of America. The result of this unparalleled freedom was that, unlike in Eastern Europe, where revolt against the rigidity of religious control was often a push toward Zionism, American Jews had little against which to revolt. Indeed, Reform Rabbi Isaac Meyer Wise, one of America's most powerful

Jewish leaders, was moved at the time of the First Zionist Congress to declare the movement to be the product of the "momentary inebriation of morbid minds."[20] From the very beginning of their history in America, Jewish immigrants to the United States were not so much concerned with preserving their identities as Jews as with fulfilling their new ones as Americans.

Despite the seeming irrelevance of Zionism to American conditions, continuing persecutions of European Jews and, paradoxically, the security and success of American Jews gave rise to a small Zionist movement. The pogroms and persecutions in Russia, Rumania, and Poland assumed a regular intensity that left no doubt that they were part of official government policy. In 1903 the worst outbreak took place at Kishinev in White Russia, where forty-seven Jews were killed and hundreds brutalized and left homeless. It is a measure of our own age's diminished capacity for moral outrage that the death of forty-seven sent shock waves throughout the world. American Jews lodged protests, collected aid for the victims, and enlisted the help of the president and Congress to prevent future pogroms. But the outrages only increased.

The reaction of the influential German American Jews who comprised the American Jewish establishment was to form a permanent organization to defend Jewish interests. Self-appointed and composed of the cream of German American Jewry, the American Jewish Committee had little connection with the vast majority of Jews in whose name it presumed to speak. Its method of promoting Jewish interests also reflected the committee's genteel origins. Rather than engaging in public political agitation that might reflect unfavorably upon Jews, the committee preferred to act as a backstage lobbyist with the American political establishment. The composition and methods of the committee alienated the masses of Eastern European Jews, who felt that such tactics smacked of the old country and were not worthy of American citizens. Some of those advocating a more avowedly political organization were attracted to Zionism. Even though Zionist ideology did not suit American conditions, Zionist-led settlement in Palestine would help relieve the suffering of Eastern European Jews. In addition, the reaffirmation of Jewish values, which was a vital component of Zionist doctrine, appealed to those who felt that the material and social success of Jews in America was eroding their spiritual identity.

The themes sounded by early American Zionists were not those of European Zionism: the ineradicability of anti-Semitism and the necessity of all Jews to settle in Palestine. While some rabbis emphasized that Zionism could serve as a spiritual bulwark against assimilation,[21] the American movement as a whole emphasized that it was the duty of secure American Jews to help their Eastern European coreligionists reach Palestine, where they could lead secure and productive Jewish lives. The total ingathering of all Jews motivated American Zionists not in the slightest. In 1898 the Zionist Organization of America (ZOA), which had been formed the year before in response to Herzl's call, explained in its first pamphlet the limited concerns of American Zionism. Written by Richard Gottheil, the organization's first president, the pamphlet sounded the theme for subsequent American Zionism. After expressing the general Zionist conviction that the oppressed Jews of the world must find a haven by settling in Palestine, Gottheil was quick to emphasize that American Jews did not fall into this category:

But if you ask if Zionism is able to find a permanent home in Palestine for those Jews who are forced to go there as well as those who wish to go, what is to become of us who have entered to such a degree into the life around us and who feel able to continue as we have begun? What is to be our relation to the new Jewish polity? I can only answer, exactly the same as is the relation of people of other nationalities all the world over to their parent home. What becomes of the Englishman in every corner of the globe; what becomes of the German? Does the fact that the great mass of their people live in their own land prevent them from doing their whole duty toward the land in which they happen to live? Is the German-American considered less of an American because he cultivates the German language and is interested in the fate of his fellow Germans at home? Is the Irish-American less of an American because he gathers money to help his struggling brethren in the Green Isle?[22]

From the beginning, then, American Zionists, while accepting the necessity of a Jewish homeland, quickly added, "but not for me." In feeling that they already had a permanent home, American Zionists disagreed totally with their European counterparts. But for the moment this vast ideological and social difference could be ignored, as both the European and American Zionist movements concentrated on the practical work of alleviating the misery of Eastern European Jewry. The humorous definition of a Zionist as "an American Jew who sends money to a German Jew so that an East European Jew could go to Palestine" was not far off the mark. Most American Jews, however, remained indifferent to even the limited aims of American Zionism. The specter of Jewish persecution in Europe made them cherish America all the more and not want to do anything that might rock the boat. Above all, they feared the accusations of dual loyalty, a charge levied (by fellow Jews) against the early Zionist Emma Lazarus, whose poetry was considered American enough to grace the Statue of Liberty.[23] The fact that Lazarus, who celebrated America as the refuge of the oppressed, could simultaneously be a Zionist reveals the gulf between the European movement and its American adherents.

* * *

It was not until Zionism was able to demonstrate its compatibility with the American patriotism that was the primary identification of American Jews that it was able to gain broad appeal in the United States. The principal architect of this change was Louis Brandeis, who provided the personal example and the intellectual formulation that reassured Jews that adherence to Zionism did not dilute their identity as Americans. The totally assimilated offspring of German Jews, the most famous lawyer of his day, political reformer, and confidant of presidents, Brandeis was the epitome of the Jewish establishment. But his championing of social causes, particularly his arbitration of the clothing workers' strike in 1906, had made him a folk hero to the *Ostjude* of the Lower East Side. In 1914, Brandeis was appointed honorary chairman of a Zionist committee to coordinate relief to the Jews of Eastern Europe caught in the ravages of World War I. To everyone's surprise, Brandeis announced himself a convert and devoted his superb intellectual and administrative skills to the Zionist movement. In recognition of his symbolic importance and actual achievements, he was elected head of the World Zionist Organization (WZO) of America in 1914.

Brandeis's most important contribution was to demonstrate the compatibility of Zionism with American citizenship. For Brandeis the Zionist ideal was but a reflection of the American spirit, of the progressive political and social programs with which he had been identified in the larger society. To desire to live in freedom was as American as the Pilgrims, and a Jew became a better American as he worked to further the principles of freedom in Palestine. A Zionist no longer need feel defensive but could take pride in the American virtues of his movement. More than anything, this formulation and Brandeis's personal conduct served to legitimize Zionism, particularly among the masses of Eastern European immigrants who had feared compromising their

American identity. The fact that Brandeis was a "German Jew" made his example all the more powerful. Ironically, the identification of Eastern European Jews with Zionism was itself a revolt against the hegemony and policies of the German Jewish Community.[24] Brandeis's subsequent elevation to the Supreme Court powerfully demonstrated that Christian America saw no inherent conflict between Americanism and Zionism and further increased the movement's appeal.

Brandeis also greatly influenced the course of American Zionism, and ultimately the world movement, by insisting on an American approach to the building of the Holy Land. With a lifetime of experience in the organization of political and social causes, he brought to the movement progressive methods of systematic recruitment and fund-raising. Moreover, Brandeis's conception of the object and methodology of Zionism resulted in a further divergence of the American Zionist movement from its European sources. Reflecting America's pragmatism, Brandeis saw not ideology, not culture, but the economic and agricultural development of Palestine as the prerequisite for all other Zionist development. The economic and social development of the Jewish national home became the overriding concern of American Zionism, and the potential effect of the movement on American Jewish life aroused relatively little interest.[25] Indeed, the narrow and secular definition of American Zionism constituted a significant part of its appeal to many American Jews. Brandeis's deemphasis of cultural matters, his concentration on the practical aspects of colonization, and his use of non-Zionist experts in Palestine was vigorously resented by European Zionists. Practical necessity, however, forced the world movement to follow Brandeis's lead a few years later.

American Jews were inspired by Brandeis's example and motivated by the suffering of European Jews during and after World War I and by the rise of anti-Semitism both in Europe and in America.[26] They were greatly encouraged by the Balfour Declaration and the establishment of the Palestine Mandate under the British. Membership in the American Zionist movement increased greatly and by 1925 reached twenty-seven thousand. Even the mandarins of the American Jewish Committee, who had long felt that Zionism compromised their position as Americans, declared themselves ready to take part in the economic and cultural upbuilding of Palestine. The committee now gave specific projects in Palestine very generous support but refused to recognize the necessity of a Jewish state, much less consider the possibility of mass

American Jewish emigration to it. In this last point, at least, the committee accurately reflected the feelings of American Jewry.

The divergence between American and European Zionism became clearer during the interwar years. The European Zionists' primary and absolute loyalty was to Zionism, whereas the American Zionists adhered to the movement only within the context of their American priorities. Chaim Weizmann, the leader of the WZO, gave up his professorship at the University of Manchester in order to devote his full efforts to the Zionist cause. When Weizmann asked Brandeis to resign from the Supreme Court for the same reason, the justice refused, saying that he could do more for Jews within the American official establishment than outside it.[27]

This difference in focus was philosophically expressed by American Jews' refusal to accept the concept that all Jews owed political allegiance to Zionism. However much they embraced the idea of a Jewish homeland, American Jews rejected with similar intensity the notion that their primary loyalty was to any future Jewish state. So strong was this feeling that when Weizmann visited America in 1927, he felt it necessary to assert to Jewish but non-Zionist potential donors that no Jewish state was contemplated.[28] While this statement was disingenuous at best, by the late 1920s the World Zionist position began to move closer to the American view—that practical work should take precedence over ideology.[29] But the basic divergence between the European conception of Zionism as leading ultimately to the settlement of all Jews in a Jewish state and the American one—that Zionism simply meant aid and refuge for the oppressed—still remained. Since Americans had perceived Zionism primarily in terms of relief for persecuted Jews, even this limited commitment waned when there were no specific crises to mobilize public support. Conflicts within the movement over Zionist policy in Palestine, which led to Brandeis's resignation as honorary president in 1921, also took their toll. The onset of the Depression turned the thoughts of many Zionists closer to home, and Zionist membership declined to less than 8,400 in 1932.[30]

* * *

The growth of Nazism and the beginning of a new and more virulent Jewish persecution, in Western as well as in Eastern Europe, revived the American movement. The severity of these outbreaks and their occurrence in such "cultured" societies as Germany seemed to confirm the Zionist thesis that anti-Semitism was ineradicable. More important in reattracting Americans to the movement was the practical help that Zionist organizations extended through charitable relief, through aid to immigrants, and through constant pressure upon Britain to permit more Jews to enter Palestine. As the persecutions of Jews became more and more violent, the need for a refuge became painfully obvious. The American B'nai B'rith fraternal organization, long a bastion of anti-Zionism, now came out in favor of the movement.

The practical necessity of saving European Jews prompted even American Reform Judaism to abandon its fundamental principles by declaring its support for a Jewish homeland. Membership in the ZOA of America rose from 8,400 in 1932 to 43,000 in 1939 and to over 200,000 in 1945.[31] Between 1932 and 1937, ZOA contributions increased sevenfold, and many other contributions were made to European Jews privately.[32] In the face of ever growing disaster, American Jews agitated for increased immigration quotas to the United States and against the 1939 White Paper by which Britain had closed Palestine to Jewish immigration at the very moment that a refuge was most needed.

In this time of extreme crisis, American Jews' support of both their coreligionists in Europe and of Zionism was still limited by their overriding priority: not to jeopardize their acceptance as true Americans. Even after the outbreak of war in Europe, American Jews were afraid that questioning the wisdom of America's isolationism would leave them open to possible charges that they had led the country into the European conflict. As one frustrated Zionist leader noted, "The American Jew thinks of himself first and foremost as an American citizen. This is a fact, whether we like it or not."[33] Even the American Zionist movement was "impotent" and refused to forward any appeals on behalf of the Jews of Europe or Palestine.[34] Only after Pearl Harbor did American Jewry give full expression to its hatred of Naziism.

* * *

The war and the Holocaust completely transformed the relationship of American Jews to Zionism. As the magnitude of the Holocaust became known, many American Jews were overwhelmed by guilt for having been unable to exert sufficient influence to save European Jews from destruction. Despite their efforts, the masses of doomed European Jewry had been unable to escape by immigration either to the United

States or Palestine. Adding to the sense of Jewish impotence was the fact that many Jews appeared to have gone to their death passively without offering any resistance. The determination to redress, as far as possible, their own guilt and to fight the image of Jewish passivity found its logical outlet in Zionism. A Jewish state would be a powerful indication of the rebirth of the Jewish people and would provide a home for those who had survived the death camps. American Jews, now the healthiest and most dynamic component of world Jewry and citizens of what was now the most powerful nation in the world, felt an increased responsibility for Holocaust-diminished Jewry, especially in the face of British intransigence and American indifference. As a result, American Jews now became among the most enthusiastic and radical elements in the world Zionist movement.

As early as 1942, American Jews were instrumental in moving the WZO away from the policy of cooperation with Great Britain, which had ultimately resulted in the 1939 White Paper that had prohibited immigration to Palestine at the precise moment when a refuge was most urgently needed. At a conference held at the Hotel Biltmore in New York, a committee representing the four largest American Zionist organizations, radicalized by the oratory of Cleveland rabbi Abba Hillel Silver, demanded that "the gates of Palestine be opened and that Palestine be established as a Jewish commonwealth integrated into the structure of the new democratic world."[35] The only major dissenting organization was the American Jewish Committee, but it was soon isolated as organized Jewry united around the idea of statehood.

The minuscule American Council for Judaism, composed mainly of assimilated Jews who feared the charge of dual loyalty, became the focus of Jewish anti-Zionism. Founded in 1942 by a group of Reform rabbis, the council's declaration of principles somewhat inconsistently combined the old universalistic ideal with fear for Jews' status in America. "We oppose the effort to establish a National Jewish State in Palestine or anywhere else as a philosophy of defeatism and one which does not offer a practical solution to the Jewish problem. [Such an effort is] inimical to the welfare of Jews in Palestine, in America, or wherever Jews may dwell."[36] Almost all Jewish organizations immediately denounced the council and demanded that it cease its activities. Despite the massive amounts of propaganda it produced, its ideas were thoroughly rejected by the mass of American Jews, who felt both responsible for the fate of their brethren and secure in their identity as Americans.

The explicit definition of statehood as the unalterable goal of Zionism marked the emergence of Rabbi Abba Hillel Silver as a dominant force in American Zionism, as well as the American movement's ascension to power within the world movement. It also marked the personal ascendancy of David Ben Gurion, who, repudiating the policy of cooperation with the British advocated by Chaim Weizmann, looked to an aggressive policy as the best means of securing Jewish statehood. After the Biltmore declaration, membership in the ZOA rose from 50,000 to 135,000, with a similar increase in the membership of Hadassah, the Zionist women's organization. By 1945, membership had reached almost 300,000, with another 2,500,000 Jews belonging to organizations that had given their blessing to the idea of a Jewish commonwealth.[37] Insight into the motivation for this mass support, even from non-Zionists, was provided by Adele Rosenwald Levy's speech to a special United Jewish Appeal (UJA) convention held in Atlantic City in December 1946. Having just returned from the European refugee camps, she told the gathering that she had heard no singing or laughter except among those preparing to emmigrate to Palestine. "Zionism or no Zionism, ideology or no ideology—that is not my concern. But if Palestine means that they will once more be able to laugh and sing, then we must help these Jews in all possible ways."[38]

*   *   *

American Jews' increased commitment to Zionism was of incalculable importance, for it was the political influence and financial resources of American Jewry that played a leading part in converting the aspirations of the Biltmore conference into the reality of a Jewish state. Spurred by the refusal of the British to permit one hundred thousand inhabitants of displaced persons' camps in Europe to enter Palestine and by their internment of former death camp inmates whose only crime was to try to get there, the American Zionist movement strongly supported Ben Gurion's call for an end to the Zionists' traditional policy of cooperation with Great Britain. This change, as well as the WZO's acceptance of American influence, was marked by the removal of the moderate Weizmann as WZO president in 1946. Out of deference to the revered leader, the office was left vacant, but henceforth the Zionist movement would depend upon its own resources and not Great Britain to achieve statehood. A small minority went even further. In an effort to force the British to withdraw from Palestine, a splinter faction of the Zionist self-defense organization inaugurated a campaign of sabotage that reached its culmination in July 1946 with the bombing of the King David Hotel in Jerusalem at a cost of ninety-six lives. Exhausted by six years of world war, unable to settle the conflict between the Jews and Arabs in Palestine, and subject to increasing terrorist violence, the British announced in late July 1946 their intention to withdraw from Palestine and to place the whole question in the hands of the UN. The Arabs of Palestine and the surrounding area refused any compromise and looked to the departure of the British as providing an opportunity to eliminate Jewish settlement once and for all. The Yishuv (the Jewish community in Palestine), while agreeing to a proposal for the division of Palestine between Jews and Arabs, declared its intention to establish a Jewish state and made preparations for its defense.

* * *

In the subsequent political and military struggle for statehood, most of the political and material support came from the United States. The amount of money raised for Palestine by the five million Jews of America was astounding. In the three years between the end of World War II and the proclamation of the State of Israel, American Jews donated more than $400 million to the relief, development, and defense of Palestine.[39] They were instrumental in smuggling in immigrants and in the illegal traffic in arms to prepare for the war that all expected as soon as the British left Palestine. Within America the political pressure brought by Jews upon the Democratic Party and President Truman was even more important.

The UN inherited the Palestine problem from Great Britain and put forth various peace plans, including partitioning the territory among its Arab and Jewish inhabitants. Since partition would result in the creation of a Jewish state, American support for the partition plan was absolutely crucial. American Jews abandoned their fears of being charged with dual loyalty and united to wage a vigorous campaign in favor of Jewish statehood. Symbolizing the new American Jewish assertiveness, Rabbi Abba Hillel Silver presented the case for Jewish statehood before the UN General Assembly.[40] The American Jewish community marshaled all of its skills and resources in rallies, newspaper advertisements, pressure on congressmen, and even the famous visit to Truman by his old friend and business partner, Eddie Jacobson. Such tactics were instrumental in counteracting the anti-Zionist stance of the State

Department and of the highest ranks in the military. American Jews desired not only that the United States vote for partition but that it use its influence to convince other UN members also to vote affirmatively.

Against the wishes of the "striped-pants boys" of the Department of State, Truman directed the U.S. ambassador to the UN to vote for partition and to use all possible American influence to convince others to do the same. By a vote of 33 to 13, with 10 abstentions, the Jewish state and an Arab Palestinian state were proclaimed on November 29, 1947. The importance of American Jewish influence in bringing about this decision can hardly be overemphasized. As Truman himself noted, "I do not think I ever had as much pressure and propaganda aimed at the White House as I had in this instance."[41] It has been confirmed by both friendly and hostile contemporary observers and by historians writing decades later that the successful UN vote would have been impossible without the political campaigns of American Jewry.[42]

What emerges from this brief discussion is that, from its very beginnings, American Zionism differed greatly from its European counterpart. Far from being a response to native anti-Semitism, American Zionism was for many a way of counteracting the loss of Jewish identity in the American environment of opportunity and acceptance. American Zionists never contemplated their own emigration but saw the movement as a means of helping their coreligionists in Europe. Yet even with this limited objective, Zionism's early growth was inhibited by Jews' fear of jeopardizing their American identity. Only when Brandeis showed how Zionism could be compatible with Americanism did the movement swell to appreciable proportions. American Jewish priorities were again demonstrated in the 1930s when, however much they hated the Nazis, they refrained from advocating war until the bombing of Pearl Harbor.

The war and the Holocaust reduced European Jewry to a small remnant and gave American Zionists a new influence within the world movement. It was a re-evocation of old themes—the desire to help European Jewry and the search for dignity and identity—that radicalized American Zionism. It was American influence in the WZO that tipped the scales in favor of a policy of noncooperation with Great Britain. It was American Jewish pressure in the United States that convinced President Truman to support statehood in the UN and use American power to convince others to do so. American Jewish material support of Palestine had been instrumental in developing the country and would soon make possible its defense. As Israeli foreign minister Moshe Sha-rett (Shertok) wrote, "Perhaps one of the most remarkable aspects of that very strenuous period was the way in which Jews of the most varied outlooks and of all ranks came forward to do what ever lay in their power to secure a favorable decision."[43] Without the support of American Zionists, who never had any intention of forsaking their adopted homeland, the Jewish state would very likely never have been born.

With this foundation the new Jewish state and American Jewry might have entered into a fruitful partnership based upon mutual re-spect and sympathetic appreciation of each other's contributions and needs. America's most important Zionist, Abba Hillel Silver, was the first of many who spoke of the "interdependence" of American Jewry and Israel.[44] But Israelis' return to the classical Zionist ideology of the inferiority of the Diaspora and American Jews' headlong retreat into political passivity soon demonstrated that the partnership was not to be an equal one. Instead. American Jewry willingly, some might say enthu-siastically, allowed itself to be dominated by the new Jewish state.

||2||

The Making of the American Jewish Consensus

The foundation of Israel potentially opened the way for a true partnership between American Jewry and the Jewish state. The political struggle in the UN and the military threat of the Arabs had demonstrated the necessity of the strongest possible American support. The old Zionist contention that a Jewish state would defend the Diaspora had been reversed. For their part, American Jews felt that support of Israel provided some compensation for their inability to prevent the Holocaust. They took justifiable pride in the accomplishments of the young state and in their contributions to them. "Israel became not only a focus for fundraising but a source of prideful identification for virtually all of American Jewry."[1] The erosion of Judaism in America, the spiritual needs of the Diaspora, and the material and cultural requirements of Israel might have led to the kind of creative and mutually beneficial partnership envisioned by Ahad Ha'am.

But a combination of psychology, ideology, and politics prevented the rise of a mutually respectful and self-renewing relationship. As long as the goal of the Zionist movement had been, first, the building of Jewish settlements in Palestine and then the creation of a Jewish state, American and European Zionists could submerge their philosophical differences in practical work. But once Israel became a reality, their differing points of view could no longer be ignored, especially since the new state gloried in expressing just those concepts that European Zionism had always underplayed in an attempt to foster unity during the pre-state period. Israeli leaders' articulation of "hard-line Zionism" was both the result of sincerely held ideological beliefs and a way of demonstrating their country's independence from its principal Diaspora supporters. The resulting conflict between Israeli and American Jewry was more than the inevitable adjustment process between utopian plans and actual conditions. It stemmed from the most basic ideological differences between American Zionism and the European Zionism that animated the Jewish state. While American Jews remained strongly tied to their Diaspora existence, Israelis looked to the total ingathering of world Jewry and the creation of a new mode of Jewish national life. In responding to the conflict and in evolving their new relationship with Israel, the great mass of American Jews gradually retreated from their position of self-assertion within the Zionist movement to one of uncritical approbation and unconditional support for the Jewish state. Whereas in 1942 the assertiveness of American Jewry had helped to redirect the course of world Zionism, in the 1970s and 1980s the vast majority of American Jews meekly and uncritically supported the policies of the Begin government despite widespread and vigorous dissent within Israel itself. Even when American Jews disagreed with Israel, they almost invariably shunned public criticism on the grounds that revealing disunity would give comfort to Israel's enemies. The profound change from intellectual and political ferment to uncharacteristic unanimity was the result of both a conscious Israeli policy and the social and political evolution of American Jewry.

* * *

The future relationship between a Jewish state and the Jewish people had long been the subject of lively discussion. In the early days of American Zionism, fear that a Jewish state would enable anti-Semites to claim that Jews had dual political loyalties had impeded the growth of the movement. Brandeis's immense prestige and his formulation that Zionism was good Americanism had stilled such fears. By 1943 almost all American Jewish organizations had united behind Zionist efforts to create a Jewish state. Even the prestigious and conservative American Jewish Committee, long an opponent of statehood, had dropped its opposition in return for a promise that Israel would not claim any loyalty from American Jews or interfere in their internal affairs. But soon after the foundation of the state, the prime minister, David Ben-Gurion, declared that all Jews should emigrate to Israel because Jewish life in the United States was doomed, a statement that drew protests from the American Jewish Committee. Ben-Gurion and Jacob Blaustein, the president of the American Jewish Committee, agreed on a set of statements that reiterated the old framework of American Jewish loyalty to their homeland and of no Israeli interference in American Jewish domestic affairs. Blaustein's statement reflected the feelings of the vast majority of American Jews, whether formally Zionist or merely sympathetic to Israel, by stressing both their unbreakable ties to America and the importance to Israel of a vital Jewish community in the United States. "To American Jews, America is home. There, exist their thriving roots; there, is the country which they have helped to build; and there, they share its fruits and its destiny."[2] Ben-Gurion, for his part, appeared to concede the American position in pronouncing that Israel would not interfere in the domestic affairs of American Jewry. "The State of Israel represents and speaks only on behalf of its own citizens and in no way presumes to represent or speak in the name of the Jews who are citizens of any other country. We, the people of Israel, have no desire and no intention to interfere in any way with the internal affairs of Jewish communities abroad."[3]

In retrospect the agreement appears to have been a tactical concession by Ben-Gurion to mollify American Jewry in view of Israel's overwhelming need for political and material support. The state of continuous war with the Arabs and the great resources needed to absorb the mass of immigrants from Muslim countries forced the Israeli government to focus more on problem solving than on ideology. But when the worst crises had passed, Ben-Gurion once again felt free to interfere by denigrating the lives of American Jews and demanding their mass immigration to Israel. At the Twenty-third Zionist Congress (1951), with the support of the Israeli delegation, Ben-Gurion launched a surprise attack upon American Zionism and American Jews in general. While recognizing the contributions of American Zionism in the pre-state era, the prime minister announced that the existence of Israel made immigration imperative for anyone who considered himself a Zionist. Indeed, the ultimate destruction of the whole Diaspora made immigration necessary for all Jews whatever their ideological bent. Even American Jews who were not as yet menaced by physical destruction should make aliyah (emigrate to Israel) because only in the Jewish state could one live a full Jewish life. All existence outside of Israel was *galut* (exile) and inferior.[4] Any Zionist who did not come to Israel was not a Zionist, and any Jew who lived in exile was similarly an inferior Jew.

The bitterness of the charismatic prime minister's attack shocked the American delegates. After all, in the forty years that Americans had been Zionists, they had never agreed that their ties to the movement involved aliyah. Despite their enormous contributions, they were now dismissed by the head of the state that many felt owed its very existence to their efforts. The attack naturally provoked a great debate both within and outside the Zionist movement, since the alleged inferiority of world Jewry implied its subservience to Israel. American Jewry tended to reply that the creation of Israel was not an end in itself but a means of fostering the health of world Jewry and Judaism. Ben-Gurion countered that the open society of which American Jews were so proud failed to provide a challenge for Jewish life and seduced and corrupted Jewish Americans. If America was not traditional exile, it was at least spiritual exile with the same consequences: Jewish inferiority.

Historians have advanced many explanations for Ben-Gurion's behavior, ranging from guilt over massive American aid to Israel to fear of the supposed ambition of the great American Zionist, Abba Hillel Silver. But the simplest explanation is that the diatribe was an expression of the prime minister's sincere and deepest beliefs. Practical considerations greatly reinforced the need for the ingathering of exiles that had long been a part of Zionist dogma. Every immigrant was another potential soldier in the war with the Arabs, who outnumbered the Israelis fifty to one. More important, American immigrants would have the education and technical skills needed to develop the country, skills not possessed in abundance by the undereducated immigrants from Arab lands.

Ben-Gurion's contention that the Jewish state's foundation completed the task of Zionism outside Israel and his refusal to distinguish between a Zionist who did not immigrate and a non-Zionist sympathizer had additional implications. By stating that there was no difference between Diaspora Zionists and non-Zionists, he both denied the leadership of the former and let it be known that Israel would welcome support from the great masses of ordinary Jews who remained outside official Zionism. This was but a prelude for the prime minister's campaign against the ZOA. Taking advantage of dissatisfaction with the ZOA leadership of Abba Hillel Silver and Emanuel Neumann, which many American Zionists considered authoritarian, Ben-Gurion encouraged a dissident faction to organize a new group to take over fundraising from the ZOA. Such a group would be controlled not by Zionists but by non-Zionist community leaders who had a much broader base of appeal, particularly to wealthy Jews who had never declared their formal allegiance to the movement. As a result of the conflict the charismatic Silver stepped down and retired to his congregation in Cleveland. Amid much publicity the new United Palestine Appeal was formed, making fundraising no longer a solely Zionist enterprise but the responsibility of the whole American Jewish community. In addition the crucial task of political lobbying was removed from the ZOA and placed in the hands of the newly created American Zionist Committee for Public Affairs.

The results were of tremendous importance to the relations between American Jewry and Israel. Having lost its most charismatic leader and having been deprived of its most important tasks of fundraising and political lobbying, the ZOA began a long period of decline. Control of fundraising and articulation of the relationship between Israel and American Jewry increasingly passed into the hands of a new generation of non-Zionist community leaders who were enthusiastic supporters of Israel and were able to mobilize a vast constituency. But their basic unfamiliarity with the issues and conflicts within the Zionist movement meant that they were unprepared intellectually or emotionally to do more than sincerely write checks in support of the Jewish state.

To coordinate and take advantage of the great increase in charitable contributions resulting from this enthusiasm, local Jewish federations were given responsibility for collecting and distributing such monies. They decided to allot to Israel 65 percent of all funds collected at the expense of domestic charity and education. While this extraordinarily high percentage devoted to the Jewish state would decrease as Israel's international and domestic crises abated, it was an indication of the new priorities of American Jewry. The emotionalism of the support for Israel and the voluntary nature of membership in Jewish organizations left little room for dissent within the Jewish establishment. Those moderates whose support for Israel was less than unquestioning very often resigned or simply became inactive, leaving the field to volunteers who totally agreed with all policies of the Jewish state.

The revolution in the relationship between Israel and American Zionism went unnoticed by the vast majority of American Jews, who had simply never viewed their ties to the Jewish state in ideological terms. Since they were mostly ignorant of Jewish history and unprepared to explore the significance of Zionist policies for Israel and the Jewish people, the mere existence of Israel was satisfaction enough. The failure of American Jews to assert themselves in relations with Israel was not an abdication of responsibility, since they had neither the inclination nor the experience to influence Israeli leaders on matters of policy. Like previous generations of American Jews, they were moved by issues, not ideology. The defense and development needs of Israel were overwhelming, and the task of providing a new life for millions of uneducated immigrants particularly appealed to the American imagination. The sheer magnitude and worthiness of these tasks were all-absorbing and left little time or energy for discussion of the larger question of the relationship between Israel and American Jews.

The one place where American Jews did resist Israel was over the question of aliyah. Despite Ben-Gurion's exhortations, American Jews simply ignored the Jewish state's call for their immigration. From 1948 until 1967, approximately ten thousand permanent immigrants to Israel came from the United States.[5] This rate of less than one thousand per year from the most populous and wealthiest nation of the Diaspora remained a great embarrassment to Israel. The rebuff to Zionist ideology and Israel's need for the technical skills possessed by potential American immigrants accounted for the increased rancor of Zionist predictions of a new Holocaust and the necessity of aliyah. But however sympathetic American Jews may have been to Israel politically and however generous they were financially, their failure to respond significantly to calls for aliyah demonstrated, as did nothing else, that their ultimate self-identification and priorities were American.

In the early 1950s, American Jews increasingly saw their role as providing the Jewish state with financial and political support. The latter became all the more necessary during the Eisenhower years, when the United States retreated from the unabashedly pro-Israel stance initiated by the Truman administration. John Foster Dulles, Eisenhower's secretary of state, felt that a military alliance with the Arab world would be the best means of assuring future oil supplies and containing communism in the Middle East. Dulles began to court the Arabs actively and even supplied Iraq with a limited amount of arms. In part to coordinate Jewish protest against such actions, the Conference of Presidents of Major Jewish Organizations was formed in 1955. Composed of both Zionist and non-Zionist organizations and of all religious branches, it represented a broad spectrum of American Jewry. Just as the creation of the United Palestine Fund had powerfully reinforced Israel's ability to raise money from the masses of American Jews, the creation of the Conference of Presidents provided for a similar increase and coordination of lobbying and propaganda. While this made Jewish pressure more effective, the creation of a single body to speak for American Jews encouraged a uniformity of opinion that would only increase as the

Conference of Presidents embraced additional Jewish organizations. Moreover, since the Conference of Presidents had strong formal and informal ties to Tel Aviv, its pronouncements often reflected not so much American Jews' grass-roots opinion but the views of the Israeli government.

The 1956 Israeli-Egyptian war was the first major test of American Jews' ability to influence foreign policy. After Egypt's president Gamal Abdel Nasser had nationalized the Suez Canal, Israel, inflamed by Nasser's encouragement of Arab guerillas, invaded Egypt. With the logistic and diplomatic support of France and England, who were angered respectively by Nasser's encouragement of the Algerian revolution and the nationalization of the canal, Israeli troops under General Moshe Dayan occupied the Sinai all the way to the canal. The United States was caught unawares by the Israeli success. Angry about not being consulted by its allies, America, joined by the Soviet Union, demanded the immediate withdrawal of Israeli troops. Israel refused. For the first time since the founding of the Jewish state, a serious dispute had arisen between the two governments. The depth of the disagreement was demonstrated by President Eisenhower's decision to terminate all American official economic aid to Israel in order to force withdrawal. The Conference of Presidents successfully lobbied to remove the economic sanctions. As the crisis went on, many American Jews began to feel uneasy about being caught between their sympathy for Israel and their American patriotism. Gradually, American Jewish support for the Israeli policy of nonwithdrawal began to weaken. As the head of the World Zionist Organization, Nahum Goldman, wrote to Ben-Gurion in early November: "I must tell you that it will be impossible to mobilize to support this position of non-withdrawal."[6] Bowing to diplomatic pressure, Israel eventually did withdraw, easing the strain on American Jews. As time went on, the pro-Israel stance of American Jews came to be taken for granted. In 1960, when Senator William Fulbright, the head of the Senate Foreign Relations Committee, stated that American Jewish policy had not been developed by American but by foreign interests and groups, the statement amounted to a direct accusation of dual loyalty. American Jewish support of Israel was by then seen as normal and patriotic, and the charge caused hardly a ripple.[7]

Nothing reflected and reinforced the new image of Israel more powerfully than Leon Uris's *Exodus* (1958) and its movie adaptation. A mammoth potboiler of a novel fictionally chronicling events surrounding the foundation of the Jewish state, *Exodus* was derided by critics for its shallow characterizations, simplemindedness, and stereotyping. Its plot was based in part on an actual historical event—the attempt of the refugee ship *Exodus* to land six hundred Holocaust survivors in Palestine in the face of a British prohibition against Jewish immigration. The novel's hero, Hagana officer Ari ben Canaan, was a new, tough, militaristic Jew who outwitted the British and whose daring, courage, and commanding presence could also carry the day against increasingly malevolent Arabs. The brave, decisive ben Canaan represented the substitution of a positive Jewish stereotype, which, of course, had no more relationship to reality than the negative one it replaced. As Yehiel Aranowicz, the real-life captain of the *Exodus* stated, "Israelis were pretty disappointed in the book to put it lightly—the types that are described in it never existed in Israel. The novel is neither history nor literature."[8] But Captain Aranowicz, for all his authenticity, missed the point. Far more pertinent was David Ben-Gurion's evaluation: "As a piece of propaganda it's the greatest thing ever written about Israel."[9]

Exodus was a new kind of Jewish novel, depicting its protagonist not as conflicted, ambivalent, ultra-introspective, and marginal but as decisive, courageous, and ultimately victorious. It presented Zionism and Israel as the Jewish people's triumph over two thousand years of persecution. In good Zionist fashion, Jews were no longer passive victims but the triumphant molders of history. Despite a limited interest in Zionism, *Exodus* struck a chord in Jews and other Americans, remaining on the best-seller list for eighty weeks and selling four million copies. For American Jews, it became a secular icon whose dust cover in blue and white—the colors of Israel—adorned the bookshelves of nearly every Jewish home. It was as if American Jews now felt comfortable enough in America to appropriate for themselves the classic and optimistic American myth of virtuous struggle and ultimate triumph. For both the American Jews and the Gentiles for whom the novel was their only contact with Jewish history, *Exodus* provided a powerful image of a new, vital, and exemplary Israel.

However influential the novel, it was dwarfed by the Hollywood version. Produced and directed by Otto Preminger, the movie *Exodus* employed an ultra-wide screen, forty-five thousand extras, and ten "name" actors, including Paul Newman as Ari ben Canaan. With a running time of almost four hours, including intermission, the movie was of epic length. Allegedly, during a preview screening, after three hours, comedian Mort Saul stood up and intoned, "Otto, let my people go!" Nevertheless, the film racked up a record $1.6 million in advance sales.

Upon the film's release in December 1960, it was described by the *New York Times* as "a massive, overlong, episodic, involved and generally inconclusive cinemarama" that nevertheless is "a fine reflection of experience that rips the heart."[10] *Time* magazine called it "a serious, expert, frightening and inspiring political theatre" despite "an irritating tendency to Zionist tirade." It also complained that "the film unequivocally blamed Arabs [and] absolutely absolves the Jews."[11]

Other aspects of the film prized neither nuance nor subtlety. Its theme song, crooned by Pat Boone, hit the top of the charts and began with words as triumphant as they were arrogant. "This land is mine. God gave this land to me." The film's advertising logo, a series of overlapping arms forming a triangle to hoist a rifle aloft, evoked the most reproduced photo in history, that of American marines raising the flag at Iwo Jima. It implicitly equated Israel's struggle against the Arabs with America's fight against similiar forces of darkness. To further drive home this point, in the movie version of *Exodus*, the Arabs were counseled and motivated by a fugitive from the Third Reich. Just as America triumphed over evil with goodness, pluck, and God's favor, the movie reaffirmed an identical view of Israel's ultimate victory.

American Jewry's relationship with Israel settled into a pattern of normalcy. According to historian Melvin Urofsky, "The initial honeymoon came to an end as American Jews no longer saw Israeli rebirth as the all consuming passion of their lives while Israelis wondered if they had been deserted."[12] Certainly by the early 1960s, Israel's existence was taken for granted, and while it evoked feelings of pride and responsibility, most Jews were too busy "making it" in the suburbs of America to relate to Israel in any but superficial terms. The cultural revival envisaged by Ahad Ha'am simply did not occur. What little religion or cultural commitment remained was often replaced by superficial identification with Israel, often taking the form of the acquisition of material objects. It sometimes seemed that for American Jews the sole purpose of the rebirth of Israel after two millenia was that suburban living rooms could sport blue ashtrays with "Eretz Yisrael" stamped on the underside. In his famous study of the "Lakeville" Jewish Community, Marshall Sklare, one of the most respected sociologists of American Jewry, found that only 8 percent of respondants had attempted any study of Hebrew and only 2 percent had attended study groups, courses, or lectures concerning Israel in the past year.[13]

Yet beneath the seemingly casual ties a more profound connection was growing. As American Jews increasingly viewed their religion in nostalgic and emotional, as opposed to spiritual, terms, the problem for Jewish professionals of all denominations was how to lead their constituencies back to a living faith. Both consciously and unconsciously Israel provided the solution for rabbis and Jewish professionals seeking to rally the troops. For the Conservatives, Israel was the most attractive and dynamic illustration of the movement's assumption that a valid and satisfying blend of Jewish tradition and modernity was possible. For Reform Jews, Israel now provided the kind of internal spiritual experience that many felt the movement lacked. Israel now became so important to Reform Judaism that the movement's theology was modified to permit immigration to Israel, and Reform rabbinical students were required to study there. But to the American Jewish public, Israel's appeal reached far beyond theology. Many middle-class Jews felt rootless in suburbia and more than a bit guilty about their new prosperity, especially in the shadow of the Holocaust, which had destroyed the old demographic and cultural centers of Judaism. For average, well-intentioned, middle-class Jews, identification with Israel provided an emotional link with Judaism without jeopardizing their newly won place in America. Even more important, the Jewish state, especially after it moved into the Western camp in 1950, provided a new means of Jewish expression for American Jews not wanting to be encumbered by religion. Instead of identifying Judaism with rituals or attitudes that seemed increasingly alien and a barrier to assimilation, how much more convenient to redefine one's Jewishness as loyalty to a progressive, courageous, modern state and a staunch American ally to boot.

In was widely reported that the Six-Day War of 1967 revealed the depth of the American Jewish attachment to Israel. The war itself raised the specter of another Holocaust. With Israel's existence imperiled, American Jews abandoned their attitude of benign indifference and casual support and came to Israel's aid with an intensity that astounded even the most optimistic Zionists. Even "non-Jewish Jews" were not immune to this passion. Glued to their radios, American Jews spontaneously came to Israel's aid. Within hours thousands had volunteered to go to Israel to fill jobs vacated by soldiers at the front. The outpouring of funds was even more impressive. Through children collecting on street corners, through founding special emergency funds, and by means of normal channels such as the Jewish Federation, American Jews pledged $430 million to the war effort.[14] Cases of individuals mortgaging their homes for Israel, synagogues divesting their building funds, Episcopalians rediscovering their Jewishness only give a hint of the emotion generated by the crisis. The astounding Israeli victory converted the fear and despair of American Jews to relief and immeasurable pride in one of the most successful military campaigns in history. *Life* magazine's cover showing an Israeli soldier holding his rifle aloft while cooling off in the Suez Canal transformed the popular image of Jews. As Theodore H. White's accompanying essay noted, "legends have been born that fathers will tell children to tell their children after them."[15] The new image of the Jew as conquering warrior proved irresistible to American Jews whose religious and cultural identities had long been waning. "Peoplehood" began to take the place of religion as identification with Israel became the lowest common denominator of Jewish identity.

*   *   *

Any number of rapturous histories have stated that American Jews' unprecedented identification with and contributions to Israel constituted a rediscovery of their roots and of the feelings they had always had toward the Jewish state. Facing the possibility of another Holocaust, American Jews discovered their real priorities. Such an analysis is correct but incomplete. The depth and breadth of emotional and financial support for Israel is also explained by the war's coincidence with the identity crisis of American Jews. How much easier to find one's identity in Israel than in a religion that had become increasingly unfashionable. How much more comfortable to invest one's emotions in Zionism, where the issue appeared to be that of simple survival, than in the complexities of the political liberalism with which American Jews had so identified. How much more reassuring to identify with the clear military decisiveness of Israel rather than with the ambiguity of the political process in America or the quagmire in Vietnam.

The resolution, activism, and incredible victory of the Jewish state in a complex world where success was increasingly perceived in relative terms had an immeasurable effect on American Jews. Given the magnitude of Israel's military success, it would have been less than human if American Jews, who felt more socially and politically vulnerable than at any time since World War II, had not strongly identified with the state and basked in its glory. The salutory change in the image of Jews from concentration camp inmates to military geniuses and heroes was well nigh irresistible. American Jews responded by adding a new myth to their stock conceptions of the Jewish state, that of the Israeli superman who could do no wrong.

* * *

The reaction of the world to the Israeli victory helped complete American Jews' new identification with the Jewish state. Having made immense territorial gains in Syria, Egypt, and Jordan, the Israelis now found themselves in the unfamiliar role of military occupiers. The Arabs, much of oil-dependent Europe, and most of the Third World, ignoring the origins of the war, increasingly condemned the Israelis as expansionist. In America much the same criticism came from those who were also attacking American Jews—the New Left, a number of Black spokesmen, and portions of the old liberal coalition. This completed many American Jews' alienation from the American Left. It also fueled in them a sense of parallel beleaguerment with Israel and provided a further basis of identification with the Jewish state. The new myth of the Israeli superman was reinforced by the necessity of solidarity in time of crisis. In the face of the breakdown of the traditional liberalism that had been such an important element in American Jews' self-image, the resulting worship of Israel became the supreme basis of American Jewish identity. When Prime Minister Eshkol at the World Zionist Organization conference in 1967 reiterated from the dais Ben-Gurion's controversial notion that Zionism and aliyah were synonymous, euphoric American delegates broke into cheers.[16] Such support was more rhetorical than real when measured against Jews' American priorities. To the great disappointment of the Israeli government, American Jewish immigration after 1967 remained embarrassingly low and indicated that despite their emotional support of Israel, American Jews' priorities remained overwhelmingly American. Nevertheless, most now identified with Israel, whose total and uncritical support had become the principal component of the "civil religion of American Jews."[17]

The years following the war saw a further increase in American Jewish identification with the Jewish state. Israel became the primary focus of Jewish emotion and activity, and its actions became almost sacrosanct in the eyes of most American Jews. American Jewish organizations sought to defend every aspect of Israeli policy despite vigorous dissent within Israel itself. After 1967 domestic Israeli criticism of their government's more debatable actions, such as its policy of bombing Palestinian refugee camps in retaliation for terrorism, the raid on the Beirut airport, and the downing of a Libyan airliner over the Negev, generated little public criticism from American Jews. The phenomenon of Jewish consensus—so rare in any other context—was more than the age-old fear of showing disunity. It was as if American Jews had expended so much psychological energy on Israel that its being subject to human error was a possibility too fearful to contemplate. As Rabbi Eugene Borowitz noted mordantly, Israel had provided American Jews with another topic that could not be discussed.[18]

After the 1967 war, the American Jewish community increased its emphasis on providing political support to an increasingly isolated Israel. The Conference of Presidents, whose influence and prestige had been greatly increased by Israel's victory over the Soviet Union's Arab protégés, worked ceaselessly to ensure that Israel would receive American weapons, a task made more difficult as America's unfolding Vietnam involvement led to increasing calls for her pullback from world commitments. As the 1973 Yom Kippur War and its aftermath imperiled the Jewish state, American Jewish lobbying and community solidarity became even more vital. During the war, in which Israel was attacked by surprise by Egypt and Syria, the Conference of Presidents worked to assure that Israel would be immediately resupplied with the weapons and ammunitions she was rapidly depleting. The fact that the American government, through its control of resupply literally held Israel's fate in the balance increased the importance of such lobbying and of American Jews as intermediaries between Israel and the American government.

The war's aftermath was troubling for American Jews. Israel's vulnerability to surprise attack and her high number of casualties had punctured the myth of the Israeli military superman. The war's political implications were even more disturbing. Spurred by feelings of Muslim solidarity, the Organization of Arab Petroleum Exporting Countries had instituted a successful boycott of Europe. Their ability to control the supply and price of oil had given Arabs the kind of world influence that they had not had for a millenium. As a result the Nixon administration began to talk of balancing traditional American support for Israel with a consideration of Arab aspirations. Indeed, Henry

Kissinger's refusal to permit Israel's destruction of the Egyptian Third Army at the end of the Yom Kippur War seemed to indicate an American willingness to control Israel. The growth of world and American pressures upon Israel further reinforced American Jews' role as the Jewish state's principal spokesmen and advocates.

The most disturbing of the pressures upon Israel was the emergence of the Palestine Liberation Organization (PLO) as a recognized world body. One year after the October war, the Arab nations met at Rabat, and all powers having a claim to the West Bank ceded their claims to the PLO. The PLO also gained acceptance as the legitimate expression of Palestine national aspirations in the world at large. PLO chief Yasir Arafat, despite his advocacy of terrorism, became a legitimate Third World hero and was invited to address no less a body than the United Nations General Assembly, where he called for the creation of a Palestinian state and a continuation of the armed struggle. This was less shocking than the rapturous response accorded him by the General Assembly, bent on showing its contempt for the West, of which Israel was a convenient symbol. The General Assembly's subsequent vote condemning Zionism as racism again had less relationship to the ostensible issue than to the need of the Third World to attack Israel and her closest ally, the United States. Jews in Israel and America considered the General Assembly vote to mark the reemergence of world anti-Semitism, albeit in the more respectable form of anti-Israeli sentiment. Now more than ever, American Jews closed ranks to defend all policies of the Jewish state.

But within Israel itself, it was precisely the fate of the Palestinians and the West Bank that generated ever greater debate. An extreme faction of the opposition Herut bloc, the Gush Emunim (Front of the Faithful), maintained that the West Bank was Israel's by biblical right and agitated for its permanent retention. The Labor government of Yitzhak Rabin did not restrict the paramilitary settlements that the Gush Emunim established in the occupied territories. By contrast many Israelis felt that, moral considerations aside, the retention within Israel of the West Bank's million Arabs would be suicidal. Given that the Arab birthrate was much higher than that of the Jews, within a few decades Israel would either lose its Jewish character or be forced to enact restrictive measures that would end its existence as a democratic state. While the debate over the settlements and the future of the West Bank raged within Israel, most American Jews simply took the hard line of the Rabin government. One American commentator noted that it became an article of faith among American Jews that Israel should not give up an inch of occupied territory. When a small number of concerned Jewish Americans breached this concensus by advocating publicly that Israel make concessions to the Palestinians, most Jewish organizations were scandalized.[19] Less scathing than most was the opinion expressed in the editorial column of *Commentary*, which characterized such actions as representing "the view of that increasingly visible faction of the American Jewish community to whom support of Israel is conditioned on Israel's good behavior as measured by the liberal pieties in fashion on any given day."[20]

Such criticism implied that Israel's policies were by definition always the best and most appropriate and that the mere act of criticism revealed the critic to be on a lower intellectual and moral level. American Jews had transferred religious associations surrounding the Jewish state and the secular charisma of its military to the world of politics. It was as if Israel's governmental leaders all combined the revelation of Moses, the wisdom of Solomon, and the moral vision of Isaiah and were not subject to such human foibles as error, lack of judgment, personal ambition, or momentary political considerations. American Jews had responded to the Zionism as racism resolution by wearing buttons proclaiming "I Am a Zionist" or "We Are One." Most interpreted the latter button to mean not only one people but one opinion.

The continuing refusal of the American Jewish community to tolerate internal dissent on Israel was demonstrated by its furious reaction to the founding and growth of Breira. Breira, meaning "alternative" in Hebrew, was founded in late 1973 "to legitimize public dissent within the American Jewish community concerning the profound issues that confront us as Jews in the Diaspora." These included the Orthodox religious monopoly in Israel, Israel's allegedly inflexible policy toward a peace settlement, and the tendency of American Jews to rubber-stamp that policy, and the unequal relationship between the Jewish state and the Diaspora. As Breira's statement of purpose noted, "We deplore the pressures in American Jewish life which make open discussion of those and other vital issues virtually synonymous with heresy."[21]

Breira soon attracted concerned Jewish intellectuals and members of the growing Jewish counterculture, as well as sixty Reform and Conservative rabbis, many from the Hillel Foundations charged with promoting Jewish life on college campuses. The organization also attracted a fair number of "stars," including Balfour Brickner, the rabbi of the Stephen Wise Free Synagogue in New York and an official of the Union of American Hebrew Congregations, and Joachim Prinz, chairman of the World Conference of Jewish Organizations. Irving Howe, editor of the journal *Dissent* and famous as the author of *World of Our Fathers*, became an important if unofficial spokesman for the organization. Although Breira was concerned with a whole range of issues, its pronouncements on the Palestinians soon overshadowed all others. Breira's position was by no means anti-Israel. In common with the Israeli government it called for negotiations with the Palestinians only on the basis of Israeli security and demanded that the PLO modify its national charter, which called for the destruction of the Jewish state. Unlike the government but along with many Israeli citizens, Breira felt that the solution to the Palestinian problem was the key to an overall peace settlement. The only realistic course, according to Breira, was a state run by the Palestinians, not one tied to Jordan as Jerusalem had proposed. Notwithstanding this divergence, Breira's real "sin" in the eyes of the establishment was to go public with its criticism of Israel and to urge others to do so, thereby destroying the illusion of unity that the mainstream organizations had labored so mightily to build.

In October 1976 a group of American Jews, including two members of Breira, met as private citizens with two PLO members touring the United States under the auspices of the American Friends Committee. Arthur Waskow, a participant and one of the founders of Breira, wrote an op-ed article for the *New York Times* detailing the meeting.[22] Waskow's account was more skeptical than optimistic, but the article set off a furious debate among American Jews concerning the propriety of meeting with representatives of an organization whose avowed goal was to destroy Israel. Taking note of the ongoing debate, on December 30, the *New York Times* ran a front-page article entitled "American Jewish Leaders Are Split over Issue of Meeting with P.L.O."[23] The reaction of these Jewish leaders was so apoplectic that the *Times* printed a correction stating that it was the rank and file, not Jewish leaders, who were divided."[24] But the cat was out of the bag—the fact that not all Jews were marching in step had been emblazoned on the pages of the most influential newspaper in America.

As a result of such publicity, many Jewish organizations subjected Breira to ever increasing criticism. The *American Zionist* warned that "defeatist Jews were rallying for an assault on historical fact and moral commitment that would be played out in the damaging arena of the mass media."[25] The president of the Zionist Organization of America was more explicit in his criticism. "This insignificant splinter is composed of new leftists, financed by mysterious sources. They have become the Jewish spokesmen of the PLO and the mythical Palestinians."[26] The most thoroughgoing attack was a pamphlet entitled "Breira Counsel for Judaism," written by political scientist Rael Jean Isaac. Published by Americans for a Safe Israel, a group tied to Israel's Gush Emunim (whose policy of planning settlements in the occupied territories had been a principal focus of Breira's displeasure), the pamphlet was marked by extremely bitter personal attacks upon the founders of Breira. Two thirds of its twenty-eight pages were devoted to an "exposé" of the alleged anti-Israeli radical past associations of leading Breira members. According to Isaac, far from being the Zionist organization that it appeared, Breira was actually a de facto arm of the PLO.[27] But what about the hundreds of Breira members whose Jewish credentials were beyond question? What of the famous rabbis and intellectuals who were attracted by Breira's contention that discussion of vital issues was more beneficial than enforced silence? For Isaac the solution was simple. If a Breira member was not malevolent, he was simply a sucker: "Breira . . . serves as a 'front' group, where the majority who join are unaware of the purposes of the minority who shape the path of the organization. If Jews want to organize on behalf of Fatah [the Palistinian revolutionary organization], that is their privilege. But let them call it 'Jews for Fatah' and not 'Breira.' "[28]

The Isaac pamphlet was merely the most virulent in an ever growing chorus of attack upon Breira. The newspaper *Jewish Week*, distributed to every contributor to the United Jewish Appeal in the New York area, engaged in a smear campaign whose personal attacks rivaled those of Professor Isaac. Articles with such titles as "Why Our Doves Are Pigeons"[29] and "Breira: Alternative of Surrender"[30] appeared in the Jewish press. An article in the mainstream *Commentary*, heavily dependent upon the Isaac pamphlet, branded Breira as a force for evil. Simple fairness forced the author to concede grudgingly that most Breira members "were not anti-Israel in any simple sense of the term."[31] Those articles attacking Breira usually followed a set pattern. A discussion of the impropriety and dire implications of public criticism of Israel was followed by an attack on Breira's founders as old-line radicals who consciously or unconsciously wished to weaken or even destroy Israel.

Other prominent members, such as Irving Howe, were then lambasted as Johnny-come-latelies to Jewish causes. Significantly, when millions of Johnny-come-latelies had come out of the woodwork in 1967 to offer total support to Israel, no one had questioned *their* Jewish credentials. The emotion-laden attacks, the ad hominem criticism, the abstract philosophical discussions all disguised an unwillingness to debate Breira on the substantive issues it raised. Was Israeli policy self-defeating in the long run? What was to be done with the Occupied Territories and with the Palestinians? What was the place of dissent concerning Israel in the Diaspora? What was the desirable relationship between the two strongest Jewish centers in the world? Since most establishment Jews found such vital questions too sensitive or painful to discuss in public, the apparent solution was to seek to drown Breira in a sea of vituperation.

Words soon begat deeds. The leadership of B'nai B'rith, one of the largest Jewish organizations, unsuccessfully tried to fire any employee who was a member of Breira.[32] Similarly, Hillel Foundation rabbis who were Breira members were subject to increasing pressures to recant or resign their posts. In an unprecedented move the Rabbinical Assembly denied seats on its executive council to two rabbis because of their ties to Breira.[33] When Breira held its first national meeting in March 1977, the Jewish Defense League broke in, overturned tables and files, and assaulted some Breira members.[34] On the local level, rabbis sympathetic to Breira were often ostracized by their colleagues and subjected to calls for their dismissal by some of their congregants.

In retrospect what was most significant about Breira was that the reaction it elicited was all out of proportion to its power and influence. While a national organization, Breira could boast hardly more than 1,500 members. Its program departed from the mainstream but was certainly not beyond the bounds of sincere dissent. Why then the hysteria, the mudslinging, the physical assualt and the attempts to punish Breira members and sympathizers? Breira's insistence on public dissent struck a raw nerve in individuals and organizations. On a personal level Breira threatened the Jews' sense of Jewish and American well-being by calling public and Gentile attention to Israeli policies with which they themselves were beginning to feel increasingly uncomfortable. Breira also caused distress by demanding that American Jews transform their relationship with Israel from that of passive giving and unquestioning approval to one of genuine concern and responsibility.

On a collective level the threat was twofold. The notion that any public dissent concerning Israel played into the hands of the anti-Semites was an article of dogma only slightly less powerful than monotheism. Breira's ability to gain a good deal of publicity for its Jewish anti-Israeli pronouncements—presumably in the man-bites-dog theory of journalism—was viewed as especially threatening. The fact that Breira began its own lobbying efforts on Capitol Hill was particularly galling to Jewish organizations that had made the American Israel Political Action Committee (AIPAC) one of the most effective lobbies in Washington. By stating that the public discussion of important issues was more vital to Israel's welfare than the maintenance of an illusionary unity, Breira threatened both the monopoly of ideas and organizational control that the Jewish establishment had long considered necessary for its own and Israel's welfare.

This was not to imply that Breira was without fault. The group's pronouncements were sometimes marked by self-righteousness and lack of empathy, which even its supporters found offensive. No matter how laudable its appeals to reason, Breira's refusal to consider the emotional needs of American Jews often cost it as much support as did the attacks of its enemies. When Yasir Arafat visited the UN in 1974, the Soviet bloc and much of the Third World united in a cynical campaign against Israel. As Israel stood almost alone, American Jews organized an anti-Arafat protest in United Nations Plaza. The one Jewish dissenting voice was Breira, which in the midst of an international anti-Israel hysteria saw fit to point out that Arafat and the Palestinians were not the same and that mass protests only increased Jewish fear and isolation.[35] Breira demonstrated a similar failure of empathy after the Israeli rescue of Jewish hostages at Entebbe, when it sought to puncture the collective euphoria by pointing out that what Israel really needed was a "diplomatic Entebbe."[36] Such pronouncements, however laudable in the abstract, were simply too coldly logical to attract mass appeal. Breira at times could also be faulted on tactics. When one hundred prominent American Jews signed a petition supporting an Israeli demonstration against Gush Emunim and further West Bank settlements, it was published in the *Jerusalem Post*. Breira then circulated the petition in America despite the fact that many of the signatories had been assured that Breira was not involved and that the document would not be circulated outside Israel.[37]

But it was not self-righteousness or questionable tactics that prevented Breira from capturing a mass following. Quite simply, for most American Jews, Breira's advocacy of moderation was marked by a fatal lack of symmetry. As long as all Arab states vowed to destroy "the Zionist entity," there was no real outlet for the Israeli flexibility that Breira advocated. Moreover, the potentially disastrous implications of the retention of the West Bank for Israel's political and cultural future were not generally evident. Those who did point out the pitfalls of West Bank settlement were often cowed by the Israeli government's contention that the settlements were vital to national security. It would take a revolution to overturn the American Jewish consensus on Israel. Within a few years, the election of Menachem Begin and Anwar Sadat's peace initiative would provide just that.

| |3| |

The World Turned Upside Down

The election of Menachem Begin as Israeli prime minister in May 1977, combined with Anwar Saddat's peace initiative four months later, seriously weakened the foundation of the American Jewish consensus on Israel. The first produced a divided Israel that could no longer provide unambiguous ideological and political direction for American Jews. The second, by providing an alternative to Israel's three decades of necessarily hard-line policies, created new choices and controversies as Israelis and American Jews sought how best to respond to the Egyptian initiative.

* * *

Initially, the reaction of American Jews to Menachem Begin's election demonstrated the persistence of the old patterns. A disciple of the rightist Jabotinsky (who had emphasized the importance of power over morality), religiously Orthodox, and a former terrorist, Begin's ideals and program were in sharp disagreement with the politics of American Jews. Moreover, he had spent the last thirty years in parliamentary opposition, where he was detested by American idol David Ben-Gurion. Finally, Begin was allied with the religious parties and with the Gush Emunim, which advocated permanent Israeli retention of the West Bank. Unsurprisingly, immediately after Begin's victory some American Jewish journals expressed fear that Israel's foreign policies would move toward a new and dangerous assertiveness. But an attack on the new prime minister by President Jimmy Carter and the generally unfavorable reaction of non-Jews directed attention away from the question of what Begin actually stood for. *Time* magazine even explained the pronunciation of his name by pointing out that it rhymed with "Fagin." Faced with the skepticism of Gentile Americans, American Jews were more willing to line up behind the prime minister. In the two months between his election and his first official visit to the United States, American Jewish organizations worked overtime to assure popular support. As a result of their sense of American pressure upon Begin, Israel's public relations effort, and Begin's old-fashioned Jewishness and undeniable personal charm, the new prime minister was given a tumultuous reception by American Jews in July 1977. The fact that Begin and Carter appeared to be establishing a warm personal relationship, based in part upon their mutual respect for the Old Testament, did much to boost his popularity.

This popularity had its price: the willful failure of American Jews to examine the substance of Begin's policies and their implications for the future. Beneath the cordiality the issue of Israel's retention of the West Bank still remained. The Carter administration felt that Israel's interests would best be served by settling with the Palestinians. It opposed Begin's refusal to relinquish control over the occupied territories and made no secret of its dissatisfaction. Yet American Jews, also increasingly disturbed by Carter's approaches to the PLO, now lined up solidly behind Begin and against Carter's attempts to pressure Israel. When, in October 1977, Carter proposed to bring the Russians into the negotiations as cochairs of a Geneva peace conference, American Jewish organizations orchestrated a national protest against what they feared would be a Great Power attempt to bully Israel into a settlement. By late 1977 a Harris poll revealed that 60 percent of Jews gave Carter a negative rating. Just when the stalemate between Israel and the United States appeared permanent, Anwar Sadat announced his willingness to go to Jerusalem.

Until the autumn of 1977 the most powerful argument that the Israeli government could marshall in favor of its hard-line policies was expressed by the popular slogan "*Ein breira*—there is no alternative." In the face of over thirty years of Arab intransigence, any softening of the Israeli position would be misplaced at best and self-destructive at worst. With whom was Israel to negotiate? With Nasser, who had regularly published the viciously anti-Semitic *Protocols of the Elders of Zion* and vowed to drive Israel into the sea? With the Syrians, who spiced the emotionality of jihad (holy war) with socialist ideology? With Yasir Arafat, whose Palestinian National Covenant promised the same annihilation as Nasser had but in terms more suited to the era of international public relations? Peace advocates could point only to Arab moderates like Habib Bourguiba of Tunisia, who was at most a peripheral player.

The overwhelming reality was that after four wars, resulting in at least one hundred thousand Arab casualties and the loss of massive amounts of territory, the Arab world had not moved one iota toward recognizing Israel's legitimacy. And since this intransigence left Israel no options but the hard line, the United States, despite its oil-bred desire to cultivate the Arab world, similarly had little choice but to support the Jewish state.

Anwar Sadat's peace initiative of November 1977 was truly revolutionary. It was sudden and unexpected, and it radically changed the entire diplomatic and psychological structure of the Middle East. By going to Jerusalem, Sadat had hoped to open the way for the long delayed Geneva peace conference on the Middle East.[1] More grandly, Sadat sought to overcome three decades of hostility and to pave the way for a peace treaty between Israel and the Arab world. The importance of such a visit by the head of the Arab world's most populous and influential country could hardly be overestimated. For the first time, Sadat provided realistic alternatives to the unrelenting policies of the Jewish state. How best to exploit this opportunity and fulfill its promise of a settlement soon led to an unprecedented gulf between the United States and Israel. At the same time, despite their deep emotional ties to Israel, an increasing number of American Jews found themselves doubting the wisdom of Israel's reaction to the peace initiative. The validity of such criticism and airing it publicly spurred lively debate within the American Jewish community.

The Egyptian peace initiative sought to provide an alternative to war not simply by declaring Egypt's willingness to make peace but by attempting to meet Israel's political, military, and psychological needs. Most significantly, Sadat was acknowledging the existence of Israel and declared himself ready to make peace. From Israel's perspective the fact that this change appeared to stem from a hardheaded appreciation of both Israel's strength and Egypt's developmental requirements argued for the Egyptian leader's sincerity. Beyond this, Sadat subsequently declared that he understood Israel's security needs. When Begin welcomed Sadat at Ben-Gurion Airport in Tel Aviv on November 10, 1977, it indeed seemed as if the atmosphere of goodwill could produce an Egyptian-Israeli peace. Sadat's presence was the strongest possible statement of the change that had occurred, and Begin declared Israel ready to make significant concessions in the service of a comprehensive settlement. In November and December the latter appeared to be a realistic possibility.

But when the cheering stopped and the military bands of each country no longer agonized over the other's national anthem, the resolution of thirty years of conflict called for much more than good intentions. As the two leaders attempted to give legal substance to their rhetorical love feast, pledges of mutual understanding soon dissolved into distrust and recrimination. The major points of conflict were relatively straightforward and negotiable. These basically involved the time and demarcation of Israel's withdrawal from occupied Egyptian territories and the precise nature of the diplomatic recognition, the peace treaty, and the normalization of relations with Egypt that Israel was to receive in return. By contrast, the fate of the Palestinians became the sticking point. Given the PLO's murderous past and its long-standing vow to destroy the Jewish state, the Israeli government was unwilling to consider any arrangement that might increase or institutionalize the PLO's power. The notion that the West Bank was Israel's by religious right exercised an increasing influence over Begin, who took every opportunity to refer to the occupied territories by their biblical names of Judea and Samaria. Israel thus refused even to consider the possibility of an independent Palestinian state. But Sadat, although not sympathetic to the PLO's political philosophy, could not afford to turn his back on his fellow Arab leaders. When he recognized Israel's right to exist, Sadat cut Egypt off from the rest of the Arab world, for whom the defense of the Palestinians, at least rhetorically, had been the touchstone of Arabism.

By achieving a just settlement for the Palestinians, Sadat hoped to regain Egypt's influence and lead a recalcitrant Arab world into recognizing and making peace with Israel. Ideologically and politically, Sadat was unwilling to abandon the Palestinians by negotiating a peace treaty that ignored their interests and aspirations. For this reason he insisted on the Palestinian right of self-determination. At the same time, Egypt sought to balance her advocacy for the Palestinians with an appreciation of Israel's rightful insistence on security. Conceding the impossibility of Israel's granting the West Bank immediate independence, Sadat simply desired an Israeli pledge that Israel would, sometime in the future, relinquish its claim to the West Bank, providing that satisfactory security arrangements could be devised. Presumably, these would include the establishment of a Palestinian regime willing to coexist with Israel and/or some sort of international guarantee of Israel's security.

The Israeli government would go no further than to propose the negotiation of a system of autonomy for the West Bank's million plus Arab inhabitants. Such a system envisaged Palestinian responsibility for domestic and municipal affairs, while Israel would retain control over security and public order. To many it appeared that the Israeli proposals, far from satisfying Palestinian aspirations, would merely simplify the task of Israeli administration. With regard to the ultimate disposition of the territories, the most the Israelis would concede was that after five years they would reassess the whole West Bank problem.[2] The seriousness of the gulf between Egypt and Israel on the future of the Palestinians was first revealed when Begin and Sadat were unable to agree on a joint statement of principles at their meeting at Ismalia on December 24, 1977.

That meeting appears to have been a turning point in the ultimate failure of the two parties to obtain a comprehensive peace treaty. From then on the euphoria degenerated into disappointment and suspicion, and the positions of both Egypt and Israel hardened. Both leaders moved from the high road of statesmanship to the political path of least resistance. Begin, who had previously resisted the pressure of the religious right, began to establish more paramilitary settlements on the West Bank and continued quoting Scripture in justification for Israel's retention of the occupied territories. Sadat, responding to the desires of the rest of the Arab world, now reverted to the notion that, in return for peace, Israel had to give up all territories captured in the 1967 war. By the first half of 1978 it appeared that, despite the mutual desire for a settlement and the sincere goodwill of the participants, the peace process was foundering on the rock of Palestinian nationalism.

* * *

Once it emerged as the key element in any regional Middle East settlement, the West Bank issue did much to determine the relationship among Israel, the U.S. government, and American Jews. After November's hopes of a quick peace had degenerated into stalemate and mutual recrimination, the differing priorities of Israel and the United States quickly surfaced. For the United States, caught between its commitment to support Israel and increased dependence upon Arab oil and petrodollars, the Egyptian peace initiative seemed heaven-sent. From the U.S. perspective, if Sadat needed a pledge from Israel of Palestinian self-determination to convince his fellow Arabs that a settlement was desirable, it was a small price to pay for a comprehensive peace. Moreover, American policy makers felt that Egypt could be kept in its unaccustomed nonbelligerency only through speedy Israeli concessions. For this reason the United States now deemed Israel's proposals for a limited Palestinian autonomy on the West Bank inadequate and pressed Jerusalem to give the West Bank a greater measure of self-determination in the future.[3] Israel considered this to be especially unfair, since it was being asked again to sacrifice vital security and political interests in return for mere verbal promises. In reply to repeated threats to suspend weapons deliveries, Israel "created facts" by establishing more paramilitary settlements in the West Bank and Gaza. In March 1978, Prime Minister Begin visited Washington, where he refused to terminate the settlements or to budge on the larger issue of the West Bank. An incensed Jimmy Carter enumerated to the media what seemed an endless series of Begin's no's.[4] Israel, in turn, was increasingly disturbed by what it felt was American appeasement of the Arab world. In pursuit of its more balanced policy the Carter administration had openly courted Syria during that period, made explicit reference to the desirability of a Palestinian entity, and proposed the sale of warplanes to the Saudis. Israelis began to fear a sell-out by an administration whose cultivation of the Arabs appeared to be more important than Israeli security.

For American Jews it seemed that their long-dreaded nightmare had come to pass: American and Israeli interests were no longer perceived as identical. Not only was Israel being pressured, but American Jews were being ignored, and they felt a united front all the more necessary. Some reflexively, others after reflection, leapt to defend Israeli policy. An ever increasing number of still others—while disagreeing with Israel's establishment of new West Bank settlements—felt that the maintenance of Jewish solidarity called for their support. Throughout the first half of 1978, American Jewish organizations and newspapers poured forth an endless stream of articles that argued the Israelis were not the ones responsible for the breakdown of the peace process. If much of the world thought otherwise, this was attributed to Sadat's public relations coup in offering negotiations. The West Bank, it was endlessly maintained, was vital to Israeli security. Moreover, as peace seemed to be slipping away, some now saw the whole process as a trap for the unwary into which Begin in his wisdom refused to fall. A number of American Jewish organizations went so far as to take out advertisements alluding to Sadat's alleged Nazi sympathies during World War II.[5] The Council of Presidents, whatever its private objections, gave Begin public support. In early February the American Zionist Organization declared that Diaspora Jews should back Israel no matter what her policies. Even a noted moderate such as Melvin Urofsky stated that American Jews should not let the settlements be used as a club against Israel.[6]

But for the first time small but significant cracks appeared in the public facade of American Jewry. Breira continued its campaign but was continually branded by the Jewish establishment as little better than a "PLO front." Thirty-six prominent American Jews took out an advertisement in the *New York Review of Books* questioning the wisdom of Israel's policy of establishing new West Bank settlements.[7] They were roundly criticized in the American Jewish press as naive idealists washing dirty laundry in public. Nevertheless, a delegation of eighty equally prominent American Jews soon took out an ad in the *Times* to tell the world how much they supported Israel.[8] More significantly, in July 1978, Senator Abraham Ribicoff, one of Israel's chief supporters, also publicly questioned the wisdom of establishing settlements that so complicated the path toward peace: "I've been deeply disappointed by so-called Jewish spokesmen who tried to throttle expression by American Jews. There could be no greater disservice to the Jewish people than to suppress the diversity of thought that has been there for 5000 years."[9]

Just when it appeared that the peace process was beyond repair, in early September, Carter invited Sadat and Begin to Camp David for one last attempt at accord. After thirteen days of extremely arduous negotiations, Carter was able to get the two leaders to agree to what was presented to the world as a comprehensive plan for peace in the Middle East. In retrospect the Camp David Agreements marked the high point of both the peace process and the Carter presidency. Like the latter the Camp David Agreements were distinguished by an evident sincerity and a high moral tone that promised much more than they actually achieved. The agreements were not a peace treaty but were described as a "framework for peace," a terminology chosen to deemphasize the fact that, as they stood, the agreements actually constituted a separate peace treaty between Egypt and Israel. A separate peace, while no mean achievement in itself, was a far cry from the comprehensive settlement between Israel and the entire Arab world toward which Camp David was designed to be a way station.

Carter at Camp David wisely concentrated on settling those issues on which agreement was possible and left the intractable ones for the future, when it was hoped that changes in leadership or simply the momentum of peace would hasten their solution. The first set of agreements delineated Israeli/Egyptian relations and formalized many of the proposals that Sadat had brought to Jerusalem almost a year earlier. With extreme reluctance, Begin agreed to submit to the Knesset the question of dismantling Israeli settlements in the occupied Sinai. The Knesset's approval made possible an agreement under which a phased Israeli military withdrawal from the Sinai would give way to a peace treaty, with Egypt providing full diplomatic recognition and normal political and commercial relations. For Israel this was a stunning achievement; it removed from confrontation the nation that had supplied 80 percent of the manpower and casualties in the four previous Arab-Israeli wars.

Without Egypt's participation the Arabs could not wage war—at least not with their traditional objective of driving Israel into the sea. But neither could there be peace and stability in the Middle East without the Palestinians' acquiescence. Hence, the second part of the Camp David Agreements sought to fix principles for the solution of the Palestinian problem. To paper over fundamental disagreements between Israel and Egypt, the language employed in this "framework for peace" was necessarily vague and subject to conflicting interpretations, but at least it set down principles that would animate future negotiations. A portion dealing with the West Bank spoke explicitly of "the legitimate rights of the Palestinian people" and of "their just requirements."[10] More specifically, the document ultimately signed by Egypt and Israel stated that, after a transition period of five years, a final agreement on the West Bank consistent with Israel's security needs would be decided by Israel, Egypt, Jordan, and the Palestinians themselves. Despite Begin's disclaimers this language seemed to recognize some arrangement that went beyond Israel's original offer of a very limited autonomy for the West Bank.[11] To many, including former UN ambassador and Israeli foreign minister Abba Eban, it appeared that Begin had agreed to eventually give up the West Bank or at least had held out the strong possibility of doing so.[12]

The very ambiguity that had made the agreement possible soon came back to haunt its authors. Once outside the spotlight of Camp David, Egypt and Israel saw the proposals for the West Bank in accordance with their own assumptions and needs. Sadat, acting on the most optimistic interpretation of what he signed, brandished the agreements as a blueprint for Israel's eventual cession of the West Bank. Only by maintaining that the agreement would ultimately result in justice for the Palestinians would Sadat have any chance of reestablishing Egypt's place in the Arab world and of reconciling his fellow rulers to peace with Israel. Begin appeared to have had second thoughts about the treaty. Although on September 28 the Israeli Parliament approved the Camp David Accords and the removal of Israeli settlements from the Sinai, Begin quickly discouraged any expansive interpretation of the "Palestinian framework." He emphasized that Israel would retain the right to maintain sovereignty over the West Bank for as long as she felt her security needs demanded it—even indefinitely. He also advanced the rather strange notion that the autonomy contemplated at Camp David was the autonomy of the inhabitants, not of the land—as if autonomy could be meaningful without control of land use, infrastructure, and water rights. More seriously, under pressure from the religious right, Begin continued to establish Israeli settlements on the West Bank. Ominously, he spoke of both a "Greater Israel" and of the nation's "historical rights" to "Judea and Samaria."

Given these differences in conception and vision, it is hardly surprising that great difficulties arose when the time came to turn the framework for peace into an actual detailed treaty. Subject to increasing pressure from the right, Begin authorized further settlements and the "thickening" of existing ones. Sadat's position similarly hardened. When the Arab League met at Baghdad, eighteen of twenty-one states broke relations with Egypt in retaliation for Camp David. Even Arab moderates like Saudi Arabia and Kuwait cut off their financial aid to Egypt, estimated at between $350 million and $2 billion.

Stung by Arab rejection and mistrustful of Begin's intentions, Egypt now maintained that there should be a "correlation" between the two portions of the Camp David Agreement: in order for Egypt to sign a peace treaty recognizing Israel, the Jewish state must carry out the "Palestinian provisions" of Camp David. But since Sadat had previously conceded that there was to be no legal linkage between the two portions of the agreement and since Begin had no interest in an early settlement of the Palestinian question, the Egyptians were forced to back down. After months of fruitless negotiations, President Carter visited Egypt and Israel in March 1979 to break the deadlock. After much cajoling and many promises of American aid to both parties, Israel and

Egypt signed their peace treaty in Washington on March 26, 1979. The text of the treaty was based on a State Department draft of the previous November. Annexes provided an agreement on Israeli access to Sinai oil and stipulated that the exchange of ambassadors between the two countries would take place in nine months instead of three years as Egypt had desired. In addition, a joint letter to Carter from Begin and Sadat was attached to the treaty reaffirming the Camp David framework and promising that "Israel and Egypt will proceed with these provisions relating to the West Bank and the Gaza Strip."[13]

Talks on Palestinian autonomy began in May. But while an exchange of ambassadors between Israel and Egypt had resulted in an atmosphere of superficial normality, leading to the climactic April 1982 withdrawal of Israeli troops from the Sinai, there was no progress on the Palestinian part of the agreement. The PLO's refusal to recognize Israel, as well as its ostensible reluctance to settle for anything less than a Palestinian state, meant that the Israelis had no one upon whom to confer autonomy. But for many even the promise of limited autonomy seemed somewhat hollow in view of Israel's policy of increasing the number of Jewish settlements on the West Bank and her new religious claims to the area. In truth the talks on West Bank autonomy between Israel and Egypt were little more than a diplomatic charade, which in any case broke down in 1980.

The Camp David Accords presented American Jews with unprecedented dilemmas. After the fall of the shah and the second oil crisis, the United States had sought ever closer strategic, economic, and political ties with the Arab world. The moment that a real settlement of the Arab-Israeli conflict became possible, it was inevitable that Israel would be subject to tremendous pressure from the United States to conclude a comprehensive peace treaty, even one that Israel felt might compromise its security. American Jews now found themselves in this unprecedented position: challenging the Middle Eastern policy of their government as detrimental to the Jewish state while increasingly yielding to private qualms about Begin's policies. Within the confines of Jewish organizations, American Jews expressed growing doubt about the wisdom of alienating Egypt with an expansionist West Bank policy. They also worried about the future implications of ruling over one million West Bank Arabs.

Meanwhile the Israelis were themselves publicly voicing their own dissatisfaction with the Begin government. Shortly after the conclusion of the 1973 war a group of reserve officers founded the organization Peace Now to protest the Rabin administration's diplomatic rigidity and its expansionist settlement policies on the West Bank. The leaders of Peace Now, who included some of Israel's most decorated soldiers, believed that Begin sought to retain the West Bank for reasons other than security. They felt that the area, with its one and one quarter million Arabs, was a demographic time bomb, which, if incorporated into Israel, would ultimately result in the nation's ceasing to be either Jewish or democratic. Peace Now argued that the most reasonable option was to satisfy Palestinian aspirations and Israeli security needs by negotiating the creation of an autonomous Palestinian state. To Peace Now the continuing planting of settlements was a provocation that meant the loss of a historic opportunity to create a comprehensive peace. In April 1978, Peace Now mobilized over thirty thousand demonstrators in Jerusalem to press its demands. American Jews could not dismiss such attacks on Israeli government policies with comments about the inevitability of anti-Semitism.

Despite their growing private doubts and public criticism of Israel, most American Jews still gave the Begin government an extremely large measure of public support. All the traditional inhibitors of Jewish public criticism remained strong: the notion that only Israelis could accurately assess what is the best for them, the idea that since Israeli lives were on the line no outside advice was morally justified, and above all, the dogma that any public show of Jewish disunity could only benefit Israel's enemies. One new factor powerfully reinforced this impulse to circle the wagons. As Jews watched the unfamiliar spectacle of continuous American and international pressure on Israel, they felt their own isolation and vulnerability. Such feelings not only confirmed their psychological ties to Israel but made public criticism seem more of a betrayal than ever. Despite an increasing distance between American Jews and the Begin government, their public criticism of Israeli diplomacy and domestic policies remained muted.

The fall of the shah of Iran in 1979 produced new diplomatic and military equations that reinforced American Jews' suspicions of the Carter administration. The removal of the shah eliminated one of the principal foundations of United States policy in the area. The United States had depended upon Iran not only to supply NATO members with oil but as a strong ally along the Soviet border and as a guarantor of stability in the Persian Gulf. After the shah's fall, American policy makers were even more eager for a friendly and secure Arabia as a vital element of stability in the Persian Gulf. The Saudi monarchy's new importance made it imperative that the United States get Israel to agree to a Palestinian settlement congenial to Saudi and Arab sensibilities. American Jews began to suspect that the architect of Camp David was not above sacrificing Israel's security interests in return for an American rapprochement with the Arab world.

Many American Jews perceived what they felt was a pattern of anti-Israeli behavior that by the 1980 election would lead to wholesale Jewish defections from Jimmy Carter and the Democratic Party. In late 1978, hoping to obtain Saudi support for Camp David and moderation of oil prices, the United States sold sixty-two F-15 jets to the Saudis. When the Saudis went on to reject Camp David at the Arab League conference at Baghdad, the State Department tried to appease the Saudis by getting the PLO involved in the West Bank autonomy negotiations. Even more serious was the unauthorized meeting that took place on July 26, 1979, between Andrew Young, the American ambassador to the UN, and Zehdi Terzi, the official PLO observer at the UN. Such contact was a violation of U.S. policy forbidding any recognition of the PLO as long as it denied Israel's legitimacy, and it directly contradicted State Department instructions. Young, a former civil rights leader and the highest ranking African American official in the Carter administration, was forced to resign. President Carter, worrying about Black political support, went out of his way to praise his old friend. Many Black leaders attributed Young's dismissal to Jewish pressure, and their wrath descended upon American Jews. The old Liberal alliance between the two minorities was all but dead, and tension between them was high, especially over the issue of affirmative action. Harris polls of 1974 and 1978 had shown an increase in Black anti-Semitism especially among the educated.[14] Many Black leaders, seeking to bolster their own positions, bitterly criticized Israel and its American Jewish supporters and openly embraced the PLO. To many Jews the sight of Jesse Jackson singing "We Shall Overcome" with Yasir Arafat was morally bankrupt. In reality the Young affair was little more than a media event, since the Black leaders' rabble-rousing had found almost no popular echo. But the possible shift in American policy signified by the Young meeting was another warning to American Jews already disillusioned by the direction of Carter's diplomacy. More important, the eruption of Black rage directed specifically against American Jews again gave rise to that sense of Jewish vulnerability that is expressed by an emotional cleaving to Israel. In such circumstances the feeling of mutual beleaguerment continued to prevent any widespread public Jewish criticism of Israeli policies.

The Young affair was merely the most spectacular in a series of incidents in what American Jews came to consider Carter's abandonment of Israel. In March 1980, the United States voted for a UN resolution condemning Israeli settlement policy since the 1967 war, even in Jerusalem. The fact that the American government reversed itself the following day, attributing its earlier vote to a "failure of communication," indicated that U.S. policy toward Israel was, if not hostile, at least in disarray. Even more disturbing was the administration's brief diplomatic courtship of Iraq, one of Israel's most uncompromising enemies. In May national security advisor Zbigniew Brzezinski stated that "we see no fundamental incompatibility of interests between the United States and Iraq."[15] American Jews could take some comfort in that in this instance at least America appeared to be betraying both Israel and Egypt. President Carter's endorsement of a "Palestinian homeland" at a town meeting and America's refusal to veto a Security Council resolution in favor of removing all foreign embassies from Jerusalem merely intensified American Jews' feeling that Israel was being sacrificed. Most American Jews continued to ignore the Begin government's determination to do all it could to make the West Bank autonomy negotiations appear to be as unpromising as possible. Begin's continued support of West Bank settlements and his removal of duly elected West Bank mayors evoked little Jewish criticism. So strong was the American Jewish establishment's commitment to solidarity with Begin's policies that it was difficult even for Israel's Peace Now to get a hearing at the convention of American Jewish Federations.[16]

* * *

Outside the organized framework, individual criticism of Israeli policies reached a point where its public expression could no longer be contained. On July 2, 1980, fifty-six well-known American Jews, including three former chairmen of the Conference of Presidents, issued a statement that received front-page coverage in the *New York Times*. Entitled "Our Way Is Not Theirs," it was inspired by a June declaration of two hundred prominent Israelis and stated that Israel's best hope of security was through territorial compromise on the West Bank. It declared:

Extremists in the public and within the Government, guided by secular and religious chauvinism, distort Zionism and threaten its realization. They advance
the vicious cycle of extremism and violence, which nurture each other. Their
way endangers and isolates Israel, under-mining the ethical basis for our claims
to a life of peace and security.[17]

The declaration produced a flurry of responses, often more concerned with the propriety of public criticism of Israel than with the issues themselves. One hundred rabbis declared their support for Begin's
West Bank policies. The reaction of Howard Squadron, the new chairman of the Conference of Presidents, perfectly reflected the American
Jewish establishment's attitude: "I find it most regrettable that American Jewish leaders should engage in this kind of public debate concerning the policies pursued by the government of Israel. Such debate is always unjustified and divisive."[18] Rather, said Squadron, American Jews
should concentrate on areas in which consensus existed.[19] These consensus points were spelled out by Morris Amitay, the chief American
lobbyist for Israel, who stated that Jewish criticism of Israel's settlement policy was inappropriate because American Jews "have more important things to do." These included "encouraging American aid to
bolster Israel's economy, limiting the flow of arms to the Arabs, and assuring the election of legislators friendly to Israel"[20]—in short, what Israel tells them to do and no more.

Unsurprisingly, in the 1980 presidential elections, Ronald Reagan
reaped the benefit of Jewish perception that Carter was betraying Israel. Having produced Camp David, Carter seemed to take Jewish support for granted. Moreover, he considered Israel "a moral obligation."
By contrast Reagan emphasized that he considered Israel to be not just
a burdensome "obligation" but a "strategic asset." Reagan's emphasis
on military spending promised increased aid to Israel. At least in part
for these reasons, the 1980 election saw the lowest Jewish Democratic
vote and highest Republican vote in recent history. Forty-five percent
of American Jews voted for Carter, compared to 64 percent in the 1976
election.[21]

American Jews had hoped that Reagan's staunch anti-Communist
stance would translate into unequivocal support for Israel, since many
of Israel's enemies were clients of the Soviet Union. But the conservative oil-rich Arab states were strongly anti-Communist and had close
ties with the petroleum and commercial interests that had been among

Reagan's principal supporters. Contrary to American Jewish expectations, Carter's tilt toward moderate Arabs continued under his successor. As early as March 1980, Reagan asked Congress to approve the sale of extra fuel tanks, multiple bomb racks, and other "offensive enhancers" for the Saudi F-15s. Congress went along with the sale despite the fact that Carter's assurances that such equipment would never be put into Saudi hands was a condition of approval of the original deal in 1978. Howard Squadron protested against "the principle that solemn assurances to the Senate, made by one President, can simply be ignored by the next President less than three years later."[22]

The Reagan administration soon afterward proposed to sell the Saudis the AWACS early warning air defense system as part of an $8 billion arms package. Both the Pentagon and the State Department felt that AWACS, which could track all aircraft within a two-hundred-mile radius, was necessary to protect the Saudis against air attack from abroad. The implicit hope was that the AWACS sale would inaugurate a very close relationship between America and Saudi Arabia, resulting in Saudi moderation of oil prices and endorsement of Camp David. The Saudis themselves declared the sale to be the litmus test of American friendship.

Although Israel maintained that the sale of such sophisticated surveillance equipment would compromise its security, Israelis may have been more afraid that the sale would threaten their special relationship with the United States. From the American perspective, many congressmen, chastened by the example of Iran, cautioned against placing so much diplomatic and strategic reliance in the hands of an old-fashioned monarchy whose stability was in doubt. Critics of the proposed sale also questioned its expected dividends, since previous shipments to the Saudis had resulted in neither oil price moderation nor support for Camp David. Against these arguments stood the considerable weight of commercial and defense interests who stood to gain $8 billion, much of which could be used to defray the costs of weapons development.

The AWACS sale and its implications were the subject of long and bitter congressional debate. For the most part, the administration chose not to argue the military merits of the sale but stressed its symbolic value both as a bellwether of United States–Saudi relations and as an indicator of the new president's ability to govern. The debate profoundly distressed American Jews. Despite the most massive and sophisticated lobbying effort in American Jewish history, the sale was approved on October 8, 1981, by a vote of 52 to 48. For all their alleged political power, American Jews could not prevail on an issue that was of central importance to the president. Internationally, the vote appeared to compromise the long-standing special relationship between the United States and Israel. The American Jewish Committee characterized the vote not only as "a breach of prior assurances that such weapons would not be provided to the Saudis" and as "a reckless repudiation of the traditional longstanding commitment to Israeli security." A letter from President Reagan to Prime Minister Begin reaffirming traditional ties between the countries did little to assuage American Jews' unease, particularly when the State Department was expressing interest in a Saudi peace plan that envisaged a Palestinian state in return for only the vaguest Arab recognition of Israel's legitimacy.[23]

However disturbing the approval of the AWACS sale, the tone of the political debate that preceded it was even more shocking to American Jews. As senators and lobbyists had attempted to influence what all conceded to be a close vote, the anti-Semitic rhetoric Jews felt had been long banished from American public life now reappeared on Capitol Hill. In an attempt to muzzle American Jews and to shift the debate away from the actual merits of the proposed sale, Ronald Reagan invoked the specter of the "Israeli Lobby," declaring, "It is not the business of other nations to make American foreign policy."[24]

Congressman Charles Matthias of Maryland elaborated on Reagan's theme. He called for a distinction between ethnicity "which enriches American life and organized ethnic interest groups which were against the national interest."[25] Less subtle and nastier was the speech of Congressman Paul McCloskey: "'We've got to overcome the tendency of the American Jewish community in America to control the actions of Congress and force the president and Congress not to be even-handed."[26] The object of such "strategic anti-Semitism" was to cow American Jews into dropping their opposition to the AWACS sale by characterizing such opposition as being solely motivated by "Jewish considerations." Yet as non-Jewish a body as the U.S. House of Representatives had opposed the sale by an overwhelming 301 to 111. A national survey taken in the spring of 1981 found that fifty-four of sixty-three major American newspapers had opposed the AWACS deal.[27] Moreover, most of those who had opposed the sale had done so because they felt it was contrary to American interests to place so much reliance upon the traditional Saudi monarchy. To the everlasting credit of American Jews, the administration's smear tactics did not deter them from exercising their legitimate political rights as Americans. But the whole debate, which was later characterized by New York senator Daniel Patrick Moynihan as "openly anti-Semitic,"[28] reminded American Jews of their political vulnerability. Jewish leaders were particularly concerned that the immoderate statements of the political elites would give new license to popular anti-Semitism. To their great relief, opinion polls showed no increase in anti-Jewish feeling. But pressure on Israel had been accompanied by a direct attack on American Jews, this time not by disgruntled minority leaders but by those at the center of power.

As the AWACS debate had gathered steam, an escalating sense of their own and of Israel's vulnerability prevented American Jews from publicly expressing their disagreement with Begin policies. The publicity surrounding the AWACS debate had transformed the American Israel Political Action Committee (AIPAC) into one of the most powerful spokesman of American Jewry. Exclusively concerned with lobbying for Israel's welfare and eschewing the liberal agenda of most other national Jewish organizations, AIPAC was ideologically comfortable with both the conservative anticommunism of the Reagan administration and the territorial expansionism of Begin's Likud and established a good working relationship with both. It devoted itself with increasing effectiveness to communicating Israel's concerns to the Republican administration. AIPAC's new power derived from its ability to quickly mobilize thousands of lobbyists across the country. Under the leadership of Tom Dine, AIPAC freed itself from control of Jewish national organizations and paid less and less attention to the opinions of the broad spectrum of American Jewry. AIPAC's rise and its perceived power inhibited grass-roots Jewish dissent from Israeli policies.

Israel soon provided fuel for the dissenters. In June 1981 precision bombing by the Israeli air force destroyed the Iraqi nuclear reactor at Osirak. The Israeli government claimed this was an act of self-defense since the reactor would soon have been producing enough uranium to manufacture an atomic bomb. Since Iraq was one of the most radical of the "confrontation states," Begin maintained that this action had to be taken to avert another possible holocaust. Most American Jews accepted the prime minister's reasoning, which in retrospect appears to have been correct, despite the raid's suspicious coincidence with the

Israeli general elections that most experts had expected Begin to lose. World condemnation of the raid again deterred any possible American Jewish criticism. The United States supported a UN resolution condemning the Israeli action and suspended the delivery of four F-16 jets to Israel. Almost all saw this as unjust in the face of an action that was often compared to the U.S. response during the Cuban missile crisis, and American Jews almost unanimously deplored the State Department actions.

Israel's bombing of the PLO headquarters in Beirut in the summer of 1981 caused much greater concern among American Jews.[29] Many were appalled by the three hundred casualties, many civilian, caused by the raid. They worried that Israel had departed from the high ethical and moral position so vital to the American image of the Jewish state. In practical terms they also feared that the massive civilian casualties, whose impact was magnified by extensive television coverage, might damage the long-standing special relationship between the United States and Israel. When the United States again suspended F-16 deliveries, American Jewish organizations were quick to defend the raid publicly and condemn the new sanctions against Israel. But so great was the private dismay that Howard Squadron, the head of the Council of Presidents of Major Jewish Organizations, flew to Jerusalem to personally convey to Prime Minister Begin the great concern of his member organizations. A Gallup Poll taken for *Newsweek* magazine showed widespread popular disillusionment with Israel's policies among American Jews. By a majority of 53 percent to 34 percent, they felt that Begin's policies were hurting support for Israel in the United States.[30] They believed that Anwar Sadat had made a greater contribution toward Middle East peace than had the Israeli prime minister. But their general support for Israel remained as strong as ever. Most said they felt more sympathy for Israel than they had five years earlier and reported that their contributions to the Jewish state had increased or at least remained at the same level. Most significantly, despite their disquiet with Begin, American Jews felt—by an overwhelming majority of 63 percent to 26 percent—that America should not put pressure on Israel.[31]

But private dissatisfaction remained strong enough to trickle up to the American Jewish leadership. As early as January 1981, Edgar Bronfman, the newly elected president of the World Jewish Congress, stated in his inaugural address that Jews should not be expected to support Israel on every matter.[32] At the same convention a film was shown in which former president and longtime Jewish leader Nahum Gold-man, too ill to attend, advocated Israeli withdrawal from the West Bank and negotiations with the PLO.[33] In June 1981, Rabbi Arthur Hertz-berg, a past president of the American Jewish Congress, advocated the creation of a Palestinian state as ultimately in Israel's best interest.[34] Former U.S. secretary of commerce and past World Jewish Congress president Phlip Klutznick added to the growing public criticism of Is-raeli policy. In a November 15, 1981, article in the *Washington Post* he wrote that the PLO was the only party qualified to speak for the Pales-tinians.[35] Klutznick followed up by coauthoring a report that called upon President Reagan to strengthen the role of the United States as a mediator within the Camp David framework. Seeking a compromise between their own consciences and their fears of showing disunity be-fore the Gentiles, 140 prominent American Jews took out an anti-Begin advertisement in the Israeli daily *Ha'aretz*, in theory limiting their criticism to the Israeli public.

American Jews who considered themselves antiestablishment pro-gressives also were mobilizing. In December 1981 a group of seven hundred met in Washington, D.C., to found the New Jewish Agenda. Organized "to foster a progressive voice within the organized Jewish community," the New Jewish Agenda's founders hoped to attract pro-gressive Jews who had been alienated by Israel's policies and by the American Jewish establishment's acquiescence to them. At its inaugural convention the Agenda called for "direct negotiations based on mutual acceptance, including the creation of a Palestinian state."[36] In the fol-lowing months the New Jewish Agenda was soon engaged in vigorous media attacks upon the domestic and diplomatic policies of the Begin government. While the vast majority of Jews and Jewish organizations persisted in their refusal to criticize Begin publicly, private misgivings over his politics and abrasive diplomatic style continued to grow.

| | 4 | |

The Invasion of Lebanon

The invasion of Lebanon inaugurated a new era in Israeli history. All of Israel's previous wars had been struggles for national survival fought against sovereign states that had the potential to drive Israel into the sea. The war in Lebanon was directed against the PLO, a savage and uncompromising but weak adversary. Its objective was not national survival but the destruction of the PLO and of Palestinian nationalism.

More profoundly, the invasion of Lebanon created a crisis in the soul and identity of Israel and called into question the meaning of Zionism. In earlier conflicts the government of Israel had enjoyed the undivided support of the people. The invasion of Lebanon resulted in unprecedented wartime civilian protests and in the previously unthinkable: morale problems in the army. Finally, the invasion's most infamous result, the massacre of at least six hundred Palestinian civilians by Christian Phalangist forces allied with Israel, led to moral revulsion within Israel and to a questioning of Israel's claim to be a special moral nation.

In the United States the invasion dispelled the long cherished illusions of many American Jews. Amid great personal agony and soul searching, American Jews began to challenge the dogma prohibiting public criticism of the Jewish state, and their traditional desire to support Israel in her moment of trouble was modified by a growing recognition that such support could legitimately involve dissent from her policies. The Sabra and Chatilla massacres, which revealed Israeli leaders not to be supermen but subject to the human faults of mendacity and self-justification, transformed American Jews' passive acceptance of Israeli policy to active dissent.

The roots of Israel's invasion of Lebanon went back at least to the Lebanese civil war. The Lebanese constitutional covenant of 1943 had attempted to reflect the conflicting claims of the country's Maronite Christians and Muslims by apportioning political power on the basis of population. But the failure of subsequent increases in the Muslim proportion of the population to be reflected in political representation, as well as their general economic deprivation, had resulted in growing Muslim discontent. The gradual introduction of Palestinians into Lebanon further upset the balance between the country's Christian and Muslim communities. The Palestinians also provided an ideology of self-assertion and the weapons to counter the private armies of the Christian magnates who sought to retain their dominance. In 1969, following clashes between the PLO and the Lebanese army, an agreement was reached that permitted the PLO to operate in some areas independent of the control of the Lebanese government. As a result, the Christians expanded their own militias.

The arrival of thousands of armed Palestinians into Lebanon in 1971, after they were expelled from Jordan by King Hussein, set the stage for civil war. Fighting broke out in the spring of 1976 between the Christian militiamen on one side and the Lebanese Muslims and the PLO, who received training and arms from Syria, on the other. Yet Syrian support had definite limits. When in 1976 it appeared that the PLO was going to defeat the Christians and create its own state in Lebanon, the Syrian government of Hafiz Assad sent in a "peacekeeping force" to defend the beleaguered Christians, thereby substituting its own domination for that of a prospective PLO state. Palestinian forces were relegated to the south, where they mounted occasional terrorist raids against Israel. In response, the Israelis entered into an alliance with the Christians of southern Lebanon, later under the command of renegade Colonel Saad Haddad who had left the regular Lebanese army to set up his own militia. In return for their policing of southern Lebanon, the Israeli government provided Haddad with arms, training, and political support.

This Israeli-Phalange connection provided the spark for the invasion of Lebanon. Israel had pledged to defend the Phalangists against Syrian air power, and in April 1981 the Israeli air force destroyed two Syrian antiaircraft missiles in the Bekaa Valley. Israel considered the presence of the missiles a grave threat to its security and drew up plans to invade Lebanon in the summer of 1981. Only the intercession of the U.S. special envoy Philip Habib prevented the invasion.[1] But Israel's plans were kept intact by Begin's military advisor and soon to be defense minister, Ariel Sharon. They were hardly a secret. The necessity and even the route of the proposed campaign were extensively and publicly debated. Eight weeks before the actual event, NBC News anchor

John Chancellor gave his audience a precise summary of Israel's war plans including a possible move to occupy Beirut.[2] Sharon felt that an invasion of Lebanon would prevent PLO shelling of Galilee and that routing the PLO and Syrians would result in a Christian-dominated state friendly to Israel. According to this scenario, the crushing of PLO military power would also free the Palestinians of the West Bank and Gaza from PLO intimidation, enabling them to accept the Israeli interpretation of autonomy in the territories.[3] In short, Israel would use the invasion of Lebanon to crush the PLO once and for all.[4]

* * *

The invasion came a year later, and Israeli spokesmen presented it wholly as a retaliation for the shooting of the Israeli ambassador to Great Britain and as a defensive operation designed to deprive the PLO of territory from which to launch military attacks on Israel. The announced objective of "Operation Peace for Galilee" was merely to establish in southern Lebanon a forty-kilometer [twenty-five-mile] zone free of the PLO. Most agreed that Israel had a legitimate right to protect itself from possible attack. Toward this end, Israel sent ninety thousand men and five hundred tanks and armed personnel carriers into Lebanon, supplemented by massive air and naval support.

No sooner had the Israeli army achieved its limited objectives than disturbing news came from the war front. Once he felt that Israel could implement its larger plans without prohibitive military or diplomatic cost, Defense Minister Sharon had moved Israeli troops far beyond the government's initial self-imposed territoral limits, attacking both PLO and Syrian forces. Although rumors circulated that Begin had lost control of Sharon, it is more likely that the defense minister had Begin's consent for the operation.[5] Much of the cabinet was probably manipulated by Sharon into consenting to a war for which it had little enthusiasm.[6]

In its rush north the Israeli army left in its wake mass destruction of property and large numbers of civilian casualties. In Sidon, Lebanon's third-largest city, there were an estimated one thousand civilian casualties, and even Israel estimated that 30 percent of its buildings had been destroyed.'[7] One reason for the high number of casualties was Israel's use of American-made cluster bombs. Designed for use against enemy troop concentrations, cluster bombs exploded just above ground level, spraying shrapnel in all directions which explained the reports that between 30 percent and 50 percent of those wounded eventually died,

more than double the expected rate.[8] Much of this devastation was due
to the PLO's deliberate policy of settling in populated areas and refugee
camps. But whatever the justification or unavoidability of such casualties, the nightly television films of burning ruins and charred bodies
had an inflammatory effect on world opinion. By the time Israeli forces
reached the outskirts of Beirut, estimates of civilian casualties ranged
between 9,500 and 18,000, with at least 250,000 left homeless.[9] Israel
maintained that it had killed two thousand PLO guerrillas and one
thousand Syrian soldiers but that the campaign had resulted in only six
hundred civilian deaths.[10] Since the Israeli government seemed to consider all Palestinians guerrillas, such an estimate was more than a trifle
suspect. In the face of mounting criticism, Israel maintained that casualty figures were vastly exaggerated and that in any case the action was
ending a civil war that in the past decade had resulted in one hundred
thousand casualties.

The initial American response to the invasion was low-key, an appropriate reaction since many felt that the United States or at least Secretary of State Alexander Haig had given tacit support for Israel's action.[11] But aside from a call by Senator Charles Percy to cancel the sale
of seventy-five additional F-16 fighter planes to Israel, there was little
overt criticism in the Senate. In the House a resolution submitted by
Congressman Nick Rahal called for Israel to withdraw from Lebanon
and for the suspension of all weapons deliveries until it had been determined whether Israel's use of cluster bombs violated agreements that
the weapons be used only defensively. The resolution attracted only
fourteen cosponsors.

On June 22, Prime Minister Begin met with the U.S. Senate Foreign
Relations Committee. Many senators expressed extreme displeasure
with current Israeli policy, but the prime minister beat down criticism
by intimating that he had the support of President Reagan.[12] The fact
that Israel had advanced American interests by routing the Soviet-
supported Syrians argued powerfully in favor of continued American
support. In the *Washington Post*, Evans and Novak declared, "The Lebanon occupation has increased Israel's influence in the United States,
not reduced it."[13]

* * *

The vast majority of American Jews accepted the Israeli contention of
the invasion's necessity. A year earlier civilian casualties resulting from

the Israeli bombing of PLO headquarters in Beirut had caused widespread American Jewish protests. Now, since the military justification appeared to be clearer, even higher casualty figures were considered an unavoidable consequence of Israel's right to self-defense.

But American Jews were dismayed by the breadth and severity of world condemnation of the Israeli action. Even a majority of Americans, according to an NBC poll,[14] disagreed with the invasion. The Jewish state in peril, even if the peril was only rhetorical, caused the usual rallying around Israel in time of crisis. Whatever the private misgivings of their members, all major Jewish organizations totally supported the invasion. Those responsible for Israeli fund drives reported greatly increased collections since the invasion.[15] On June 18, Prime Minister Begin addressed an Israeli bond fundraiser at the Waldorf Astoria. The prime minister drew the loudest applause when he spoke of Israel's determination "to resist American pressure to withdraw from Lebanon before non-aggression was assured."[16] The image of Israel victorious but beleaguered and pressured by an ungrateful America had a galvanizing effect. The affair raised over $27 million. "Never in the past," Begin *kvelled*, "was the great Jewish community of the United States so unified around Israel, standing together."[17] Ironically, Begin's view was seconded, though from the opposite perspective, by columnist Nat Hentoff, whose *Village Voice* essay entitled "The Silence of American Jews" condemned those who were opposed to the invasion but refrained from saying so publicly.[18]

Both Begin's hyperbole and Hentoff's lament ignored the growing Israeli and American criticism of the war. As the Israeli army moved northward, there was increasing confusion about the objectives and conduct of the war. In a striking deprture from the past, many Israelis turned to European radio stations rather than official military reports to get what they felt was a more trustworthy account of events. A joke making the rounds in Jerusalem cited "the idiot in the ordnance corps who must have put all Israeli cannons back to front. Each time one opened fire, the army spokesman announces we're being fired at."[19]

The gallows humor marked a growing disillusionment. Rumors (later confirmed) circulated that some Israeli reserve divisions were not mobilized because of widespread opposition to the war within them.[20] Soldiers on leave from the front demonstrated against the war at Begin's office. On July 3 almost one hundred thousand people attended a Peace Now rally, which demanded an end to the war, negotiations with the Palestinians, and the dismissal of Defense Minister Sharon.[21] For a vulnerable people so conscious of the perils of disunity, such a demonstration in the midst of war indicated the degree of national concern. The dissenters were convinced that the defense of northern Galilee was a pretext to break the power of the PLO and force the West Bank Arabs to accept the Begin-Sharon concept of autonomy, which amounted to little more than outright Israeli annexation. Such a course did not enjoy a national consensus, and many Israelis feared that Sharon's ambition and Begin's extremism could lead to the ultimate downfall of Zionism and Israel.

A growing number of American Jews felt similar worries. The specter of massive civilian casualties, however justified by Israel, was contrary to the American Jewish image of Israelis as moral supermen. An official representative of the Israeli government reported that the most common reaction among American Jews to the high number of reported civilian casualties was to ask, "How could Israel do this to me?" This loss of Israel-based *nachas* (joy) expressed a deeper suspicion that such casualties had occurred as a result of the decision by Israel to push on to Beirut. To some American Jews, Israel's actions seemed to reach beyond the right of legitimate self-defense, which had provided the moral basis for all her previous campaigns. And the negative American reaction to the Israeli push toward Beirut brought the possibility of a decisive break between the United States and Israel closer than at any time in recent memory.

A poll commissioned by the American Jewish Committee (AJC) found American Jews evenly split, 41 percent to 40 percent, over the question of whether the West Bank should be returned to some form of Arab control in return for peace and secure borders; 18 percent were undecided.[22] Many of those who objected attributed Israel's policies to the excessive but forgivable zeal of Menachem Begin, whose overt religiosity legitimized him in the eyes of many American Jews. Some of those who felt strong disagreement rationalized their lack of criticism by maintaining that Israel would regain its virtue once Begin was no longer in power. The reason for such rationalization was evident. Their disagreement with the Begin government did not diminish by one whit their fierce emotional attachment to Israel. The AJC poll also found that 93 percent of American Jews considered themselves pro-Israel, 50 percent strongly so. Even more significantly, 83 percent of the respondents felt that if Israel were to be destroyed, it would "be one of the greatest personal tragedies in my life."[23] When combined with the traditional taboo on public criticism as only helping Israel's enemies, these emotional attachments ensured that even the relatively high level of public criticism of Israel would fail to reflect the internal dissatisfaction of the American Jewish community.

Mainstream Jewish leadership now had fewer inhibitions about questioning Israeli policy. Both Philip Klutznick, a past president of the World Jewish Congress, and Nahum Goldman joined former French premier Pierre Mendez-France in calling on Israel to lift its siege of Beirut and to negotiate with the PLO on the basis of mutual recognition. On July 4, sixty-six prominent American Jews, including seven rabbis, published a full-page advertisement in the *New York Times* in support of Israel's Peace Now movement. Entitled "A Call to Peace," the ad expressed "grave misgivings over the fighting in Lebanon" and advocated "national self-determination" for the Palestinians. "It is now the time for us as supporters of Israel to speak out critically about those Israeli policies which we know to be mistaken, self-defeating, and contrary to the original Zionist vision."[24] Signers of the statement included author Saul Bellow, critic Alfred Kazin, and sociologists Nathan Glazer and Seymour Martin Lipset. The last two had also contributed a piece to the *Times* op-ed page that warned that the continuing silence of American Jews encouraged the Israeli government's mistaken impression that they supported all aspects of the war.[25] These were but the opening shots in a campaign of advertisement and counter-advertisement by groups as diverse as Americans for Peace and Democracy in the Middle East, Americans for an Undivided Israel, the Ad Hoc Committee for Lebanese Freedom, and American Jews Opposed to Israeli Aggression. A resolution of the Central Conference of American Rabbis, the national organization of the Reform rabbinate, that condemned "the tragic loss of life in Lebanon" and expressed concern for "the soul of Israel and of the Jewish people" received one third of the assembly's votes.[26] After bitter debate the minority settled for a compromise that endorsed the Israeli incursion into Lebanon while expressing "deep concern" over the loss of life on both sides.

The spiral of public dissent continued after Begin brusquely rejected Reagan's Middle East peace plan as ultimately leading to a Palestinian state. Although the Conference of Presidents of Major Jewish Organizations followed Begin's lead by rejecting the plan as contrary to the spirit of Camp David, Reagan's attempt to bring Jordan into the peace process gained official approval of the American B'nai B'rith. In a similar vein, Tom Dine, the head of the American Israel Political Action Committee, Israel's lobby on Capitol Hill, declared that he "saw a lot of value" in the plan. When questioned about this unprecedented divergence from Israel, Dine replied, "We are an American organization. I see my job in strengthening American-Israeli relations. Begin sees his in strengthening Israeli security, and Reagan in strengthening American security."[27] Even the AJC, while stating that the proposal violated the spirit of Camp David, nevertheless saw some merit in it.[28] Most organizations, already uneasy as a result of the invasion of Lebanon, selectively distanced themselves from Begin by deploring the tone and speed of Israel's rejection of the Reagan initiative. A growing number of critics felt organizational half-measures were not enough. For those who felt that Israel's survival depended upon the public airing of criticism, the problem was how to break through the wall of illusions and rationalizations and make the mass of American Jews realize that the Israel they so cherished was in great danger. Unfortunately, it took the Sabra and Chatilla massacres to initiate this process.

Symbols evoke strong emotions. They serve to summarize whole series of events and to render abstract conditions concrete and graspable. In eighteenth-century France the fall of the Bastille, the royal fortress and prison, symbolized the end of Louis XVI's authority and issued a call to political revolution. In modern times the vast power of the media has greatly increased the potency of symbols as expressions and agents of change. Like the fall of the Bastille, the Sabra and Chatilla massacres were an extremely powerful symbol. But in Beirut it was a moral fortress that fell. The massacre of at least six hundred Palestinian civilians by rightist Christian forces under the very nose of the Israeli army, which had taken responsibility for their safety, produced one of the greatest upheavals since the founding of the state. The massive Israeli trauma was reflected in an equally intense soul-searching among American Jews, whose agony produced new boundaries, new rules of engagement, and a new willingness to legitimize criticism within their relationship with Israel.

* * *

On June 10 the Israeli army (IDF), surrounded the PLO guerillas who had taken refuge in the Muslim western part of Beirut. The IDF had hoped that the forces of the Lebanese front would occupy West Beirut.

But the Phalangist leader, Bashir Gemayel, felt that such action would jeopardize his chances of success in the coming Lebanese presidential election.[29] Israel was now in a dilemma. To let the PlO remain would negate their war aims at a time when the Israeli public was withdrawing support for the Lebanon invasion. To take West Beirut would involve hand-to-hand fighting with substantial Israeli casualties and a greater number of civilian deaths, which would further strain Israel's already poor public image. Rather than invade West Beirut, the Israelis besieged it.

For ten weeks the IDF shelled and bombed the city and cut off its food, water, and electricity. The bombing reduced substantial parts of the city to rubble, and in one day in March air raids killed three hundred civilians. World criticism of Israel and native Lebanese unwillingness to absorb punishment for the sake of the PLO enabled U.S. special envoy Philip Habib to mediate an agreement providing the PLO guerillas with safe passage out of Lebanon to any Arab country that would take them.

This withdrawal agreement was a tremendous victory for Israel: it avoided increased casualties and the bad publicity that would have accompanied the inevitable destruction of Beirut. The agreement deprived the PLO of the military and political base it had so laboriously built up in the past decade. By September 7 the PLO and the Syrians had completed their withdrawal from West Beirut. According to the UN, 8,300 PLO guerillas and 3,600 Syrians departed. Palestinian civilians were now left without military protection in a country that had experienced seven years of extremely bitter civil war.

On September 16, the morning after the newly elected Christian president of Lebanon, Bashir Gemayel, was assassinated, Israeli troops occupied Muslim West Beirut to "prevent possible grave occurances and to insure quiet."[30] This action, directly contrary to a firm promise that Israel had given to American envoy Philip Habib, reflected Israel's desire to control subsequent political developments[31] and was taken by Sharon and Chief of Staff Rafael Eitan without consulting the Israeli cabinet.[32] The next day the cabinet approved the decision to allow Christian rightist forces to rid the Palestinian refugee camps of any remaining guerillas.[33]

Accordingly, on September 16, as Israeli flares lit the night, Phalange forces entered the Sabra and Chatilla camps. Many of the Phalangists were natives of Damur, a Christian town destroyed by the PLO in

1976,[34] and they engaged in wholesale slaughter of defenseless civilians. The orgy of killing went on from Thursday evening until Saturday morning, when the Phalangist troops were finally ordered to leave the camps.

The massacre was a human tragedy for Israel; it was also a political disaster. Newspapers compared Sabra and Chatilla with My Lai and the Katyn Forest. At least six hundred civilians were butchered in cold blood. Israeli military intelligence later put the death toll in the two camps at between seven hundred and eight hundred; some estimates ran as high as two thousand.[35] The massacre did what nearly twenty years of Palestinian agitation had failed to do: it elicited a growing sympathy for the Palestinians and their dream of a Palestinian homeland.

Though the Israeli government blamed the massacre on the Phalangists, who, they said, were independent of any control, the Israeli public, along with the rest of the world, began to ask a number of discomforting questions. Why had the Phalangists, known to be spoiling for a fight—the same Phalangists who had massacred up to three thousand Palestinians at the Tel Zatar refugee camp in 1976—been allowed to enter the camps at all?[36] As opposition leader Shimon Peres stated in the Knesset, "You don't have to be a political genius or a famous commander. It was enough to be a country cop in order to understand from the outset that those militias which were emotional more than ever following the murder of their leader were likely to commit atrocities also among innocent people."[37] An equally disturbing question was why nothing was done once the killing started, since there was an Israeli army observation post only two hundred yards away that had received indications of violence soon after the Phalangists entered the camps.[38] And after the massacre became known and the Phalange refused the Israeli army's order to leave the camps, why did the IDF not move to expel them until Saturday morning, especially since the Israeli rationale for entering West Beirut was the maintenance of order?

The response of the Begin government was not reassuring. The prime minister maintained that the IDF had no inkling of possible trouble and when it occurred, did everything possible to put a stop to the killing. Characterizing charges that Israel was indirectly responsible as a "blood libel," he retorted, "When goyim kill goyim they come to hang the Jews."[39] Such a self-serving assertion sought to shift the alleged burden of responsibility from Begin's cabinet to the entire Jewish people. The prime minister's response to the anguish of Jews all over the world on that Yom Kippur weekend was to assert his own moral superiority. "No one will preach to us ethics or respect for human life."[40] And initially, he refused to appoint a commission to investigate who was responsible for the massacre, claiming that such a step would be an admission of guilt. Defense Minister Sharon's reaction was no more reassuring to American Jews, telling the Knesset that "we did not imagine in our wildest dreams that the Phalangists would act thus."[41] He branded demands for a panel of inquiry as irresponsible and dangerous and equated Israelis who pressed the government for an accounting with traitors.

Others disagreed. The daily *Ma'ariv*, which usually supported Begin, commented on the government's refusal to order a full judicial inquiry. "We must have enough integrity and strength of character to admit first of all to ourselves that by our entry [into West Beirut], by our presence, by our exaggerated confidence in the Phalangists, we are indirectly responsible for the terrible pogrom that took place there."[42] On September 25, over four hundred thousand, or close to 10 percent of the population, demonstrated in Tel Aviv in protest of the massacre and in favor of the appointment of a commission of inquiry.[43]

American Jews experienced the same emotions. Newspaper headlines alluding to their "anguish, "revulsion," and "worry" barely hinted at the turmoil the massacre produced in American Jews. Before Sabra and Chatilla the worry of those dismayed by Begin's rejection of the Reagan peace plan and by Israel's refusal to end the siege of Beirut had largely subsided with the conclusion of the agreement that permitted the withdrawal of the PLO guerillas. But the massacre confirmed the worst fears of those who distrusted Begin's policies and devastated those who had supported them. Such anguish had many roots. The massacre called into question the cherished notion that Israel was somehow qualitatively different from other countries. It was inconceivable that a nation of Jews with a five-thousand-year-old heritage of respect for human life and a history of suffering almost as long could be even indirectly involved in a massacre of defenseless civilians.

Ever since the earliest days of Zionism the state—whether dream or reality—had been seen as a light unto the nations. Yet this was more than a dream. In its three decades of existence, Israel had gained world praise for her concern for human welfare, her advocacy of social progress, and her simple devotion to justice. Its army of citizen soldiers, respected as one of the most efficient in the world, was felt to be committed to the same elevated vision. Beyond self-image or the fulfill-ment of its Zionist design, this moral vision was a vital component of the support Israel received from both Jews and non-Jews. As nothing else did, the Beirut massacre called Israel's moral stance into question. For some it symbolized the decay of Israeli public morality and the de-generation of classical Zionism into Israeli expansionism. At the least, it demonstrated the troubling growth of racism embodied in Menachem Begin's reference to Palestinians as "beasts with two legs."[44] While it was a vast overstatement to claim, as did the *Philadelphia Inquirer*,[45] that the massacre had resulted in a moral symmetry between Israel and the PLO, it did strip the mantle of righteousness away from Israel. Ameri-can Jews, who had bent over backward to justify all aspects of the Leba-non invasion, could not easily evade the implications of the massacre. Out of American Jewish agony and despair a new, more assertive but increasingly divided American Jewry would emerge.

* * *

The major American Jewish organizations reacted with the predictably vapid statements, deploring the massacre while supporting Israel. These were so carefully crafted that one could sympathize with the au-thors as they labored to express the depth of their dismay without say-ing anything that could be remotely construed as critical of Israel. The statement of the Conference of Presidents chairman, Julius Berman, was notable for its combination of faith and chutzpah. Given the Jews' own history, he declaimed, "any suggestions that Israel took part in [the massacre] or permitted it to occur must be categorically rejected."[46] The massacre, Berman and Rabbi Joseph Glaser of the Central Con-ference of American Rabbis (CCAR) argued, "illustrated the epidemic nature of terrorism."[47] From the opposite perspective, the American Jewish Congress stated that Israel must withdraw from Beirut and sever all ties with the right-wing Christians who were "as depraved as the PLO."[48] Responding to popular pressure, many Jewish organizations called for Begin to impanel an impartial commission to establish whether Israel was implicated in any way. After the prime minister's in-itial refusal to investigate the massacre, Alexander Schindler, former chairman of the Conference of Presidents, flew to Jerusalem to impress upon Begin the importance American Jews attached to such a step.

When speaking individually, Israel's critics went far beyond the consensus-bound moderation of the organizations. Edgar Bronfman of the World Jewish Congress advocated full support of the Reagan Middle East plan.[49] In a *New York Times* op-ed piece, Irving Howe called upon American Jews to condemn publicly Israel's recent policies. The course pursued by Begin and Sharon, he said, was more dangerous to the Jewish state than any possible use of public criticism by Israel's enemies.[50] Arthur Hertzberg demanded Begin's and Sharon's resignations; they had "squandered Israel's fundamental asset: its respect for itself and the respect of the world."[51] These views were echoed by a *New York Times* advertisement signed by several hundred Jewish intellectuals. As "Friends of Peace Now," they maintained that by allowing the Christians to enter the camps, the Begin government had some responsibility for the massacre.[52] The most stunning change in attitude was that of Martin Peretz, editor of the *New Republic*. A strong supporter of Israel's original move into Lebanon, Peretz characterized the Israeli decision to allow the Phalange into the camps as "a moral, political, and military enormity." Alluding to the mass demonstrations in Jerusalem, Peretz now took pride not in Israel's actions but in Israel's shame. Begin had to resign. "He can no longer speak for Israel's soul."[53]

A *Newsweek* poll found that 65 percent of American Jews considered Israel at least partially responsible for the killings, while 78 percent felt that Begin's policies were hurting American support for Israel.[54] In response to this unprecedented concern, Israel's president, Yitzhak Navon, told visiting members of the National Jewish Community Relations Advisory Council that they should not engage in public criticism; but if they had anything to say, they should do so quietly through proper channels.[55] When public pressure in Israel forced Begin to form a commission of inquiry, headed by Supreme Court president Yitzhak Kahan, American Jews were mollified, as this was "in keeping with Israel's moral and democratic traditions."[56]

The debate would grow more bitter still. Supporters and detractors of Begin alike were appalled at the magnitude and severity of world criticism of Israel. Equally disturbing was its asymmetry. While all joined in the clamor against Israel, few criticized the actions of the Phalangists or the PLO. Even worse, many of those who gleefully led the abusive tirades regularly committed far worse atrocities as a matter of national policy. Russia's carpet bombing in Afghanistan, Syria's brutal repression of domestic opponents, and Libya's encouragement of international terrorism hardly qualified them as moral arbiters. Against this background it was especially wrenching for American Jews to join a chorus at least partly composed of those who wished Israel ill. But the fact that the policies of Israel that they considered misguided were providing such potent fuel for anti-Semites made Jewish criticism all the more vital.

Begin's supporters detested such criticism as desertion in Israel's time of need. The old themes were again replayed, this time with a new emotional intensity and in full view of the media. In Chicago a group of Reform rabbis and synagogue presidents called for Begin's resignation.[57] In response, fifty-four other area rabbis condemned their colleagues' action as "promoting anti-Israel and anti-Semitic feelings on the part of the general population."[58] In Boston a self-appointed religious court of three rabbis attempted to excommunicate seven local Jews who had signed a New Jewish Agenda advertisement critical of Israel.[59] A kind of secular excommunication was attempted by Norman Podhoretz, editor of *Commentary* and one of Israel's most ardent supporters. In a long and bitter article entitled "J'accuse," he railed against those who held the world at large to one standard and Israel to a higher one. In such circumstances, he stated with more emotion than logic, "criticism of Israel deserves to be called anti-Semitic even when it is made by Jews or for that matter Israelis."[60] Rabbi Alexander Schindler forcefully admonished that "dissent should never be equated with disloyalty."[61]

In early February the Kahan commission of inquiry, so reluctantly empaneled by Prime Minister Begin, issued its report. It concluded that although the Phalangists alone were directly responsible for the killings, Israeli military and civilian leaders nevertheless bore an "indirect responsibility" in at least two ways. Top Israeli officials should have known that the violent history of the Phalangists and the assassination of their leader made a massacre likely to occur: "The decision on the entry of the Phalangists into the refugee camps was taken without consideration of the danger—which the makers and executors of the decision were obligated to foresee as probable—that the Phalangists would commit massacres and pogroms against the inhabitants of the camps, and without an examination of the means for preventing this danger." Second, "When the reports began to arrive about the actions of the Phalangists in the camps, no proper heed was taken of these reports, the correct conclusions were not drawn from them, and no energetic and immediate actions were taken to restrain the Phalangists and put a stop to their actions. This both reflects and exhausts Israel's indirect responsibility for what occurred in the refugee camps."[62] The commission recommended the dismissal of Defense Minister Ariel Sharon for "non-fulfillment of duty" and the removal of three senior generals.

American Jews' response to the Kahan report was strangely muted. General reaction went little beyond praising the report as illustrating Israel's democracy at work and deploring the lack of any similar inquiry on the part of the Lebanese. Most official spokesmen did agree that, for the good of Israel, Sharon should resign. The public positions that only a few years before had made pariahs of Breira advocates were now being expressed by members of the establishment. The invasion of Lebanon and the refugee camp massacres overturned the traditional patterns of American Jews' relationship with Israel. Near-universal faith in Israeli wisdom gave way to widespread skepticism and a great deal of activist protest. Henceforth, American Jews would subject Israeli to an increasingly critical scrutiny.

| | 5 | |

The Pollard Affair

Sabra and Chatilla unleashed a torrent of public criticism by American Jews. But that storm paled before the fury elicited by the Pollard spy case. As never before, the Pollard affair highlighted the tension underlying the tripartite relationship among American Jews, Israel, and the United States. It also laid bare the ideological gulf between Israel and American Jewry. Characterized by Abba Eban as Israel's "worst moment" in foreign policy, it completed the overturning of old conceptions and underscored a new set of cleavages between American Jews and Israel that neither side hesitated to play out in public.

On November 21, 1985, Jonathan Jay Pollard, an American Jewish civilian analyst for the navy, was arrested outside the Israeli Embassy in Washington, where he had unsuccessfully sought refuge. He was accused of being the most prolific spy in American history. From April 1984 to November 1985, Pollard used his high-level security clearance "to make virtually the entire U.S. intelligence gathering apparatus available to Israel."[1] At Israel's specific direction he allegedly stole 360 cubic feet of top-secret documents. Many of these concerned the state of Arab military preparations and their defensive alignments. Such information allegedly made possible Israel's October 1985 air raid on PLO headquarters in Tunis. While Secretary of Defense Weinberger's contention that it was impossible to conceive of greater harm was overstated, the damage to American intelligence was considerable. After Pollard's arrest, Israeli prime minister Shimon Peres adamantly disclaimed all knowledge of the affair. He characterized it as "a rogue operation" even though it was planned and carried out by a special intelligence unit attached to the prime minister's office. Peres then apologized and promised that those responsible would be "brought to account."[2]

Israel's mounting of a spy operation against the United States profoundly disturbed American Jews, who reacted with anger, incomprehension, and embarrassment. As the affair unfolded, their customary refusal to criticize Israel in public, already eroded by the Lebanon adventure, was replaced by a precisely directed rage against the Israeli government. American Jews were not simply stunned by the sheer stupidity of the operation—after all, allies may sometimes spy upon each other in the normal course of events—but Israel stole secrets from the one ally upon whom it had a nearly absolute dependence, on whose goodwill Israel's very existence might actually rest. Could any intelligence gathered by Pollard be so important as to put in peril the special relationship? Israel's use of an American Jew to carry out this dirty work was particularly abhorrent, since it gave substance to the old anti-Semitic charge of dual loyalty. At the very, least Israel's use of Pollard demonstrated contempt for American Jewish sensibilities; the old Zionist notion that the Diaspora is, as Hillel Halkin noted, "a depletable resource"[3] achieved a dramatic realization.

Israel's mistakes were compounded by the notion that the affair could be easily controlled. After all, was not the Reagan administration the most friendly in Israel's history, combining generosity with a political vulnerability that enabled Israel to convince a coterie of presidential aides of the wisdom of arms for Iran? Could not Israel count on the absolute support of American Jews and the Israel lobby, which in time of crisis invariably rallied to whatever cause happened to be the order of the day? That some of the most severe criticism of Israel would come from American Jews taking the side of the U.S. government probably never even occurred to Israeli policy makers. If Ronald Reagan was the "Teflon president," Israel saw itself as the Teflon country, immune from being called to account by either the United States or American Jews.

The Jerusalem government assumed that Peres's apology and promise to punish those responsible would suffice to defuse the affair. But rather than make a clean breast of the scandal, Israel persisted in stonewalling. The government was less than candid with a State Department delegation dispatched to Jerusalem to investigate the case and returned only a minuscule number of the stolen documents. The new prime minister, Yitzhak Shamir, who occupied his post though a power-sharing agreement with the Labor Party, strenuously resisted Israeli and American calls for an investigation of who was ultimately responsible. Even more serious was Israel's apparent failure to make good on its promise to punish those whose culpability was known. The special intelligence unit that had mounted the operation was disbanded and its head, Rafael Eitan, was forcibly retired. Eitan, however, was now given the lucrative post of director of Israel's largest state-owned company. Colonel Aviem Sella, the much-decorated air force officer who was Pollard's recruiter and first spymaster, became commander of Israel's second-largest air base. This was hardly punishment for the "rogue operation" that the government had claimed it was. The magnitude of the theft, the amount of payment to Pollard, and the sophistication of the requests for information all pointed to a single conclusion: the government was in on the plot from the beginning. And the public rewarding of Eitan and Sella added insult to injury and acted as a kind of diplomatic version of "I dare you to knock this chip off my shoulder."

The different political cultures of the two countries added to Israel's failure to appreciate American sensibilities, as the Jerusalem government simply didn't realize how profoundly disturbing the Pollard case was to relations with America and its Jewish community. For Americans, the rule of law is an absolute value, guaranteeing "liberty and justice for all." By contrast, Israel's most basic concern is the defense and welfare of the state as the guarantor of Jewish survival. Toward that end, Israelis developed a casual attitude toward the rule of law—first during the corrupt Ottoman period and later when they increasingly perceived British rule to be illegitimate. Through bribery, arms smuggling, and illegal immigration, the law was something to be gotten around. Correspondingly, in the post-state era, pragmatism often eclipsed legalism.[4] In some of their most famous foreign exploits, Israelis stole the blueprints for the French Mystere jet, illegally obtained tons of fissionable nuclear fuel, and commandeered a squadron of French patrol boats.

Since this chutzpa was often applauded by American Jews, some Israelis were genuinely mystified by the level of American shock elicited by their employment of Pollard. Clearly, as the general reaction demonstrated, the American government was not so malleable nor American Jews so supine as Israel had assumed. The Reagan administration was so incensed at the promotions of Eitan and Sella that it revoked the immunity from prosecution granted earlier to four Israelis implicated in the affair. Colonel Sella was now indicted on charges of espionage, and American military personnel were forbidden to have any contact with him or the air base under his command. It was within this acrimonious atmosphere that, on March 4, 1986, Pollard was given a life sentence, despite the fact that he had alledgedly cooperated with the prosecution. Crucial to the judge's decision was a forty-six-page memorandum submitted by Secretary of Defense Caspar Weinberger, stating that it was difficult "to conceive of greater harm to the national security than that caused by the defendant."[5] The severity of the sentence in part reflected American frustration with Israel's failure to take responsibility. Public reaction toward Israel was equally condemnatory. The *New York Times* wrote: "Every diplomat, whether in friendly or unfriendly capitals, assumes his phone conversations may have unlisteners. But for senior officials to conduct a major espionage operation against a close ally is a breach of trust of a different magnitude."[6] If relations with America were not bad enough, Pollard's sentencing had come less than a week after the Tower Commission's investigation of the Iran Contra scandal, which revealed Israel's role in inducing America to sell arms to Iran. The *Boston Globe* editorialized, "It's hard to decide which Israeli action is more outrageous—playing the United States for a fool in the Iran arms swap, or mocking us with deceitful conduct in the Pollard spy case."[7]

The two instances of Israel's alleged misdeeds provide an illuminating contrast. The issue of the Israeli role in instituting the Iran arms deal was allowed to die. That American foreign policy was determined by a country one fiftieth her size profoundly embarrassed the Reagan administration. Moreover, the Israeli government, the Israel lobby, and the American Jewish public were united in their determination to prevent Israel from being made a scapegoat for Irangate. The Pollard affair was a different matter. In the past, when Israel faced criticism from all sides, American Jews swallowed their private doubts and circled the wagons. Now, American Jews led the chorus, often raising their voices louder than anyone else. This was in part because the Israel that cooked up the scandal didn't conform to American ideas of morality or intelligence. Jonathan Pollard also represented some of the most unsettling nightmares of American Jews—a turncoat whose loyalty to Israel caused him to betray his native country. Pollard's statement that he was motivated by extreme Zionism and his assertion that Israeli vulnerability justified "situational ethics" seemed even more damaging to American Jews sensitive to the accusations of dual loyalty. What made this especially distressing was that this anti-Semite's dream personality was the direct and calculated creation of Israel.

The Pollard affair called into question the judgment, intelligence, and sensitivity of Israel's leadership. As William Safire, conservative columnist and an American Jew, wrote in the *New York Times*, "Jewish Americans feel doubly betrayed. Most of us are offended first as Americans at the spectacle of having our foreign aid dollars used to buy U.S. secrets. We are betrayed again by the easy exploitation of Mr. Pollard's Zionism by Israeli spymasters blind to the immorality of inducement to treason and the consequences of getting caught."After condemning the "moral cowardice" of Israel's leaders for failing to punish Eitan and Sella, Safire suggested that unless those responsible were punished, a likely consequence would be a "Pollard fine"—a cut in American aid. He then got to what, for him, was the heart of the matter. "American supporters of Israel cannot support wrongdoing here or there. In matters of religion and culture many of those supporters are American Jews, but in matters affecting national interest and ultimate loyalty, the stonewalling leaders will learn to think of us as Jewish Americans."[8]

Safire's condemnation was typical. Conservative rabbi and leading Jewish intellectual Jacob Neusner wrote in the *Washington Post* that America, "the freest and most open society Jews have ever known, is not only good for the Jews but better, for the Jews, than the State of Israel."[9] American Jewish leaders were unanimous in their support of Pollard's life sentence. The Israeli embassy in Washington and the five American consulates were deluged with phone calls from irate American Jews. So negative was the American reaction that many Jewish leaders flew to Jerusalem to express their dismay and to impress upon Prime Minister Shamir the importance of opening an official investigation. Referring to the Iran-Contra investigation in Washington, the head of the Anti-Defamation League explained that "the United States cannot ask of its friend and ally to do less than the American people, the American media, and the American institutions are asking of themselves.[10] The Conference of Presidents characterized the promotion of Aviem Sella as an 'irresponsible act" that left "a deep wound" in the relationship between Israel and America.[11] Hyman Bookbinder of the American Jewish Committee declared, "[Pollard is] a criminal found guilty in our system of justice. It's as simple as that. If it was perceived in America that we had come to the defense of Pollard because he's a Jew, our credibility as a Jewish community would be down to zero overnight and Israel would be the loser."[12]

Israelis reacted bitterly to American Jewish criticism. Zionist ideology had not prepared them to accept lectures from their American cousins. There also seemed to be a deep resentment of Israel's dependence upon America. Many Israelis considered Pollard a national hero. According to one survey, 90 percent of Israelis felt that their government should do something to help Pollard and his wife.[13] Ariel Sharon typically argued that the affair would not have occurred had the United States given Israel all the secret information it needed. Yitzhak Shamir, offended American Jews by maintaining that the United States should deny refugee status to Soviet Jews, thereby forcing them to immigrate to Israel. On a less ideological level some Israelis accused the Jewish leaders who came to Israel as merely trying to curry favor with the Reagan administration. As one official noted, "We have an embassy in Washington that talks to all of them and we are perfectly aware of the seriousness of the situation. But they come here to spit on us when we're in trouble because they want to be in good with the United States government."[14]

But it was Shlomo Avineri, well-known political scientist and former director of the Israeli Foreign Ministry, who raised the dispute to unprecedented levels of nastiness. Building upon the classical Zionist ideology that had animated Shamir's desire to close the United States to Soviet Jews, Avineri penned an article in the *Jerusalem Post*, "Letter to an American Friend" that paid homage to Hillel Halkin's similarly named Zionist polemic. American Jewish leaders' condemnation of Pollard, wrote Avineri, demonstrated "narrowness, insecurity and even cringing on the part of the American Jewish community." It was even comparable to Jewish leaders running for cover under Nazism or Khomeni. For all their protestation that America is the promised land, American Jews still had that old *galut* mentality—the condition of psychic insecurity inseparable from the Diaspora. "The test of really belonging and of real equality is when the going is tough. And when the going got tough your leaders acted like trembling Israelites in the shtetl, not like the proud and mighty citizens of a free democratic society."[15]

Outrage was too mild a word to describe the reaction of American Jews to Avineri's article. One Jewish leader called it an "intellectual temper tantrum." Reform leader Balfour Brickner fumed, "Of all the things that erupted, that was perhaps the most angering. I'm not some crypto-Israeli living with an exile mentality here in America, waiting for some opportune moment to pack my bags and run off."[16] Hyman Bookbinder was especially offended by Avineri's contention that American Jews abandoned Israel when the going got tough. "We've been on the battlefield too long for Israel—even been subjected to physical attacks—for anyone to throw that crap at us."[17] Suzanne Garment noted on the op-ed page of the *New York Times* that American Jews "have managed to help build a stable supportive relationship between America and Israel that could not have been imagined in 1948. . . . When American Jews condemn the Pollard affair so loudly, it is this accomplishment they see threatened."[18]

Abraham Foxman, Anti-Defamation League (ADL) head and one of the leaders accused of trying to ingratiate himself with the Gentiles, fired back one of the most articulate of the many "replies" to Avineri. Also appearing in the *Jerusalem Post* and entitled "Israeli Hutspa" (nerve), Foxman's reply noted that Avineri's misreading of American Jews was astonishing. "We raised our voices out of concern for Israel's security and not as you suggest, to ingratiate ourselves with the *goyim*." The Pollard case was a great breach of trust and Israel's cavalier reaction "borders on contempt for American sensibilities." It was not fear of anti-Semites but Israel's monumental stupidity that so disturbed American Jews. But the core of Foxman's offensive was a frontal attack on Avineri's basic contention that American Jews reacted like shtetl inhabitants.

You accuse us of behaving like "trembling Israelites in the *shtetl*" now when the going got tough. How quickly you forget, Shlomo, how tough it was in the past, defending the Suez invasion, coping with the attack on the Liberty, defending settlement policy, challenging the president over AWACS and the Reagan Plan, and getting caught by surprise over the annexation of the Golan Heights and East Jerusalem.

Do you think it was easy making the case for Israel while the IDF bombardment of Beirut was driven home nightly in vivid colour on American television newscasts? However much we were disconcerted by these policies, we neither shrank from our Jewishness nor did we waver in our support for Israel. And we aren't "cringing" when we disavow Israeli espionage against the U.S. in the strongest terms.

The real problem, Foxman said, was Israel: "If there is any collective neurosis among Jews over the Pollard affair it exists in Israel and not the United States" and comes from declaring the scandal a "rogue operation and then rewarding the rogues and from using and abandoning the Pollards. If there is any soul searching to be done it is in Israel."[19]

Foxman's reply was less noteworthy for the intensity of his public criticism than for his admission of disagreement with many of Israel's past policies. His recitation of past grievances demonstrates the breadth, depth, and duration of the gulf between many Jewish leaders' private reservations and their public support of Israel. But for all his indignation Foxman's critique omitted one awkward fact. If he and other leaders had not had a history of swallowing their pride, had not often suspended disbelief, and had not chosen to support policies that "disconcerted" them, then Israel might have hesitated before launching the Pollard fiasco.

In the short run, Israel appears to have been lucky. The Pollard affair did not result in either a diminution of public support for Israel or in an increase in anti-Semitism. A *Washington Post*/ABC poll taken shortly after the scandal broke showed the same level of support for Israel as in the spring of 1982 before the invasion of Lebanon. Another survey demonstrated that only 18 percent of the respondents even knew that Jonathan Pollard had spied for Israel. For the majority of Americans, Israel's political and moral shortcomings still paled in comparison to the bombings, hijackings, and kidnappings committed by her Arab enemies. In short, the Jewish state was viewed as "like us" and as a reliable ally.

The major damage to Israel wrought by the Pollard affair was among American Jews. While less than one in five non-Jews knew that Pollard had spied for Israel, almost two of three American Jews did.[20] For them the spy case was simply the last and most intolerable of a long line of scandals and cover-ups that demonstrated beyond the least doubt that Israeli leaders were not only human but at least as incompetent as anyone else. Animated by the growing perception that "Israel was too important to be left to the Israelis," American Jewish leaders became actively involved in the determination of its policies. Their vigorous condemnation of Israeli spying, their public disagreement with Prime Minister Shamir over Soviet Jewish immigration, and their extreme opposition to change in the "Who is a Jew" law bespoke a new willingness to join the political fray. A great taboo was broken as they engaged in the kind of public criticism of Israel forbidden for almost forty years. To their surprise, the sky did not fall, Israel did not appear to be any weaker, and their own position within the American Jewish community was similarly unthreatened.

* * *

For a half decade after his incarceration, Jonathan Pollard all but disappeared from the consciousness of American and Israeli Jews. Both were anxious to bury the traumatic episode, which was soon supplanted in immediacy and importance by the Intifada and the Gulf War. During this period only a small but vociferous group of religiously Orthodox and politically conservative supporters campaigned for the commutation of his sentence. They argued that Pollard's prosecutors reneged on a plea bargain because Secretary of State Caspar Weinberger, allegedly an anti-Semite, feared that Pollard knew too many secrets potentially damaging to the Republican administration.[21] The desire to shut him up, not the heinousness of his crimes—after all "he spied for Israel and not against the United States"—explained the severity of his punishment.

Pollard's supporters also took refuge in the claims of situational ethics. Confronted by the failure of the American government to fully implement an agreement to share intelligence with Israel, including the fact that Iraq was producing poison gas, Pollard chose to ignore his allegiance to America in favor of the higher morality of saving the Jewish state from its archenemy.[22] Disregarding that much of what Pollard stole had no connection to Israeli security,[23] they depicted Pollard not a traitor but a hero of the post-Holocaust age, abandoned by Israel, misunderstood by supine American Jews, and condemned to rot in jail by an anti-Semitic defense establishment. Some even called him "an American Dreyfus"—neatly sidestepping the fact that Dreyfus, unlike Pollard, *was* innocent.

These arguments had little effect on American Jews, for whom Israel's reaction to the Palestinian Intifada produced more than enough anxiety and contention. In the era of coalition building between the United States and Israel preceding the Gulf War, the Pollard affair was the last thing anyone wanted to remember. A 1991 American Jewish Committee poll showed that only 27 percent of American Jews felt that Pollard's life sentence was excessive. An even smaller number, 22 percent, felt that Jewish organizations should press for his release. Reflecting massive indifference, 57 percent of American Jews said they had no opinion on the question.[24]

The passage of time and the improvement of relations between America and Israel led to greater sympathy for the convicted spy. The monumental damage inflicted by Pollard's resuscitation of the old canard of dual loyalty existed almost exclusively in the Jewish mind, not in the American body politic. Israeli self-restraint during the Gulf War, which helped hold the anti-Saddam coalition together, restored the image of the Jewish state from oppressor of Palestinians to heroic victim of scud attacks. Pollard's advocates alleged that the information he had passed five years earlier had enabled Israel's civil defense to prepare for those attacks.[25] Additional focus on Pollard was provided in March 1992, when a divided federal appeals court, including future Supreme Court justice Ruth Bader Ginsberg, upheld his life sentence. But the dissenting judge, Stephen Williams, supplied ammunition for Pollard advocates by characterizing the government's disregard of its plea bargain as a "miscarriage of justice."[26]

In September 1992, B'nai B'rith called on President Bush to grant clemency to Pollard,[27] as did an October 25 full-page advertisement in the *New York Times* signed by 560 rabbis of all denominations. The text of this first major public request for a presidential pardon demonstrates the mentality of his new supporters: "We in no way condone acts of espionage. We nonetheless call upon you, Mr. President, to recognize that the lifetime sentence imposed upon Jonathan Pollard is unduly harsh and grossly inconsistent with the punishment given to other Americans convicted of similar and even worse crimes."[28] By shifting the terms of appeal from questions of Pollard's guilt or motivation to the narrower one of fairness of his sentence, they submerged their ethnic motivation into a universal concern for American justice. The American Bar Association maintained that disparity of sentence—the fact that other spies for friendly countries had received shorter sentences—provided the best grounds for any Pollard appeal.[29]

The new iniative met with only limited acceptance. Phil Baum, chair of the National Jewish Community Relations Committee, declared on the subject of Pollard: "This is not a Jewish issue and the ad does not make it one."[30] While Hadassah and the American Zionist movement pressed for clemency, the National Jewish Community Relations Council voted not to bring up the case in its first approach to newly elected president, Bill Clinton. In what would become a common theme they declared that "issues like health care, poverty, social justice, urban affairs—these were felt to be more pressing."[31] Probably reflecting an internal compromise, both the American Jewish Committee and the American Jewish Congress decided to request not clemency for Pollard but merely a presidential review of his case.[32] Two of the most influential Jewish organizations, the ADL and the Council of Presidents, maintained their policy of nonintervention.[33]

The era of good feeling that followed the signing of the Israeli-Palestinian peace accord in October 1993 sparked optimism among

Pollard supporters. They hoped that President Clinton would act favorably upon an appeal for clemency that reached his desk near the end of the year. As Abraham Foxman, earlier one of Pollard's severest critics, stated, "There is a new feeling in the American Jewish community. After the Israeli-Palestinian peace treaty the world and the Jewish community reconciled with Yassir Arafat. In the light of that we should be able to consider commuting Pollard's sentence."[34] Foxman's personal turnaround was robbed of some of its impact when the ADL still refused to support Pollard. But a clemency petition by one thousand rabbis, including the president of Yeshiva University and the chancellor of the Jewish Theological Seminary, demonstrated growing grass-roots support.[35] A substantial number of American Jews agreed with Michael Ledeen, a Jewish advisor on security to Clinton, who declared, "The man deserves everything he got, and more, both for the despicable acts he committed and for the damage he did to the American Jewish Community."[36] For Rabbi Avi Weiss, a principal Pollard advocate, the issue was equally clear cut. "He is sitting in jail because the Pollard case is an example of the cowardice of the American Jewish establishment."[37]

As Clinton pondered his decision, *Time* magazine revealed that Pollard had done untold damage by stealing a compendium of radio frequencies used by foreign military and intelligence sources and that these might have found their way to Russia.[38] Pollard's supporters condemned the story as a Pentagon-inspired leak designed to inflame public opinion against a presidential pardon.[39] Less easily dismissed was a letter from Secretary of Defense Les Aspen, long known as a strong supporter of Israel, that Pollard had on fourteen occasions tried to pass classified information from prison.[40] Citing "the grave nature of his offense and the considerable damage that his activities caused our nation,"[41] President Clinton rejected Pollard's appeal for clemency in March 1994. The shallowness of American Jewish institutional support was demonstrated by the silence that followed the president's decision. Indeed, the day after he rejected the appeal Clinton met with eighty leaders of the Conference of Presidents of Major Jewish Organizations, who not once raised the issue.[42] As the *New York Jewish Week* lamented, "250 organizations have spoken up on Pollard's behalf but his proponents have shown a glaring lack of passion."[43]

The arrest and conviction of CIA executive Aldrich Ames in early 1994 on charges of spying for Russia revived interest in the Pollard case. Ames, whose crimes were acknowledged by the Justice Department to have done much greater damage, received the same sentence as did Pollard. In addition, Pollard supporters speculated that Ames, while still occupying his CIA position, had tried to cover his tracks by attributing the damage he caused to the convicted naval spy.[44] On both grounds, Pollard's sentence was excessive and inhumane. This argument, which combined the American preoccupation with equal justice under the law with the quintessentially Jewish virtue of *rachmones* (compassion), attracted a new band of supporters. Milton Viorst wrote in a typical formulation, "Like most Jews I have no sympathy for Pollard, nor do I identify with the segment of my community that extols the purity of his motives. And yet as an American I have concerns about the sentence. This issue is not Jewish, it is an issue of elemental justice."[45] This argument attracted non-Jews as diverse as Theodore Hessberg, Pat Robertson, Carole Mosley Braun, and Benjamin Hooks. Prominent Jewish supporters now included Elie Weisel[46] and, in a triumph of symbolism, Mrs. Oskar Schindler.[47] But *rachmones* aside, most organized mainstream Jewish groups seemed reluctant to do more than go through the motions on Pollard's behalf. Ambivalent at best, they were unwilling to invest their prestige and political capital in a man they had castigated as a traitor, an embarrassment, and a nightmare. Recognizing this was Jonathan Pollard himself, who now decided that his path to freedom lay not through New York or Washington but through Jerusalem. Shortly after Clinton rejected his appeal, he applied for Israeli citizenship.

The success of his request depended on the Israeli government's public acknowledgment of its responsibility for the convicted spy. After his arrest, Israel had abandoned him and turned over crucial evidence in a futile attempt to assuage American and American Jewish wrath. But most of the Israeli public considered him a hero. The government secretly doubled his salary while he served his jail time.[48] An unrelenting campaign by Pollard's relatives and sympathizers, his alleged contributions to Israel's' civil defense during the Gulf War, and Israel's guilt about abandoning one of her "soldiers" led to a public outpouring of support for Pollard. In January 1993 eighty Knesset members signed a petition to President Clinton requesting clemency.[49] A year later the government's senior cabinet secretary publicly admitted that Pollard's spymasters were employed by Israel and that the state had "a moral duty if not a formal obligation to help bring about his release."[50] In November 1994, Prime Minister Yitzhak Rabin again requested presidential clemency. Henceforth, discussion of Pollard became a regular item of discussion at meetings between American and Israeli officials.[51] In November 1995 a popular play opened in Tel Aviv that criticized the Israeli government for using Pollard and then abandoning him.[52] It was reported that the prime minister's office was secretly funding Israel's Free Pollard Committee,[53] and a poll in *Maariv* found that 77 percent of Israelis favored the immediate granting of citizenship to Pollard.[54] Israel's granting of citizenship to Pollard on November 21, 1995, signified both an acknowledgment by the state that it had directly employed the American as well as an implicit promise to use its power to gain his freedom. Because it coincided with the outpouring of world sympathy following the assassination of Yitzhak Rabin, Israel's action elicited little notice or comment from the American or Jewish press.

Thus far Israel's increased efforts to free Pollard have borne no fruit. Its suggestion that President Clinton free the spy as a last gesture to Yitzhak Rabin fell on deaf ears even though the request was seconded by the Conference of Presidents, whose policy of nonintervention had been overturned by the assassination.[55] The fact that Israel had not fully absorbed the lessons of the Pollard affair and the opposing perspectives of Israeli and American Jews was demonstrated in an interview that Israel's ambassador to Washington, Itamar Rabinovich, gave to the daily *Maariv* in January 1996. Combining equal parts of chutzpah and unintended irony Rabinovich blamed Pollard's continued incarceration on "American Jews failure to speak in a unified voice."[56] Echoing the notion that somehow American Jewry had a duty to support Pollard, a *Maariv* editorial complained that "the militant fight for [Pollard's] freedom has been all but absent from American soil."[57]

Yet Israel's commitment to its new citizen seems beset with its own ambivalence. Pollard's supporters had hoped that newly elected prime minister, Benjamin Netanyahu, personally untainted by the Pollard scandal, would provide the final push for the spy's release. But when Netanyahu met President Clinton for the first time in July 1996, he did not even bring up Pollard, presumably because there were so many more important issues dividing them.[58] In addition, the freeing of Pollard and the welcome he would receive in Israel would reopen old wounds at a time when American-Israeli relations had reached a recent low point. This was a double defeat for Pollard advocates. If Israelis, who perceived Pollard as a hero, were unwilling to give his appeals priority, how could American Jews, whose perception of the spy was much more negative, be expected to do more? It was hardly surprising that, in August 1996, Clinton rejected for the second time a petition for clemency. Again there was almost no reaction from mainstream American Jewry.

As American Jews have become increasingly concerned with the Israeli-Palestinian peace process and the "Who is a Jew" question, Jonathan Pollard once again began to disappear from their collective consciousness. Most remaining support comes from the religious right. In January 1997, Alexander Schindler, past president of the Reform movement's Union of Hebrew Congregations and Israel Singer, the secretary general of the World Jewish Congress, visited Pollard to show "that Jews who are associated with the political center and left support Pollard's release on humanitarian grounds as much as those on the right."[59] Schindler's hopes aside, Professor Jack Wertheimer, provost of the Jewish Theological Seminary, was more on the mark when he wrote that on Pollard "the public policy arms of the American Jewish community remain largely indifferent. The current leadership of the Conference of Presidents of Major Jewish Organizations, the voice of American Jewry on international matters, appears unwilling to invest its prestige to press the governments of the United States and Israel to work out a deal."[60]

It was Jonathan Pollard himself, who had become an Orthodox Jew while in prison, who again provided the most telling commentary. In November 1997 he sued the Conference of Presidents in rabbinic court, claiming that "their unprincipled indifference toward me" constituted a refusal to honor the mitzvóht (religious obligations) of *Pidyon Shvuyim* (redemption of captives) and *Pikuach Nefesh* (saving of a life).[61] Whether Jonathan Pollard is a true captive and whether freeing him from prison would constitute saving a life is certainly open to debate, but the relative indifference of the American Jewish community toward him has long been demonstrated. American Jews' public and vociferous disagreement with recent Israeli policy has diverted much of the remaining support for the convicted spy. It is therefore ironic that it was the Pollard affair itself that did so much to legitimize and encourage such criticism.

Pollard's supporters in both Israel and America continued their efforts. In December 1997, Prime Minister Netanyahu sent a letter to Pollard expressing the hope that he would soon be a free man. For the first time the Conference of Presidents of Major Jewish Organizations sent a letter to President Clinton asking him to release the convicted spy. But reports that the letter was forced upon the conference leaders, who sent it three weeks later than promised—too late to coincide with a Netanyahu meeting with Clinton—indicated that the unanimity and zeal were more apparent than real.[62] At the same time the Central Conference of American Rabbis, an umbrella group of Reform rabbis, called for Pollard's release.[63] Having failed with previous arguments that his spying for an ally had done no real harm or that his sentence was disproportionate to those given others convicted of the same crime, Pollard's advocates now argued that he was guilty and had "paid his debt," and they pleaded for mercy on humanitarian grounds. As Rabbi Avi Weiss has noted, "Even Arafat, who murdered American diplomats in Khartoum, has been forgiven."[64] President Clinton remained firm, sending a form letter reply to the Conference of Presidents and refusing to meet with representatives of the Central Conference of American Rabbis.

In May 1998, after thirteen years of stonewalling, Israel, responding to public opinion, finally admitted that the Pollard operation was not a rogue affair but had had the sanction of the highest echelons of government. "The State of Israel announces that Jonathan Pollard acted as an Israeli agent" and "acknowledges its obligation to Mr. Pollard and is ready to accept full responsibility accordingly."[65] How seriously Israel took its responsibility was revealed when the issue of Pollard's release allegedly almost derailed the interim peace agreement between Israel and the Palestinians concluded at the Wye summit in October 1998. After a deal had been brokered to give the Palestinians control of 40 percent of the West Bank, Prime Minister Netanyahu insisted that President Clinton had promised to free Pollard. The Israeli prime minister threatened to bolt the conference, and it was allegedly only Clinton's counterthreat to recognize a Palestinian state that dissuaded him.[66] According to some sources, Clinton had been indeed ready to free Pollard, but a revolt by the intelligence community—most notably, CIA chief George Tenet's threat to resign—had caused the president to change his mind.[67] The most Clinton would do was to promise to review the case again.

Fearing that he might actually be freed, anti-Pollard forces, led by the military and intelligence establishment, came out of the woodwork. In December seven former secretaries of defense urged Clinton not to release Pollard and four past directors of naval intelligence called him a "traitor whose release would be totally irresponsible from a national security standpoint."[68] Sixty senators wrote to the president against clemency, including Jewish senators Frank Lautenberg, Diane Feinstein, Herb Kohl, and Joseph Lieberman.[69] The explanation given by Lieberman, an Orthodox Jew, was particularly revealing. His spokesman noted, "The Senator has been in several highly classified briefings on Pollard's actions and the repercussions of those actions and he feels pretty strongly that Pollard is guilty of serious crimes against the people of the United States.[70]

Apparently relying on information from the intelligence community, the *New York Times* and CBS News reported that Pollard had stolen secret codes and vital radio signals and compromised agents abroad.[71] These allegations were made more explicit in an article in the *New Yorker* magazine by Pulitzer Prize–winning reporter Seymour Hersh. Entitled "The Traitor" and, according to the *New York Times*, based on CIA leaks,[72] the article maintained that the damage done to American security was much greater than had previously been revealed. Pollard allegedly turned over to the Israelis not simply the reports of American intelligence but its sources and methods.[73] The information passed by Pollard included methods of data collection by satellite, a ten-volume code for the collection of electronic data from all over the world, a daily task list for intelligence services, and even the U.S. attack plan on the Soviet Union. Much of this material, alleged Hersh, was then traded by Israel to the Soviets in return for permission for Jewish nuclear scientists and others to emigrate to the Jewish state.[74]

In the face of the anti-Pollard cacophony the mass of American Jews remained quiet. The efforts of celebrities like Elie Weisel, Edgar Bronfman, and Alan Dershowitz simply did not resonate with the mass of American Jews. As Lawrence Rubin, executive vice chairman of the Jewish Council for Public Affairs, a pro-Pollard group, noted, "There are some people for whom Pollard's fate is a matter of intense concern, but it would be hard to say that it's a major priority for the organized Jewish community."[75]

The Pollard affair has served as a great barometer of Jewish communal security. The vociferousness of those who fight for Pollard's freedom despite his admission of "dual loyalty" demonstrates as nothing else the sense of security of contemporary American Jews. It is that sense of security that enables Pollard's Jewish detractors to condemn him as a traitor. On a personal level, Pollard's fate reveals the pitfalls of accepting the extreme Zionist line that American Jews must support Israel unconditionally, that the United States and Israel have the same interests and that Israel is the sole basis of Jewishness. For Pollard, whose politics appears to have become increasingly right-wing, there is a final irony based on Israel's continuing political and social evolution. If and when he is released, the possibly more pluralistic and liberal Israel to which he will immigrate may have little resemblance to the beleaguered and exclusivist state whose image had motivated him to spy in the first place.

| |6| |

The Intifada

The Intifada may be the most important event in the past twenty-five years of Israeli history. Armed with little more than their own appalling misery, the Palestinian youth of the occupied West Bank, Gaza, and even Israel proper engaged in a mass revolt against Israeli authority that transformed the relations between the two peoples. The revolt made it clear that the Palestinians would no longer be intimidated by the Israelis and gave rise to a new self-respect that ultimately enabled them to engage in fruitful negotiations with the Jewish state. The revolt also destroyed any Israeli illusions that they could occupy Gaza and the West Bank indefinitely with little cost to themselves and forced Israeli politicians and the public to examine the hard questions concerning the future of the territories that they had studiously ignored for two decades. Ultimately, this revolutionary transformation of both Palestinian and Israeli would lead to the Oslo Peace Accord.

* * *

The Intifada produced a second, less noted revolution. Whereas the first was fought in the streets with rocks, bottles, and Molotov cocktails, the second was fought by American Jews against a long history of Israeli psychological domination, and the battlefield was in synagogues, Jewish organizations, lobbying groups, and the Jewish press. American Jews' reaction to Israel's response to the Intifada was itself a mass revolt that forever changed their relationship with Israel. For the first time, mainstream Jewish American organizations, galvanized by the rank and file, not only criticized Israel for its past conduct of national defense but presumed to prescribe future courses of action.

Even before the outbreak of the Intifada, Israel's invasion of Lebanon and the Pollard affair had given rise to a new militancy among substantial portions of American Jewry. A 1987 American Jewish

Committee (AJC) poll found that a majority of American Jews (63% vs. 22%) felt it was permissible to criticize Israel. In September 1987 the American Jewish Congress criticized the failure of the Shamir government to engage in a peace conference concerning the future of the occupied territories. The Congress stated that the twenty-year occupation of Gaza and the West Bank was likely to cause "repressive measures and in the long run can only corrupt the values which are associated with the Jewish state."[1] It then called upon Israel to seek realistic alternatives to the military occupation.

Israel's reaction was immediate and predictable. Shamir termed the American Jewish Congress's initiative "a regrettable attempt to circumvent Israel's democratic process by appealing to friends abroad who do not vote in Israel."[2] Opposition leader Shimon Peres lauded the Congress and called on all American Jews to back his call for a peace conference. "Do you think that if you do not express a view, the United States government will not know there is a difference of opinion in Israel?"[3] Other American Jewish organizations were not yet ready to follow the lead of the American Jewish Congress. The American Jewish Committee stated that, while American Jewish criticism of Israel's aid to South Africa or of its conduct in the Pollard affair was permissible, discussion of security issues should be left to the Israelis. The Congress of Presidents of Major Jewish Organizations complained that "restraint in giving public advice to Israel on matters of security has been the tradition."[4]

Division among the leadership reflected the increasingly restive mood of the rank and file. At the Thirty-First World Zionist Congress in Jerusalem they engaged in a full-scale rebellion against Israel's political establishment over control of the Jewish Agency—the organization charged with distributing money for Israel collected throughout the world. Disenchanted by the agency's long record of inefficiency and corruption, the American representatives rejected two candidates backed by the Israeli government in favor of their own choice, a candidate who was unsupported by Israeli officialdom. Pressing for the religious rights of Reform and Conservative Jews in Israel, the American delegates called for the "complete equality of all streams within Judaism."[5] As one Jewish leader noted, "Israelis have always suggested we're in a partnership. If they really mean it, there should be no objection to our expressions of concern."[6] With the Intifada, American Jewish criticism soon became denunciation, and American Jewish assertiveness became a full-fledged revolt.

The Palestinian uprising, which so changed the history of the Middle East, began with an ordinary automobile accident. On December 8, 1987, an Israeli truck hit a van carrying Palestinian workers from their jobs in Israel to the Gaza Strip, killing four and injuring eight others. Immediately, the rumor spread that it was a premeditated murder in response to the killing of a Jewish settler the day before. That riots began in Gaza's Jebalya refugee camp was hardly unusual; that the rioters could not be intimidated was unprecedented. Troops sent to put them down faced stones and rocks thrown by otherwise unarmed teenagers, who refused to disperse and bared their chests, daring the soldiers to shoot them. The Arab citizens of Israel joined a ten-day general strike in the territories, and rioting soon spread to Nazareth, Jaffa, and East Jerusalem.

The auto accident only provided the spark. Arab defiance had been growing in recent weeks. Two weeks earlier, a PLO guerrilla had used a hang glider to breach the defenses of the IDF and kill six soldiers. His audacious action ignited emotional celebrations in the territories and helped break the myth of Israeli invulnerability. More immediately, the Arab summit meeting in Cairo, preoccupied with the Iran-Iraq war, had totally ignored the plight of the Palestinians.

But all of these precipitating factors paled before the root causes of the disturbances. During twenty years of Israeli occupation, the lives of many of the one and a half million Palestinians of the West Bank and Gaza had become nearly unendurable. While Israelis pointed with pride to the rise in aggregate per capita income, this was more the result of the appalling baseline than of any great advance from poverty. For most Palestinians, life in the territories was one of extreme deprivation, with little educational opportunity. For those who managed against all odds to receive a college degree, there were almost no appropriate jobs. Gaza's population of 750,000 Palestinians lived in an area twenty-five miles long by twelve miles wide, making the territory one of the most densely populated in the world. Many lived in misery and squalor, exacerbated by Israel's despotic control of the economy. For those who worked in Israel, there was the daily humiliation of passing through checkpoints, where they were often abused and insulted by military and bureaucratic authorities. For many observers the question was not why the revolt broke out but why it had taken so long. Israel's initial attempt to blame the revolt on external incitement and internal subversion ignored the mass misery of the Palestinians lest it be considered as evidence of Israeli shortsightedness and neglect.[7]

Twenty years of complacency kept the Israeli army and government from grasping the momentousness of the disturbances. Shortly after the riots began, Defense Minister Yitzhak Rabin left the country on a trip to the United States. The same week, Shmuel Goren, the coordinator of government activities in the territories, told the cabinet that "the situation will return to normal within a matter of days."[8] Israel's confusion and, to some extent, denial was shown by the government's inability to find a word to characterize the disturbances. Given the demonstrators' numbers and their military targets, the reflexive use of the term *terrorism* was plainly inaccurate. The disturbances' intensity, duration, and size also made the word *riot* inadequate. Nor did riot clearly describe a popular movement in which old men urged on participants and in which old women distributed onions to offset the effects of tear gas. Nor did it do justice to the rage that led young Palestinians, armed with stones, to refuse to disperse before the uzis of the IDF and to defy Israeli soldiers to shoot them. In the first weeks of the riots, twenty-two Palestinians were killed and twelve hundred were arrested.[9] Finally, the army began to talk of a "civil revolt against Israeli occupation."[10] But to so label the disturbances had unsettling implications, and official and unofficial commentators turned to the Arab term for the disturbances, *intifada*, or shaking off.

American Jews, no better able to assess the implications of the riots then were the Israelis, initially fell into old patterns. Shortly after the rioting began, the head of the Conference of Presidents, Morris Abram, said the disturbances were planned by the PLO. But after two weeks of mass violence, some criticism of Israel was voiced by liberals within organized American Jewry. Seymour Reich, head of the B'nai B'rith, publicly blamed Israel's continued occupation for the rioting, and Alexander Schindler, president of the Union of American Hebrew Congregations, stated that at least the violence had shocked Israel into realizing that it could not continue the occupation indefinitely. "The status quo sows the seeds of endless conflict . . . and it is a time bomb ticking away at Israel's vital center."[11] When the U.S. government condemned Israel's tough tactics in dealing with the riots, particularly its use of live ammunition, American Jews became increasingly divided and demoralized.

On the one hand, Israel itself had declared that it was engaging in an "iron fist" policy. Simultaneously, Morris Abram, the chairman of the Conference of Presidents, was trying to convince the State Department of Israel's use of restraint. On the other hand, many Jewish leaders warned that continued force could demoralize the Jewish community and erode support for Israel. For American Jews, the nightmare of being caught in the middle between Israeli actions, and American and world criticism was again occurring. Throughout the world the media increasingly compared Israel to South Africa. Most journalistic discussions of the Intifada failed to present a long-term view of the conflict, which, while not exonerating Israel, at least would have provided some balancing perspective. In early January the United States endorsed a UN resolution urging Israel to drop its plans to deport nine Palestinians whom it considered leading activists and organizers of the disturbances. The United States had abstained from the UN condemnation of Israel on December 22 that deplored the shooting of civilians. This was the first time since 1981 that America had joined the world body in a formal condemnation of the Jewish state.

Daily confrontations, filmed by Israeli and international television crews and broadcast throughout the world, continued to grow. New Israeli tactics for suppressing them—imposing curfews on entire Palestinian districts for days at a time—had little effect. On the contrary, such measures tended to unite Palestinians of all classes. Rubber bullets, arrests, and tear gas were all similarly ineffective in cowing the Palestinians. One Israeli officer quoted in the daily *Yediot Ahronot* said of the situation in the Gaza, "The residents control the main road. There is not a car that goes into the strip without getting stoned. Stones are also thrown on soldiers and not just civilians."[12] A pamphlet distributed by the Islamic Holy War Organization exhaulted, "God has frightened the enemy. They have run from children and been repelled by women. Their bullets have failed to repel your stones."[13] Hirsch Goodman, the military correspondent for the *Jerusalem Post*, was in agreement: "The mood of the high command can best be described as one of confusion, even dejection at its failure to end the unrest."[14]

As Israel's frustration grew, the military constantly sought an effective means to put down the riots. Classic riot-control tactics had been ineffective. The use of live bullets by soldiers untrained in riot suppression had resulted in an inordinate number of deaths but had failed to intimidate the Palestinians. Israel's desire both to limit civilian deaths and to reinstill fear in the Palestinians led to Defense Minister Rabin's infamous statement on January 19 that the Intifada would now be suppressed with "force, might, and beatings."[15] From the Israeli point of view, the replacement of bullets by beatings seemed to make enormous sense. Beatings would reduce the death rate, be more effective than arrests, and rekindle in the Palestinians the fear of authority that was necessary to suppress the rebellion. As General Avram Mitzna, the chief commander of the Israeli Defense Forces (IDF) on the West Bank put it, "when young people go into the streets and prevent merchants from opening their stores, we will grab whom we can and some of them will be beaten. They have to understand that they . . . can't make stone throwing and tire burning their national sport and expect no consequences."[16]

While rational in the abstract, Rabin's formula was a policy and public relations disaster of unprecedented magnitude. It permitted Israeli soldiers, frustrated by their inability to deal with young stone throwers, to engage in sanctioned mass violence. Deployed not against the military enemy for which they had been trained but against civilians their own age and younger, who daily subjected them to taunts and stones, young IDF members were increasingly humiliated by their inability to suppress the Intifada. Given their feelings of impotence and rage, the official policy of beating gave official sanction to a violence that soon became indiscriminate. In the first three days after the initiation of the new policy at least three hundred Palestinians were treated for broken bones or other severe injuries. One observer characterized the conduct of the IDF as "one riot chasing another."[17]

The beatings were a disaster for army morale and for Israel's sense of itself. The army sent teams of psychologists to units in the Gaza Strip because it was worried about the effects of new crackdowns on the mental health of the troops."[18] Yet however great, the internal disaster was minimal compared to the negative effects of the beatings internationally. With an estimated thousand journalists on the West Bank and Gaza, the beatings and victim interviews provided searing television images that humanized the violence. Meanwhile they did nothing to place Israeli conduct in perspective, giving neither the long-term reasons for the occupation nor the short-term provocations to the Israeli soldiers. All that mattered was the incredible power of the video clips and their built-in bias toward the underdog: teenagers against soldiers, stones against guns, and women against personnel carriers. These images did more to cement the view of Israel as a brutal occupier than twenty years of Palestinian propaganda. They made the abstract concrete and individualized mass actions so that people could emotionally identify with the rioters. The fact that the victims, fully cognizant that they were fighting a "television war," had often initiated these brutal encounters made not a whit of difference to the camera nor to most of the viewers.

Within Israel, Rabin soon became a lightning rod for criticism from both the left and the right. On January 24 in Tel Aviv, between twenty thousand and fifty thousand people protested against the Rabin's "iron fist" policy, the largest antigovernment demonstrations since the Sabra and Chatilla massacres. Others supported the policy but were appalled that Rabin had called attention to it by announcing it to the world. In America both Jews and non-Jews were upset by the beatings, which appeared to negate everything that Israel had stood for since its foundation. American Jews, approximately three-fourths of whom considered themselves liberals, were particularly upset. On January 4 the Council of Presidents' head, Morris Abram, an early supporter of Israel's response to the Intifada, telephoned Rabin to express "sharp criticism" and "shock" over the new policy. Obviously uncomfortable in his new role, Abram stated "that while it was not his business to tell the Defense Minister what to do, American Jewish organizations would no longer be able to defend Israel's actions in the territories."[19] Privately, most Jewish organizations burned the telephone lines between New York and Tel Aviv to express similar sentiments.

A public cable to Israel's president, Chaim Herzog, from Alexander Schindler, head of the Union of American Hebrew Congregations (UAHC), highlighted the mass concern. The beatings were "an offense to the Jewish spirit that betrays the Zionist dream. We plead with you to bring this madness to an end."[20] While Schindler was heavily criticized by many fellow Jewish professionals for going public with his criticism, he reflected, far more than his detractors did, the stance of American Jewry as a whole. Other Jewish Americans characterized Rabin's policy as inhumane and indefensible or complained that "Israel used to be a light unto the nations—now it is like the nations."[21]

The *New York Times*'s A. M. Rosenthal, long a fervent supporter of Israel, noted in an editorial entitled "Jews Must Not Break Bones" that the government's handling of the Palestinian demonstrations had "been tragically wrong." "The policy of trying to beat the demonstrators down with fist and club can break not only Palestinian bones but

Israel's respect in the world and in herself."[22] Since the world did not accept such behavior from Jews, he called upon Defense Minister Rabin to resign. Even Israel's strongest American Jewish supporters characterized the beating policy as "one of the worst mistakes you've ever made."[23] Assessing the ire of both Jewish and non-Jewish Americans, Israel's ambassador to the United States engaged in a classic diplomatic understatement when he said the riots "had hurt Israel's image of being an enlightened country."[24]

The old soldier Rabin was unrepentant. In a published reply to Alexander Shindler he challenged him to find an alternative policy. Rabin further maintained that measures were being taken that would control indiscriminate beatings, and in any case, no one had died from them.[25] But reports from human rights groups documenting cold-blooded beatings seemed to many to be even more chilling than the image of a military out of control. According to a report by the Boston-based Physicians for Human Rights organization, beatings were now administered to injure, not kill, and there was medical evidence to indicate that most were administered methodically, not in the heat of conflict.[26] The fact that many casualties admitted to hospitals were direct neighbors implied a plan of indiscriminate searches and beatings. Moreover, new information soon proved Rabin's assertion to be incorrect. Whatever the purpose and methodology of the beatings, Palestinians began to die from them.

Rabin's contention that new measures would control indiscriminate beating was similarly flawed. In late February, CBS News broadcast videos showing IDF soldiers beating two Palestinian youths caught throwing stones. The videos, shot through telephoto lenses, caught the soldiers pounding the arms of the captives as they were held down, kicking them, and striking one in the head with a helmet. Israelis were shocked, not only at the brutality—the beating lasted a half hour—but by the fact that one of the soldiers was from a kibbutz, traditionally the repository of Israel's highest values. The appalled commanding general, Avram Mitzna, required all officers above the rank of captain to watch the videotape. In the meantime, beatings continued at the rate of one or two dozen per day. Nor was this the worst. The new policy had evidently communicated to some Israeli soldiers that it was open season on Palestinians. In one incident, four soldiers were accused of attempting to bury young Palestinians alive, using a bulldozer—and this was only after the bulldozer driver had refused a direct order to run over them. All of Israel, even the far Right was shocked by this latest atrocity. As General Mitzna said, "Even in my wildest dreams, I would never imagine such a thing."[27] As world condemnation reached an ever higher pitch, Prime Minister Shamir's reaction recalled Menachem Begin's response to criticism stemming from the Sabra and Chantilla massacres. Refusing to acknowledge any wrongdoing on Israel's part, Shamir maintained that most of the criticism came from enemies of Israel or from anti-Semites. "Nations that didn't open their mouths when we were brought to slaughter were now going crazy at the sight of rioters getting their punishment. It is nothing but the fact that they love to see us beaten and knocked down and hate to see us defending ourselves with strength forcefully and remaining alive."[28]

But it was not only "the nations" but American Jews who were "going crazy." In late February, Israel called an assembly of American Jewish organization representatives to a meeting in Jerusalem to hear presentations by Labor and Likud concerning the Intifada and the future of the territories. After hearing the two opposing views of Labor and Likud, Council of Presidents' head Morris Abram came down firmly on the side of the opposition, who endorsed Secretary Shultz's idea of convening a multinational peace conference in November. "I have the strong feeling that now is the time to get the peace process on track. I have made it perfectly clear that the status-quo is not indefinitely acceptable to American Jews."[29]

While the contention of a *New Republic* essayist that "identification with the Zionist enterprise has become a source of anxiety and shame" was a bit extreme, Jewish journals were now filled with articles entitled "Should American Jews Publicly Criticize Israel?" and "Israel's Moment of Truth."[30] The answers to the former were ever more affirmative. Many said public criticism of Israel was permissible only on issues that concerned Americans directly. But for an ever increasing number, fear of the results of remaining silent had overcome the traditional reluctance to speak out publicly on issues of Israeli security. Those who argued against any public criticism of Israel fell back on the arguments of the past three decades—that any such discussion would give aid and comfort to anti-Semites and weaken the Jewish unity that was so vital to Israel. An op-ed article in the *New York Times* by Woody Allen, criticizing Israeli conduct—"I am appalled beyond measure by the treatment of rioting Palestinians by the Jews"[31]—became a particular target of conservative criticism. The actor/director was accused of superficiality and of directing his criticism not so much at Israel but at his gentile friends before whom he found himself embarrassed. Even Elie Weisel condemned those who criticized Israel but who had not been notable supporters earlier.

Such objections to Jewish criticism of Israel neglected two important points. Criticism can be a product of engagement and bespeaks the critic's caring about the object of his or her ire. Moreover, the motive of a critic, even if ignoble, does not mean that the criticism might not be correct.

Commentary magazine devoted a whole issue to the relationship between American Jews and Israel. Maintaining that "never perhaps has criticism of the state of Israel by American Jews been so open, so wide-spread and so bitter as it is today,"[32] the journal hosted a symposium to investigate the origin and implications of the upsurge of Jewish criticism of Israel. Given *Commentary*'s conservative orientation, it was not surprising that the majority of the symposium's forty-nine participants had a distinctly rightist bias. Many of the participants variously blamed the new open criticism of Israel on the psychic residue of the 1960s, the culture of narcissism, and a bankrupt liberalism. Some had particular contempt for the media, which they blamed for the crisis, thereby removing the necessity of focusing on the real problem— namely, the origin of all those devastating negative images. Somewhat more cogent was the case they made that the world's focus on Israel's transgressions was a displacement of Holocaust guilt—that some critics took comfort in the fact that Israel's oppressive acts showed that Jews too, given the chance, could act ignobly. Indeed, the *Boston Star* expressed just this kind of hyperbole when it wrote that "the horrors in the territory evoke Czarist pogroms, Babiyar and Nazi death camps." But it was impossible to delegitimize all critics.

Those in the symposium who criticized Israel simply stated that it was the Jewish state's policies and nothing else that elicited public criticism. Many spoke of their fear for Israel's soul, a stance some conservatives lampooned as pretentious posturing, masking an embarrassment before the non-Jewish world at Israeli action. Pretentious though it might have been, the expression of fear for the Jewish soul bespoke a genuine turmoil, the origin of which was not fear nor embarrassment before the Gentiles but the deepest American Jewish impulses. In poll after poll a majority of American Jews had long maintained that a commitment to liberal values and social justice were a vital component, perhaps *the* vital component, of Jewish identity. Indeed, it has been argued that a continuing commitment to liberal values is the key to Jewish continuity.[33] If American Jews were obsessed with Israel's image, it was not so much out of concern with how it played in Peoria but because it was seen as a reflection of themselves. And if this kind of obsession with image was the product of unrealistic expectations, Israelis had for three decades trumpeted the notion that Israel was truly a special state.

What was especially noteworthy about this Jewish criticism of Israel was that it persisted alongside the kind of general criticism of the Jewish state that had long caused American Jews to reflexively rally around Israel. In early March thirty U.S. senators, including some of Israel's strongest supporters, sent a letter to Secretary of State George Schultz criticizing Prime Minister Shamir's "reluctance to trade land for peace and to support Secretary of State Shultz's effort to convene an international peace conference."[34] What made the letter extraordinary was not only its public nature but the fact that it had been circulated by two Jewish senators and signed by some of Israel's strongest supporters, including Senators Edward Kennedy and Howard Metzenbaum. The fact that American politicians, a breed most sensitive to public opinion and to the Israeli lobby, could engage in such actions demonstrated more than any poll how far American Jewish support for Shamir's policy had fallen.

Shamir visited the United States, where he rejected the main points of the American peace initiative and lashed out at American Jews who sought to push him toward a peace conference. In a speech to the Conference of Presidents he evoked a familiar theme. "We believe that only those who must bear the consequences of agreements on their flesh, those who must shed their blood to defend their country, can decide what risks to take in pursuit of peace."[35] While his speech was applauded by most delegates, some, including Albert Vorspan of the UAHC, confronted the prime minister by maintaining the right of American Jews to disagree with Israeli policy. Shamir's firmness reflected the hardening of positions in Israel following a bus hijacking that killed three Israelis and the killing of a fifteen-year-old girl, allegedly by Palestinians but later proven to be the result of a stray bullet from an Israeli bodyguard. Yitzhak Rabin, the man behind Israel's policy of "force, might and beatings," was now Israel's most popular leader, and Shamir was merely reflecting public opinion when he announced in April that the rioters would be "crushed like grasshoppers."[36]

At the time no one knew how literal the prime minister was being. A few days later the Israeli Secret Service killed Khalil al Wazir who, under his nom de guerre Abu-Jihad, was the PLO military commander who planned the 1978 commuter bus bombing in which thirty-five Israelis had been killed. But Wazir had been targeted not for past crimes but for allegedly directing the Intifada.[37] So anxious were the Israelis to put down the revolt that they abandoned their policy of not assassinating top PLO leaders. The news of Abu-Jihad's death set off the worst rioting of the rebellion. Fourteen Palestinians were killed.

As Israel marked its fortieth anniversary with a three-day holiday, the mood was anything but celebratory. The country's deep divisions were symbolized by the contrasting statements of the Right and the Left. Former chief military rabbi Shlomo Goren stated, "We are fulfilling the vision of our prophets of the messianic era." The other national view was expressed by leftist gadfly Yeshayahu Leibowitz: "On the seventh day the State of Israel turned its victory in the six-day war into a historical disaster. On that day we decided the war was a war of conquest, not a war of defense, and we changed the direction and even the meaning of the State of Israel."[38] Whether to protest Israel's policies or out of fear of the violence of the Intifada, American Jews canceled their anniversary trips, and hotel occupancy dropped by 50 percent. Tourism Minister Avraham Sharir directed his ire at American Jews. "The heart hurts that the Jews were the first to turn their backs on us and not come."[39]

As U.S. pressure on Israel intensified, American Jews continued to express their own growing doubts. In early May, Rabbi Albert Vorspan, the vice president of the UAHC, published in the *New York Times Magazine* his personal diary dating from the beginnings of the Intifada. Entitled "Soul-Searching," the excerpt was a devastating attack upon both Israel's policies and the failure of American Jewish organizations to make public the depth of their dissatisfaction with them. The problem, said Vorspan, a man at the very center of organized Jewry, was that American Jews "have made of Israel an icon—a surrogate faith, surrogate synagogue, surrogate God."[40] As a result, "We in the field of Jewish Community Relations have lost sight of our role. We have ceased to be champions of social justice and become cheer leaders for failed Israeli policies."[41] Vorspan ended by noting that he had been derided as unrepresentative for confronting Shamir. Public opinion polls now demonstrated that it was Vorspan's critics who no longer reflected the rank and file. By spring 1988 fully 30 percent of American Jews felt that the occupation would "erode Israel's democratic and humanitarian character," compared to 11 percent before the Intifada. The fact that, three years later, Vorspan would receive one of organized Jewry's highest humanitarian awards would reflect the acceptance within organized Jewry of the notion of a "loyal opposition." When Secretary of State Shultz met with American members of the PLO National Council, the American Jewish reaction was muted because they still hoped for a peace conference and because they had such trust in George Shultz, "who has not and would not put Israel in jeopardy."

The Intifada now evolved from large-scale demonstrations to arson and Molotov cocktails. Particularly shocking was a firebomb attack on Dizengoff Center, a popular mall right in the center of Tel Aviv. Rabin ordered that Palestinians carrying fire bombs could be shot on sight, even by civilians, the latter order earning him a rebuke from the U.S. State Department. The gap between Israel, Americans, and American Jews was highlighted by the Israeli attitude toward Defense Minister Rabin, the architect of Israel's harsh response to the Intifada. Rabin, as the most popular politician in Israel, was called by the daily *Ha'aretz*, "the real prime minister."[42] In late June he traveled to the United States to meet the leaders of American Jewish organizations. In his direct laconic style he assessed his prospects: "I am not expecting much applause."[43]

As the summer wore on, criticism of Israel continued, increasingly augmented by American Jews. Israel sought to deport a Palestinian apostle of nonviolence, Mubarak Awad, whom they considered responsible for the Intifada's tactics of civil disobedience and refusal to pay taxes. Since Awad was an American citizen, the State Department warned of "damage to our bilateral relations." Amnesty International issued a scathing report accusing the Israeli military of killing hundreds, beating thousands, and detaining five thousand Palestinians in a harsh desert prison camp.[44] American Jews were becoming similarly alienated. The liberal journal *Moment* ran a debate on the previously unthinkable—the desirability of a Palestinian State. Support for Israel was also eroding in the center. In early Septemeber, Ismar Schorch, chancellor of the Jewish Theological Seminary and a leading figure of the Conservative movement, decried "the romantic mind set of the national camp in Israel and its unwillingness to trade land for peace. The consequences of this have been nothing less than a catastrophe—a misguided adventure into Lebanon, a government held hostage on the West Bank, the privatization of arms, brutalization of Israel's youth and the refusal to address the Palestinian problem."[45]

What made the chancellor's criticism especially significant was that, while the Reform movement tended to support labor and the Orthodox supported Likud, the Conservatives had occupied a centrist position. But now Schorch spoke for his movement, as 84 percent of Conservative rabbis were willing to give up land for a secure peace, although many were still hesitant to criticize Israel publicly. Disenchantment with Israeli policy now also reached the heart of the American Jewish establishment. In October the leaders of the three most eminent Jewish organizations, the American Jewish Committee, the American Jewish Congress and the B'nai B'rith Anti-Defamation League stated that the American Israel Political Action Committee (AIPAC, which generally supported Israeli policy) was out of step "with the consensus of the organized Jewish community."[46] They called upon AIPAC to coordinate its lobbying activities with them and announced the formation of their own joint political committee with the clear implication that it would lobby independently. The desired coordination did not take place.

American Jews looked to the coming Israeli election to replace Likud with Labor, which had promised to convene the peace conference upon which so many had focused their hopes. The Labor Party raised an estimated $10 million in the United States, while Likud raised about half that amount. But the election produced a stalemate, with neither Likud nor Labor able to gain more than one-third of the Knesset seats. The frustration and humiliation brought about by the Intifada had led to mass defections from the major parties. The electorate moved to the right, strengthening the religious parties who now seemed to hold the balance of power. As Shamir tried to form a government with the religious parties, he made all sorts of promises, including a pledge to change the conversion law so that only conversions made under Orthodox auspices would be legally recognized. This change, long desired by the Orthodox religious establishment, led to the first "Who is a Jew" crisis.

American Jews saw the proposed law as an attempt to delegitimize their own brand of Judaism, and they erupted with unprecedented fury. For almost two months, enraged American dignitaries visited Israel to express their extreme concern. Jewish intellectuals and laymen filled newspapers with polemics against Shamir. Individuals and organizations daily announced their withdrawal of financial support from the Jewish state. Some of this vitriol might have been displaced rage against Shamir's Intifada policy, a security concern that some American Jews had been reluctant to discuss publicly. But whether politically or religiously based, division between the mass of American Jews and Israel's official policies was now wider than it had ever been. When combined with the fact that Israel now had a caretaker government, the fluid political situation was ripe for new initiatives.

The first came from an ad hoc group of American Jews, including Rita Hauser, former representative to the UN General Assembly; Menachem Rosensaft, chairman of the Zionist labor movement in America; and Abraham Udovitch, professor of history at Princeton University; on December 7 they met with a seven-member PLO contingent for three hours. After their discussion, they announced that the PLO was sincere about peace and that the United States should end its ten-year ban on discussion with them. Udovitch noted, "A historic change has taken place in the attitude and the analysis by the PLO of the situation in the Middle East.[47] The Israeli Foreign Ministry pronounced itself astonished. Most American Jewish organizations criticized the American representatives and felt they had become a tool for Arafat's propaganda. While a few characterized the participants as "renegades," the thrust of most criticism was not that the meeting should not have taken place but that it would have been better had elected Jewish representatives engaged the PLO. The participants replied that they were perfectly ready to be exploited if it were to advance the cause of peace. Indeed, the meeting with the PLO appears to have been an important catalyst, at least in the short run. The following day, Yasir Arafat issued a statement rejecting terrorism. While it fell short of the explicit assurances demanded by the United States, and Morris Abram characterized the statement as "a thinly disguised version of the same old propaganda line," the majority agreed with Alexander Schindler that it "appears to be a step in the right direction and merits further study and consideration."[48]

The Reagan administration embraced Arafat's trial balloon. On December 14, after the PLO chairman said he would recognize UN resolutions 242 and 338 (which laid the basis for a negotiated Mideast settlement), the State Department announced the start of a "substantive dialogue" with the PLO. It named Robert Pelletreau, the American ambassador to Tunisia, as the conduit for the new discussions. Hardly a coincidence, the United States took this revolutionary step at the low ebb of Israel's relations with American Jews. The Shamir government expressed "shock and disappointment" at the "PLO's monumental act of deception." "In our estimation," said Shamir, "the PLO isn't capable of accepting the American conditions which contradict the very essence and the very reasons for the existence of the PLO."[49]

American Jews refused to follow Israel's lead on what was potentially the most significant security decision in decades. Morris Abram said that deeds, not words, mattered but did not criticize the United States' offer to talk with the PLO. Most major Jewish organizations were similarly silent. Caught between their dissatisfaction with the Intifada, worried about changes in the status quo, and enraged by the "who is a Jew" crisis, American Jews were no longer willing to kowtow to Israel even on issues of security. Thirty-eight percent of American Jews, according to one survey, agreed that "it was good that the United States decided to talk with the PLO," while only 28 percent disagreed.

In late December, Yitzhak Shamir sought to broaden the political base with which to resist expected American pressure. Abandoning his courtship of the religious parties, he formed another coalition with Labor. Since the exclusion of the religious parties ended the "who is a Jew"crisis, American Jews were ecstatic. Many believed that their protests had prevented Shamir from forming a coalition inimical to their interests. The new government, still headed by Shamir, remained as hard-line as before. In an effort to dampen Palestinian euphoria over U.S. recognition, the army authorized soldiers to shoot any Palestinian erecting a roadblock, throwing a stone, or burning a tire and to destroy the homes and confiscate the property of stone throwers. The State Department now issued its own report on Israel's violations on human rights. While conceding that it was able to get so much information because of Israel's open and democratic society, it strongly condemned unjustified killings by the IDF. "Israeli soldiers allegedly used gunfire in situations that did not present mortal danger to troops, causing many avoidable deaths and injuries." In most cases, the unjustified killing did not even result in disciplinary action or prosecutions. American congressional leaders warned Israel that its anti-Intifada tactics jeopardized its $3 billion annual aid package.

In an effort to counter the pressure against it, Israel convened a Jewish solidarity conference in mid-March to which it invited fifteen hundred leaders to Jerusalem to express support. No sooner had the conference opened than a top secret report from Israeli intelligence to the cabinet was leaked to the press. It was blunt in its appraisal: The Intifada could not be controlled. The government would find a political solution only by talking to the PLO. Within the PLO some elements were truly ready to work for a real peace. In a speech to the solidarity conference, the prime minister reiterated his opposition to talks with the PLO even as some members of the audience urged him to reconsider.[50] If this were not embarrassing enough, *Ha'aretz*, one of Israel's most respected newspapers, now became the first major publication to call for direct talks with the PLO. Even when subject to government pressure at the scene, the assembled conference delegates, most of whom were Americans, would do no more than express a general support for Israel while making clear that they did not always agree with Israeli policies.[51] Like much of the Israeli population, the assembled delegates, although hand-picked by the Shamir government, were themselves divided on the desirability of direct talks with the PLO.

Meanwhile, American Jewish supporters of peace were working to build grass-roots coalitions and to establish contacts with Palestinians, some of whom were closely identified with the PLO. Around the same time that the Jewish solidarity conference met in Jerusalem, Columbia University hosted "The Road to Peace," a gathering planned and sponsored jointly by the Israeli journal *New Outlook* and the Palestinian newspaper *Al Fajr*. It was endorsed by the Friends of Peace Now and the American Committee for Palestine Affairs. Its participants included Israeli peace activists, high-ranking PLO executives, and many prominent Arab and Jewish Americans. All stressed the imperative need for immediate talks between Israel and the PLO. In the nation's capital, a similar interfaith conference, held at Washington Cathedral, also brought Israelis, Palestinians, American Jews, and Arab Americans together to emphasize the need for negotiations. It was sponsored by the U.S. Interreligious Committee for Peace in the Middle East, a coalition of Jewish, Christian, and Muslim leaders, including at least one thousand clergy. Its forty-member board of directors boosted no less than fourteen rabbis, including such luminaries as Arthur Hertzberg, Balfour Brickner, and Marshall Meyer. Brickner's address to the conference encapsulated the changes taking place in the larger community: "Many people in this room remember when meetings like this were held in secret—some thought it was dangerous . . . now we are out of the closet and the doves are flying—not high enough but we're airborne and visible."[52]

To increase such visibility, American Jewish advocates of territorial compromise formed Nishma—the Hebrew word for "Let us listen." Chaired by Theodore Mann, former chairman of the Conference of Presidents; Earl Raab, a noted social analyst of American Jewish Affairs; and Henry Rosovsky, dean of Harvard College, Nishma saw its task as disseminating the views of those Israelis who sought withdrawal from the territories as part of a secure peace agreement. Toward this end, it distributed the report of Tel Aviv University's Jaffee Center for Strategic Studies which concluded that the status quo was untenable and called for the eventual creation of some form of Palestinian state. A significant number of American Jewish elite "opinion makers" were galvanized by Arafat's new moderation to envisage the possibility of a new relationship with the Palestinians.

In an attempt to deflect the welter of criticism, Shamir, during a visit to Washington, offered elections to the Palestinians of the West Bank and the Gaza Strip for the purpose of electing of non-PLO representatives to discuss the future of the territories. But the offer carried a condition: the Intifada had to be ended. That was as unacceptable to the Palestinians as the Palestinians' counterstipulation that Israel must first end its occupation was to the Israelis. Shamir's sincerity was rendered suspect by an accompanying threat—that if the Palestinians did not accept the elections Israel would restrict their freedom of movement and end their employment within Israel.[53] In an attempt to elicit a more flexible stance, Secretary of State Baker, in a speech to AIPAC, urged the Shamir government to give up "the unrealistic notion of a greater Israel."[54] Significantly, American Jewish critics disagreed not so much with the substance of his speech as with its blunt tone, which only gave fuel to Shamir's opponents on the right."[55]

AIPAC, the Shamir government's most powerful American supporter, prevailed upon ninety-two senators to send a letter to Baker urging him to fully support Shamir's election proposal. AIPAC then sent a letter to the Bush administration stating that Israel still had much congressional support—and proved it by attempting to restrict U.S. contact with the PLO.[56] Yet AIPAC itself was under fire. A group called the Jewish Peace Lobby, composed of at least one hundred rabbis and several dozen well-known academics, moved to form their own lobbying organization. "Up to now a single organization has presented itself as speaking for the Jewish community. Their view of what it is to be pro-Israel is to give largely uncritical support for any action of the Israeli government. We have a different conception."[57] While rejecting the use of American Jews as a lever against Israel, the new organization proposed to lobby for an Israeli discussion with the PLO leading to the eventual formation of an independent Palestinian state. The organization seemed to reflect a growing dissatisfaction. According to an AJC poll, more than half the American Jews stated that Israel had "acted wrongly" in its response to the Intifada, and one-third said that it was a good thing that the United States had opened the dialogue with the Palestinians. Clearly, AIPAC no longer spoke for at least a substantial minority of American Jews.

By September, six months after Shultz's original proposal, American and American Jewish frustration with Shamir's refusal to accept a peace conference reached a boiling point. Secretary of State Baker told Israel to either be more flexible or simply admit that it had never been interested in a peace conference in the first place. Shamir remained obdurate and bluntly rejected the U.S. proposal for a peace conference, saying that even though Israel was "on a collision course with the United States," he would stand firm.[58] In a most telling instance of public dissent, forty-one past and present officials of major Jewish organizations told the prime minister that he must trade land for peace. They also admonished Shamir, who was in the United States to address the General Assembly of the Council of Jewish Federations, not "to mistake courtesy for consensus or endorsement of all the policies you pursue. . . . We owe you honesty and clarity as well and it is in this spirit that we write this letter."[59]

The leadership reflected pressure from below. In a poll for the AJC, Steven Cohen found a high level of support for Israel in general but less in younger groups and perceived "a growing gap between what is Jewish in Israel and what is Jewish in the United States."[60] On the specific political situation, the polls revealed a similar ambivalence. A national survey of American Jewish leaders found that 76 percent favored Israel's trading of land for credible guarantees of peace. While a majority was still deeply suspicious of PLO intentions, 73 percent favored Israel's talking with the PLO if they renounced terrorism. Furthermore, the leaders, who included Jewish Federation professionals, volunteers, rabbis, and organization heads, maintained (by a 43% to 35% majority) that the Palestinians had a right to their homeland.[61] Arye

Naor, a former cabinet minister who spent a month in the United States, concluded that "more and more [American] Jews are keeping aloof from Israel's politics, and they do not participate in discussions and other activities, as they always used to do."[62]

After the failure of Labor to form a new government in March, following the fall of the Shamir government over the peace process, the relationship between Israel and American Jews deteriorated further. Many Americans felt that Shamir had misled them with a proposal for a peace conference that he had never intended to implement. When his caretaker government greatly increased the number of settlements it was building and moved fundamentalists into the Christian quarter of Jerusalem adjacent to the Church of the Holy Sepulchre, even AIPAC criticized these moves. A *Jerusalem Post* correspondent noted of his recent visit to the United States, "Everywhere I turned Americans, particularly American Jews, were stunned by the cumulative events of utter stupidity and moral insensitivity (their description) that seemed to seize the Israeli body politic."[63] Moreover, American Jewish leaders were criticizing Israel, not to ingratiate themselves with the American public, as Shamir maintained, but in reflection of the majority opinions of American Jews. As the article concluded, "The days of Diaspora Jewish subservience are over." Indeed, the latest polls showed that half of American Jews worried that the Intifada was eroding Israel's moral character. Furthermore, half of American Jewry now felt that criticism of Israel on all issues was legitimate.

A dispute among mainstream Jewish leaders demonstrates how far things had evolved. In early July, Henry Seigman of the American Jewish Congress criticized his fellow Jewish leaders for not telling Shamir that the United States–Israel relationship was "becoming undone." "American Jewish leaders have failed Israel when they say things the Israeli government wants them to say."[64] Other American Jewish leaders quickly defended themselves publicly by maintaining that the American Jewish organizations had been communicating their concerns to Israel's leadership about areas of erosion of U.S. support."[65]

Just when it appeared that things could not possibly get worse, they did. Since the outbreak of the Intifada the IDF had struggled to avoid any conflict with the Palestinians that could be construed as religious. If Israel were seen as suppressing Islam, it would further inflame both Arabs and world opinion. On October 8, nineteen Palestinians were killed by Israeli soldiers at the Haram al Sharif in Jerusalem, one of the holiest sites of Islam. Given that this area, also known as the Temple Mount, contains the Al Aqsa Mosque, the Dome of the Rock Mosque, and the Western Wall, it has been since the 1920s a focus of communal tension between the Arabs and Jews. In recent years, during the festival of Succoth, the Temple Mount Faithful, a radical Jewish fundamentalist group, had sought to lay a foundation stone to rebuild the Great Temple. Such a rebuilding would necessarily entail demolishing the Al Aqsa and the Dome of the Rock. Even though the police had always prevented the Jewish demonstrators from going anywhere near the holy sites, on the morning of October 8, Muslims were summoned to defend the two mosques. When the Muslim demonstrators began showering rocks down on twenty thousand Jewish worshipers gathered at the Western Wall below, the police allegedly panicked and opened fire on the Muslim demonstrators. Nineteen Palestinians were killed and 140 wounded, the highest single-day death toll since the beginning of the Intifada.

The Temple Mount killings highlighted the recent conflicts between the United States and Israel, as well as new divisions stemming from America's efforts to build an Arab coalition against Iraq, which had invaded Kuwait on August 2. Israel maintained that stores of rocks and bottles found at the riot scene showed that the demonstrations had been planned as a deliberate provocation. The Shamir government denied that it had used excessive force even though the police had employed live bullets for crowd control. The United States, already angry at Shamir's refusal to agree to a peace conference, endorsed a UN resolution condemning the killings. Maintaining that the riot was part of a plot by Palestinians to divert world attention from the invasion of Kuwait, Shamir declared that "Israel will not pay the price for Western hypocrisy."[66] A few days later the United States endorsed a second UN condemnation of Israel for its refusal to cooperate in an investigation of the killings.

As world criticism of Israel intensified, American Jews' basic solidarity with Israel reasserted itself. The riots and the magnitude and intensity of world condemnation, along with Saddam Hussein's threat to "burn half of Israel" and a PLO raid on a Tel Aviv beach convinced American Jews that the time had come to defend the Jewish state despite differences with her specific policies. American Jewish organizations almost unanimously condemned the first UN resolution, which had ignored the Palestinians' initial attack upon Jewish worshippers.

The Rabbinical Council of America declared its "sharp dismay at the behavior of the American administration in this crisis" and proclaimed a "Sabbath of Protest."[67] The new chairman of the Conference of Presidents, Seymour Reich, said of UN actions, "We are deeply disappointed in the vote and in the role of the United States in supporting the censure of Israel."[68] His organization then had a "brutal" meeting with American UN representative Thomas Pickering, which a participant described as "one of the toughest confrontations with any administration official."[69] To many American Jews, the Bush administration was sacrificing Israel's interests on the altar of the anti-Saddam coalition. Condemnation of Israel was an easy way of distancing America from the Jewish state as it sought to rally the Arab world.

Even Jewish Republicans wrote to Bush complaining of "the cold relationship between Washington and Jerusalem" and of the "pattern of indifference toward Israel."[70] On the other side of the political spectrum, the *New Republic*, a sharp critic of Shamir, characterized American policy as incoherent and as playing into the hands of Iraq and Palestinian radicals.[71] The combination of the Intifada, Saddam's war mongering, world condemnation, and increasing American hostility had reached a point where the perceived existential threat to Israel caused American Jews, despite their disagreements with the Israeli government's policies, to once again rally to the defense of the state. In the short run they courageously assumed their old role, even though there were major contradictions between Israeli and American policy. But on the Intifada and prospects for peace, they remained as deeply divided as ever.

Israel and American Jews were eventually rescued by external events. The American buildup against Saddam Hussein switched the world's focus from the Intifada to Kuwait. Moreover, the Palestinians, again manifesting their by now legendary political stupidity, negated all the sympathy they had built up through the Intifada by backing Saddam and his invasion of Kuwait. Saddam's belligerence reminded the world how vulnerable Israel was externally, while the Palestinian actions alienated them from the vast majority of world opinion.

The Gulf War did much to restore Israel's image. Since the United States, fearing for its anti-Saddam Arab coalition, prevented Israel from defending herself, the Jewish state was forced to passively accept attacks by Saddam Hussein's missiles. World television now worked to Israel's advantage. The image of Israeli women and children huddling in shelters and wearing gas masks could not but evoke the Holocaust and produce world sympathy. When Saddam's scud missiles fell on Tel Aviv, the normal 3,000 phone calls between the United States and Israel escalated to 750,000. Israel's extremely reluctant consent to the American demand not to retaliate against Iraq, for fear of breaking the Arab alliance, more than rehabilitated the image of the Jewish state in American and world opinion.

The Intifada itself entered a new phase in which the IDF reduced casualties by not confronting rioters. There were now very few large demonstrations, as individual and often random attacks against Israelis replaced mass action. The revolt, so distinguished in its early years by community unity, now broke down into internecine warfare. Palestinians fought each other over ideology, religion, or simply to settle personal scores under the cover of politics. Within any given month the number of Palestinians killed by other Palestinians as "collaborators" often exceeded the number of Palestinians killed by the IDF. The Intifada experienced a loss of energy, only occasionally revived by political or military events, but demonstrations never diminished to the point of actual extinction. However, the Gulf War and the subsequent Mideast peace efforts gave Israelis, Palestinians, and the world a new focus, directing sympathy and interest from a revolt that had become yesterday's news. Nevertheless, the Intifada, despite its seeming torpor, had transformed the consciousness of both Palestinians and Israelis. In the end it would make possible a peace agreement between the two.

| |7| |

The Perils of Peace

The Intifada vastly expanded the permissibility of American Jewish dissent. The collapse of Soviet Union and the defeat of Iraq in the Gulf War enhanced Israel's security and presented her with new and controversial choices in both domestic and foreign policy. Yitzhak Rabin's election and his conclusion of a peace treaty with the Palestinians galvanized conservatives and gave rise to an ideological civil war between Left and Right and Orthodox and non-Orthodox. In both Israel and America activists at both ends of the political spectrum did not hesitate to overturn the ground rules governing the entire American Jewish–Israeli relationship.

In the aftermath of the cold war and the American victory over Iraq, Israel was no longer at risk nor perceived by United States policy makers as America's bastion of democracy against a Soviet-dominated Arab world. The Gulf War demonstrated that Israel was not necessarily the strategic asset that most had assumed. Taking note of these changed circumstances and animated by his vision of a New World Order, President George Bush sought to make peace in the Middle East by shifting the American position from automatic ally of Israel to an "honest broker" between the disputing parties. In the wake of the Gulf War he sought to use American influence to convene an Arab-Israeli peace conference. But a principal obstacle to such a conference and to a peace settlement in general were the 140 settlements that Israel had established in the occupied territories since 1967. By "creating facts on the ground" these settlements marked Israel's determination to hold onto the occupied territories. They also created a constituency of 150,000 settlers and their supporters unwilling to withdraw at any price.[1]

Even before the Gulf War, Prime Minister Shamir had linked the settlements question to the hundreds of thousands of Soviet immigrants flooding into Israel following the collapse of the Soviet Union.

Putting a new spin on the Likud Party dogma of the West Bank as part of a God-given greater Israel, Shamir declared in January 1991 that a "big Israel" was needed to absorb Soviet immigrants.[2] The United States had long considered settlements in the occupied territory to be, if not illegal, at least a needless provocation to the Palestinians and the Arab world. In an effort to create a more neutral stance in the Middle East, President Bush made the extension of $10 billion in loan guarantees to Israel for the absorption of Soviet immigrants contingent upon Israel's freezing of settlement activity in the occupied territories. Israel desperately needed the guarantees in order to borrow at favorable rates to build housing and create jobs and infrastructure for the 350,000 Soviet immigrants who had already arrived and for the half-million or more additional immigrants expected.

From Israel's point of view the president's action was unjust in the extreme. During the Gulf War, Israel maintained an uncharacteristic and humiliating passivity at the behest of the United States so as not to break up America's anti-Saddam coalition. Even as scud missiles terrified the population of Tel Aviv, Israel refrained from retaliation. Instead of being grateful, the United States now engaged in economic coercion and threatened withdrawal of what Israel considered to be humanitarian aid.

The American Israel Public Affairs Committee (AIPAC) pledged to fight for the loan guarantees "with all of our being."[3] In September it mounted a massive lobbying campaign in both houses of Congress. In the midst of the legislative battle, President Bush declared that he wanted a four-month moratorium on the passage of any loan guarantees because they might discourage the opening of the peace conference he was trying to assemble. In a hastily called news conference, in which he promised to veto any aid passed before that time, he took on the Israel lobby in a scathing and nasty personal attack: "I heard today that there were something like a thousand lobbyists on the Hill working the other side of the question. We've got one lonely little guy down here doing it. The Constitution charges the President with the conduct of the nation's foreign policy and now there is an attempt by some in the Congress to prevent the President from taking steps central to the nation's security."[4] Such intemperate language was unprecedented and chilling. The president seemed to be using his "bully pulpit" to suggest that lobbying for Israel was somehow disloyal and un-American.

Bush pulled out all the stops because he considered the question of loan guarantees to be symbolic of nothing less than the whole tenor of the American relationship with Israel. In attempting to sway Israel's policy by threatening to withdraw aid, Bush sought to demonstrate to potential participants in a peace conference that America could be evenhanded. He also attempted to combat the Arab perception that American Near East policy was formulated not in Washington but in Jerusalem. Equally important was the ultimate fate of the territories themselves. Since the United States had long disapproved of Israel's settlements as a major obstacle to peace, the provision of loan guarantees without a moratorium on settlement building would serve to undermine America's own policies.

Yitzhak Shamir, whose personal relationship with George Bush was of mutual detestation and mistrust, refused to back down. Perceiving the moratorium demand as a capitulation to the Arabs, a Shamir spokesman referred to Bush's news conference as a "declaration of a war against us."[5] The prime minister's reaction was only slightly less hyperbolic. "This administration has decided to cut Israel down to size—we fear they have in mind cutting us down to a size that won't enable us to survive."[6]

American Jews were shocked by Bush's vehemence and by what they felt was the injustice of his attack on their lobbying efforts. As Malcolm Hoenlein, the executive director of the Conference of Presidents wrote, " It was not a thousand lobbyists descending on Capitol Hill but 1200 Americans fulfilling their constitutional right and responsibility on an issue that is of concern to them."[7] What was particularly galling was that, only a few months earlier, Bush, like most presidents before him, had not hesitated to use the "Jewish lobby" in the pursuit of his own policies, specifically asking for the help of Jewish organizations in persuading Congress to give him the authority to prosecute the war against Iraq. But since Bush now evidently saw lobbying "on the other side of the question" as illegitimate, American Jews felt doubly betrayed.

The American Jewish community would normally have responded to such attacks by rallying to the defense of the Jewish state, as they had done during the AWACS fight. Saddam's scud attacks and Palestinian support for him had turned American Jews more hawkish on the Arab-Israeli conflict in general.[8] They were dismayed, however, by Bush's tactics and tone as well as by the many anti-Semitic letters of support the president reportedly received. But many agreed with the substance of his argument: Likud's continuing establishment of settlements *was* an obstacle to peace. A November poll demonstrated that even Israel's most committed supporters were willing to publicly dissent from the Shamir government's policies. Eighty-five percent of the board members of the Council of Jewish Federations rejected Shamir's vow never to give up an inch of land. No less than 78 percent of the same sample endorsed a settlement freeze.[9] In the same week two hundred American rabbis wrote to the prime minister asking him to suspend the building of settlements.[10] One semiofficial Israeli complained to the *Jerusalem Post* that during a three-week trip to America he was met "with indifference and barely concealed hostility."[11]

American Jews, whose strength in any conflict derives from community unity, were paralyzed by a lack of consensus. While some supported Shamir, new factions arose over what to criticize. An American Jewish Committee (AJC) poll released in early October revealed that 80 percent of American Jews opposed any reduction in aid to Israel, and 54 percent said that the United States should stop criticizing Israel's settlement building. An October 21 *Jerusalem Post* editorial accused American Jewish leaders of being "court Jews of the worst kind, becoming administration apologists." One day later the same *Post* ran a headline proclaiming that American Jewish leaders were tilting toward Shamir. The National Jewish Community Relations Council, representing 13 national and 117 community organizations, overwhelmingly opposed Shamir's settlement plans but took no formal vote since "we have an obligation to avoid the impression that there is consensus back home."[12] Even Tom Dine of AIPAC, the loan guarantee's fiercest proponent on Capital Hill, told Shamir that he risked a major rift with American Jews if he chose settlements over immigrant aid. In the same vein the AJC demonstrated its very intense commitment to Soviet Jewish immigration. "I don't think American Jews are going to comprehend a decision that says settlements are more important than immigration."[13]

Here may lie a clue to what seemed an apparent disparity in the opinion polls. Even those who strongly supported retaining the settlements found it hard to accept Shamir's refusal to stop their expansion for the sake of helping the Soviet immigrants for whom American Jews had worked so long and hard. When the guarantees came up again in Congress after the four-month moratorium, there was hardly a pro-Shamir lobbyist in evidence. Bush's rejection of the guarantees in mid-March generated few protests beyond Tom Dine's statement that this "signaled the death of the peace process."

* * *

While some in America and Israel stated that American Jews had been cowed by Bush's attack, the explanation was both simpler and more complicated. On the one hand, American Jews had remained on the sidelines because the majority appeared not to agree with the Shamir government on the merits of the issue. Those who supported the loan guarantees soon found that the poor American economy had produced a congressional aversion to any new foreign aid. To keep fighting a lost battle risked angering Congress and might have put Israel's annual $3 billion aid package at risk. But the fact remained that for the first time since 1956 an American administration had chosen to coerce Israel by withdrawing aid. Because Bush had chosen an issue upon which Israel and American Jewry were divided, he was able to prevail. American Jewish sentiment against Shamir did not, however, translate into support for the president. Despite his repeated attempts at rapprochement, American Jews would, in the 1992 election, give Bush their lowest rate of support in a quarter century.

The new divisions among American Jews over Shamir's West Bank policies were also indicated by the reception given by the mainstream to the New Jewish Agenda, whose advocacy of a Palestinian state was much more radical than Breira's program of two decades earlier. A national organization with over five thousand members, the New Jewish Agenda had long cooperated with radical and pro-PLO groups. It had even advocated a PLO-Israel peace conference without requiring that Arafat either renounce terrorism or explicitly recognize Israel's right to exist. Whereas Breira, some of whose members had helped found the New Jewish Agenda, was seen as a subversive organization to be totally rejected and isolated, the New Jewish Agenda's profession to be "the loyal opposition" was largely accepted at face value. Its members were permitted to make presentations to mainstream Jewish organizations, and in major cities like Los Angeles, Hartford, Detroit, and Kansas City it was allowed to join Jewish community councils. On a national level, Americans for Peace Now, dismissed and reviled a decade earlier, received membership in the prestigious and influential Conference of Presidents. Dissent from Israel's policy was becoming accepted, mainstream, and institutionalized.

The election of Yitzhak Rabin in June 1992 led to the widespread alienation of many of Israel's most enthusiastic American Jewish supporters. This was due to Rabin's own attitude toward his American Jewish supporters, the way in which the implications of his election were perceived by his opponents, and the actions of his Likud opposition in exporting Israeli political battles to American shores. The result was the destruction of much of the conceptual framework by which American Jews and Israel had related to one another and a wholesale rewriting or even discarding of the accepted boundaries of the relationship between them.

One of the principal rewriters was Rabin himself. In August 1992 he visited President Bush at his vacation home in Kennebunkport, Maine, where, in contrast to Bush's relationship with Shamir, all was sweetness and light. But upon arriving in Washington it seemed that Rabin had saved his bitterness for his American Jewish supporters. One of his first meetings was with the executive board of AIPAC, which had long and justifiably considered itself to be Israel's American voice on Capitol Hill. Many AIPAC officials had formed close relationships with Israel's ministers and personnel during the previous fifteen years of Likud domination. The assembled gathering certainly expected a continuation of their close ties to the Israeli government. But Rabin, known for his directness, excoriated AIPAC for getting Israel involved in a needless no-win conflict with the Bush administration over the loan guarantees. He allegedly told the assembled executives, "You've aroused too much antagonism, you make too many enemies for yourselves, and your record is poor."[14]

Rabin's spleen may have been in fact an expression of old resentments. When Labor had been in opposition or even part of a unity government with Likud, AIPAC had been unreceptive to its ideas and programs. In particular it had refused to support the Peres plan for an international peace conference in 1984—even when Labor had held the post of prime minister. But Rabin's diatribe was also the result of deeply held beliefs, as well as a product of his experience in the 1970s as Israel's ambassador to Washington. In a 1978 account of his years as ambassador, Rabin noted that he disliked the use of American Jews as diplomatic intermediaries: "I believe the Israeli Embassy should assume the principal role in handling Israel's affairs at all political levels and that it was entitled to avail itself of Jews and non-Jews alike as it saw fit."[15] He had tried with uncertain success to change the system. Now he evidently believed that as prime minister he was in a position to do so. Rabin further told the assembled executives that AIPAC had overstepped its boundaries in seeking to be an intermediary between Israel and the American government. From now on diplomacy would be conducted exclusively by Israel's official representatives.

AIPAC's leadership was, to put it mildly, displeased by the prime minister's attack. Nor did he accept their claims that they had been pushed into the confrontation with Bush by the Shamir government, which had not heeded AIPAC's own warnings. After two decades of extremely effective advocacy on behalf of the Jewish state, AIPAC was being told that it was, in effect, irrelevant. Rabin may also have been motivated by traditional Zionist ideology of "negation of the Diaspora," The next day he told a meeting of the Conference of Presidents that "Israel will make her own decisions when it comes to settlements and peace."[16] He later added that he welcomed Diaspora criticism since what American Jews said didn't matter anyway.

The demeaning of American Jews was not confined to the prime minister. In July, Cabinet Minister Avram Burg told an American Jewish audience not to waste their time lobbying ; they should keep their money for their own domestic charity.[17] Six months later, Deputy Foreign Minister Yossi Beilin told another American gathering that since Israel was no longer a poor country it no longer needed American Jewish charity. American Jews should devote their money to saving their own Jewish identity.[18] The words of Rabin, Burg, and Beilin were a knockout punch directed at the most crucial point of contact between Israel and American Jewry. Lobbying on behalf of the Jewish state had become a principal and extremely successful activity for Jewish elites. "Checkbook Judaism," though often maligned, was considered by many to be the glue that held the whole American Zionist enterprise together. By striking at the key expressions of community activism the Labor Party risked alienating the great mass of American Jews at the political center, whose total support it would later need to counteract the violent criticism of the American Jewish Right.

In July, Rabin announced his intention to promote the American-sponsored peace process and to halt the massive Jewish settlement program that was so vital to Likud and so threatening to the Palestinians. The prime minister's desire to reach some sort of accommodation with the Palestinians was so threatening to both the American and Israeli Right that they abandoned the time-honored rules of engagement concerning Jewish conflict over Israel. The opening shot in the campaign against both Rabin and the rules of the game was fired by one of the rules' principal architects, Norman Podhoretz. As editor of *Commentary*, perhaps the most influential American Jewish journal, he had strenuously maintained all through fifteen years of Likud's ascendance that American Jews had no right to criticize Israel's security policies. His arguments had long been a staple of the American Jewish establishment. Living in peace and security in America, not paying Israeli taxes, and above all not having to live with the consequences of their decisions, American Jews had no right to interfere on issues of peace and security. Besides being morally abhorrent, such criticism would give comfort to anti-Semites and provide political cover for Israel's enemies. This argument had become an eleventh commandment for American Jews. Podhoretz had become one of its principal enforcers, using the pages of *Commentary* to castigate as misguided, self-hating, and deluded any American Jew who had the temerity to criticize Israel—even after the invasion of Lebanon, the Sabra and Chatilla massacres, and the Intifada.

But in a stunning volte-face, Podhoretz himself joined the ranks of Israel's American Jewish critics. From his office on Park Avenue he took up the cudgels because he detested Labor's willingness to enter negotiations with the Palestinians that were not a sham and to seriously contemplate trading land for peace in both the Golan Heights and the West Bank. For Podhoretz, Labor's actions were terribly dangerous; he was convinced that any apparent Arab moderation was a mere tactic employed in the service of the continuing goal of driving Israel into the sea. Therefore, the "peace process is the trap from which it will be very hard for Israel to escape."[19]

Podhoretz's article reflected a growing anxiety on the Right about Labor's peace efforts. Part of the problem was the inevitable resistance to conceptual change. After decades of being told that Arabs were murderers, that the chief culprit was Yasir Arafat, and that land could never be abandoned, American Jews were now asked to support the possibility of Israel's giving up substantial territory to the very man who had been so demonized. The actions that American Jews were now being asked to support were sophisticated and nuanced rather than the simplistic slogans of no recognition of the PLO and no relinquishing of territory. To its great consternation the Israeli Labor Party found that it was much easier to rally people around specific threats than around abstract opportunities.

But some of the blame was Rabin's for insulting and dismissing American Jews. It is an indication of his poor public relations that, four months after his election, 51 percent of American Jews were unaware that he was Israel's prime minister.[20] At the very least, Labor did not produce an ambassador to American Jewry such as Likud's Benjamin Netanyahu had been during the Gulf War. As Henry Siegman, the head of the American Jewish Congress, complained, "The Labor government has done a very poor job in bringing its message to the American Jewish public."[21] Seymour Reich, the chief executive of the American Jewish Committee (AJC) went even further, "The Israeli government is taking the American Jewish community for granted. There's a perspective that the American Jewish community is not needed."[22] As the center of American Jewry became increasingly alienated, confused, and passive, those who objected to any possible peace activity became more assertive. The peace process now centered on an international conference in Madrid, during which, for the first time, Palestinians and Israelis sat at the same negotiating table. But Israel's ambassador to the United States, Itamar Rabinovich, regularly found himself in the unfamiliar position of having "to explain to a skeptical minority of our own supporters that there is merit in the peace process."[23] Despite Labor's hopes, the Madrid conference dragged on with little positive result. Israel's right-wing politicians now moved to co-opt the dissatisfied minority into the rough and tumble of Israeli politics. Many came to America to raise funds and build new constituencies who were only a fax transmission away.

The now public display of intra-Jewish conflict at times assumed the quality of an opera buffa. In July 1993, Tom Dine was forced to resign for referring to Orthodox Jews as "smelly and low class." Two weeks later one of his vice presidents met a similar fate for calling dovish Deputy Foreign Minister Yossi Beilin "a little slime ball."[24] Those who valued community discipline above all could only look with nostalgia on the recent past, when the prohibition against washing dirty laundry in public was enough to keep conflict private. But evidently, American Jews had become secure enough in their own position and in Israel's so as not to worry so much about "what will the Gentiles say?"

It was a seriously divided community that in late August received the unbelievable news that Israel and the PLO, after months of secret talks in Oslo, Norway, had concluded a peace agreement. The negotiations were so secret that even Israel's ambassador to the United States was not aware of them. The agreement provided for mutual recognition, for the PLO's renunciation of terrorism and acceptance of UN resolutions 242 and 338, and for Israel's withdrawal from Gaza and Jericho with autonomy to be given to a "Palestinian Authority." Further withdrawals and political concessions would depend on the successful implementation of the first phase of the agreement. Likud's reaction was swift and unambiguous. In an indication of the growing importance of American Jews to the Israeli Right, opposition leader Benjamin Netanyahu chose the op-ed page of the *New York Times* to condemn the proposed treaty as another Munich. Within Israel, polls showed 60 percent for the treaty, 40 percent against it.

American Jews once again were confronted by a divided Israel: this time over one of the most important developments in the state's history. Most greeted the treaty with a mixture of elation and apprehension. (I remember arriving at my office the morning after the peace treaty was announced to find a group of students demanding reassurance that this did not portend the end of the Jewish state.) Initial polls revealed that 90 percent saw mutual recognition as a positive development, while 74 percent endorsed giving up Gaza and Jericho.[25] Among the Orthodox there was much less support. Almost immediately after the treaty's official signing on the White House lawn on September 13, right-wing groups opposed to the accord began to proliferate. Mainly Orthodox, they considered the famous handshake between Rabin and Arafat to be not the symbol of hope but the harbinger of the destruction of the Jewish state. At the very least the proposed relinquishing of territory dashed the hopes of religious Zionists for the imminent appearance of the Messiah.

The dissenters may have lacked the numbers—the anti-treaty forces drew support of only 10 percent of American Jewry—but they made up for that in volume and vehemence. The Lubavicher movement took out advertisements in the *New York Times* accusing Israel's leaders of selling the country's security for a Nobel Peace Prize. Rabbi Aaron Soloveichik, one of the most respected Orthodox rabbis in America, declared that the treaty undermined the sanctity of the land and that he would join West Bank settlers in nonviolent resistance if at any time in the future the Israeli government should try to remove them.[26] West Bank settlers began to employ their own fund-raisers in the United States, who now reported the response to their national campaign to be "off the charts." A number of Orthodox congregations began the policy of "adopting a settlement." Americans for a Safe Israel, a near-fringe organization advocating a "Greater Israel" policy, reported an 18 percent increase in contributions, and in December a slate of candidates opposed to the peace accord took over the Zionist Organization of America.

Even as the great majority of American Jews supported the treaty, they agonized over it. Debates over its advisability and implications dominated the Jewish press. All phases of the accord were the subject of endless discussion, including the implications of Yasir Arafat's appearing at the signing ceremony without a gun but dressed in military fatigues, which the Israelis euphemistically referred to as a green suit. Critics of the treaty maintained that the Middle East was not yet ripe for peace; that Palestinian moderation was only a tactic to get back lost territory; and that even if Arafat were sincere, the unreliability of successor regimes and the rise of fundamentalism made ultimate Palestinian adherence to the treaty unlikely. The accord would therefore inevitably lead to a Palestinian state, which would be a launching pad for terrorism and a mortal threat to Israel's existence. Advocates of the treaty maintained that it would be a tragic error not to test the sincerity of the Arab world since the only alternative was the short-term threat of terrorism and the long-term threat of being overwhelmed by the burgeoning Arab population in the territories. In any case, Rabin was not an impractical dreamer as his critics claimed but an intensely pragmatic military hero more qualified than any to deal with the threats and opportunities presented to the Jewish state. What gave the controversy a somewhat unreal quality was that the normal debating tactic of appealing to the past could not suffice; the whole question was whether, in fact, old patterns, about which there was relatively little disagreement, could be broken and a new start made.

For opponents the answer was a resounding and unequivocal *no*. For advocates it was a hopeful but somewhat tentative "maybe." The sometimes ambivalent support of the majority paled before the ferocious condemnation of those who, often motivated by religious or political dogma, considered the treaty a disaster. This disparity in confidence and emotion between the pro- and antitreaty forces helps explain why those against the treaty were much more effective in making their case. Although the Jewish press was filled with vehement antitreaty articles, the protreaty majority simply could not summon the same enthusiasm in its defense. Moreover, the Labor Party, which seemed to assume the automatic support of American Jews, never mounted a sustained campaign in favor of the peace process. Indeed, it was during the struggle to gain acceptance for the Oslo Accords that Deputy Foreign Minister Yossi Beilin made his infamous statement that Israel did not need American Jewish charity. Rabin himself later conceded that "tremendous damage was wrought to Israel in the wake of the statement that we don't need American Jews."[27] Insulted by the Labor Government and paralyzed by a lack of consensus among its officers, AIPAC and the Council of Presidents did not attempt to enforce community discipline, and their relatively tepid support of the treaty was insufficient to counteract the attacks of its opponents.

Within Israel the implications of ideological extremism had become a terrifying reality. In February 1994, Dr. Baruch Goldstein, a religiously observant American immigrant who had graduated from Yeshiva University and was a well-known follower of racist politician Meir Kahane, massacred twenty-nine Palestinians as they prayed in the Ibrahim Mosque in Hebron. Goldstein was an ally of the extreme religious nationalists who advocated the "transfer" of Palestinians and who only one month earlier at a Brooklyn rally had called for violence and even civil war to support the Jewish settlers. Appalled by the American origins of the murderer, there was a predictable wringing of hands even by the Orthodox. The American Jewish community was nearly unanimous in applauding Israel's apology to the victims' families, its granting them compensation, and its launching of an investigation to determine how further attacks could be prevented.

There were, however, some notable exceptions. Orthodox radicals began to collect for a memorial to Goldstein. The Brooklyn Kahanist organization dubbed the murderer a hero and provided the following evaluation of Israel's compensation to the families of the victims: "If Rabin were not such a self-hating timid wimp, he would have told Arafat, 'Sit down and shut up. You finally got a taste of your own medicine.'"[28] Even in the wake of such statements the American Jewish center and the Orthodox did little to fight such extremism in there midst. It was evidently much easier to issue vague and impotent suggestions that the Israeli government disarm settlers. The fact that 15 percent of West Bank settlers, including many of the most radical, had come from America was not an issue that American Jews were ready to confront.

After a brief period of reflection following the Hebron massacre the rhetoric and conflict over the peace accords again became heated. The signing of a specific agreement that called for Palestinian self-rule in Gaza and Jericho and the creation of a "Palestine National Authority" was profoundly distasteful to the Israeli Right. It was now Likud that made further breaches in the long-held practices governing the relationship among Israel's officials, American Jews, and the American government. The old convention had been that political disputes within Israel stopped at the border. It was long felt that lining up Diaspora allies on specific intra-Israeli issues would destroy the community unity that had made American Jews such a potent political force. For similar reasons, American Jews, however they might criticize Israel, usually refrained from lobbying Congress against her policies. While these prohibitions had sometimes been breached in isolated instances—most recently during the fight over the loan guarantees—Likud made the use of American Jews to lobby Congress against Israel's government an explicit policy. In September, Likud leader Benjamin Netanyahu came to America to publicize his objections to the peace treaty and told American Jews, "I will lobby in Israel and American Jews will lobby in America. I think that's a good division of labor."29

To help his American allies along, he dispatched to Washington three Likud political operatives to raise opposition to the peace treaty in any way they could. Dubbed the "gang of three" by Labor, they sought to create an antitreaty coalition of American Jews, cold warriors, and fundamentalist Christians. Their campaign had three objectives, all designed to make the implementation of the peace accords impossible. The first was to convince Congress of the dangers of sending American troops on any possible peacekeeping mission in the Golan Heights, thereby sabotaging any future agreement with Syria. After a visit from American Jews, who told him that he would be helping Israel by introducing a bill asking for an evaluation of the risks of such a mission, Representative Thad Cochran submitted his bill to the House. He soon withdrew his proposal after a call from the Israeli ambassador.

Likud's other initiatives, directed against the Palestinians, illustrated the new political combinatios resulting from the fragmenting of American Jews. Despite the decision of Rabin not to worry about every Palestinian violation, Likud formed an antitreaty alliance with the right-wing Zionist Organization of America. Together they lobbied Congress to set up a panel to monitor the compliance of the Palestinian Authority with the peace accords. Their hope was to find sufficient violations to induce Congress to cut off the $500 million it had promised to the

Palestine Authority over the next five years. The peace accord monitoring group included fifteen senators and thirty-one House members. If it were to succeed in cutting off aid, it would most probably end the peace process.

The most significant achievement of those American Jews who lobbied against the Israeli government was to convince Senator Robert Dole to sponsor a bill to transfer the American embassy to Jerusalem by May 1999. The transfer had long been desired by Israel as affirming that an undivided Jerusalem was Israel's capital, and presidential candidate Dole was eager to ingratiate himself with Jewish voters. But since control over Jerusalem symbolized the whole dispute between Israel and the Palestinians, to move the embassy now would be another way to scuttle the peace process. Dole's initiative was thus opposed by the Rabin government. But among American Jewish organizations there was no consensus, and the bill to move the embassy was endorsed by AIPAC. The change in the boundaries of permissible activity was noted by Henry Siegman of the American Jewish Congress, who stated that although criticism of Israel by American Jews was permissible, lobbying against the Jewish state was out of bounds. As usual, Yitzhak Rabin was more explicit. He later complained, "Never have we witnessed an attempt by American Jews to lobby against the policy of a democratically elected Israeli government."[30]

As the summer wore on, the disparity between the polls and the public expression of support for the peace process continued. Although only 9 percent of American Jews opposed the treaty and two-thirds felt that American Jewish organizations should do "a lot" to support the peace process, the opposition grew louder while its supporters remained silent.[31] Advertisements placed in the Jewish press told of the horrendous deterioration of Israel's security as a result of the peace treaty. One even said it was time to try Rabin for treason. The moderate center remained immobile. The attempt of the Israeli consul general, Colette Avital, to put together an ad for the Jewish New Year, expressing the backing of the mainstream organizations for the peace process, became the subject of debate. After lengthy discussions the only consensus that the Conference of Presidents could reach was to wish Israel a happy new year.[32]

Even today there are still a great many people with deep misgivings. As an AJC official explained in November 1999, "Many in this organization believe in the treaty more with their minds than with their hearts."[33] Accustomed to dealing with threats to Jews abroad or with combating anti-Semitism at home, the mainstream Jewish organizations found it hard to campaign against other Jews. As Ms. Avital would later complain after the assassination of Yitzhak Rabin, "There are Jewish newspapers that week after week had a campaign to portray the Israeli Government as Nazis. For almost two years no American objected to it. I would tell people something has to be done. This is indoctrination. But they would say, 'nobody reads it.'"[34] The only sustained campaign for the treaty came from the American Reform movement. Responding to an appeal from Ambassador Rabinovich to counteract "an enormously vocal minority" that "gave the false impression that the Jewish community was not behind the peace process,"[35] Reform leaders mailed a letter to 860 congregations, urging rabbis to use their high holiday sermons to urge support of the treaty.[36] They also sent out an information packet containing sample sermons, a letter from Yitzhak Rabin, and a resource guide.

Such a campaign was necessary; as the months passed, even the most devoted optimists were beginning to trade euphoria for gloom. Violence in the territories continued, 150 Israelis died in terrorist attacks, and Yasir Arafat failed to either condemn the attacks or unequivocally revoke the parts of the PLO Charter that called for the destruction of Israel. The deadlines for both elections in the territories and Israeli troop withdrawals came and went. In speeches to Arab audiences the PLO chairman referred to the jihad with Israel and praised the actions of terrorists. But support for the treaty remained high. In September 1995, 68 percent of American Jews still supported the peace process, down from the 84 percent that had done so immediately after the announcement of the Oslo agreement. But among the American Orthodox fully 64 percent opposed the treaty, with only 31 percent supporting it.

The same survey also demonstrated that in the last decade American Jewish attitudes toward criticizing the Jewish state had undergone a revolutionary change. In contrast to past notions of *beshri nicht* (don't talk about it), 71 percent of the respondents felt they had a right to speak out against Israel's policies. Whether such criticism would be informed was another question since the survey also revealed that 64 percent of the respondents could not tell what year Israel had taken control of the territories, and 47 percent did not even know what year Israel had become a state.[37]

* * *

Even as Rabin, alarmed by the continuing violence in Gaza, talked of slowing down the peace process, his militant opposition grew more frenzied. In June 1995 a group of Orthodox rabbis in New York City issued a halachic ruling that Israeli soldiers should disobey any order to withdraw from army bases or settlements in the West Bank. This was too much for the old soldier Rabin. "I have heard strange calls from a small group of rabbis in the United States—for whom the name ayatollah is perhaps better suited than rabbi."[38] The rabbi of a Brooklyn congregation went even further when he said it would be religiously permissible to kill Rabin. Shlomo Gazit, the former head of the Israeli army intelligence, complained of letters he had received from Brooklyn calling Rabin "a betrayer who lays Israel's head on the block. Such letters," he said, "express the brainwashed mentality and extreme manner in which a certain group within the Jewish community chooses to express itself."[39]

But blanket condemnation ignored both the diversity within the Orthodox community and the fact that the extremism of which suburban middle-class Jews were so fond of accusing the Brooklyn Orthodox could often be found much closer to home. In May 1995, Shulamit Aloni, a left-wing cabinet minister known for her vigorous anti-Orthodox and antisettler views, attended a breakfast preceding New York City's thirty-first annual Salute to Israel parade. As she began her speech amid heckling, she was attacked by a member of the audience. The attacker was wrestled off the podium, and Aloni finished her speech before leaving to see a doctor. In the afternoon, when Israel's chief consul, Collete Avital, arrived at Fifth Avenue to march at the head of the parade, she discovered to her shock that the man marching in the front row with her was none other than Aloni's assailant—who had donated enough money to have been designated an honorary parade marshal.[40]

The actions of Abraham Foxman, the head of the B'nai B'rith Anti-Defamation League, also demonstrated the pervasiveness of extremism within the Jewish community. Foxman resigned from his suburban Orthodox synagogue in New Jersey to protest his rabbi's reference to the "Rabin *judenrat*" (Jewish councils that cooperated with the Nazis). Foxman did not question the rabbi's right to criticize the prime minister, but objected to the "hate and vitriol" expressed.[41]

On November 4, Prime Minister Yitzhak Rabin was assassinated by a Jewish fundamentalist as he left a Peace Now rally in Jerusalem. If Israel's security forces were unprepared for a Jewish assassin, they only reflected the world Jewish community as a whole. But they should have realized, especially after the Hebron massacre, that the anathemas, imprecations, and Aramaic formulations distributed in Jerusalem synagogues that put a price upon Rabin's head, helped power the bullet that killed him as surely as did the explosive charge it contained. The assassin, a young Israeli named Yigal Amir, had been trained to believe in the immanence of the Messiah and that Rabin was a destroyer. He explained his action by stating that God had told him to commit the murder. Secular Jewry was not, however, without its own responsibility. The Likud slogan, "The nation did not sign" (the peace treaty), was a way to delegitimize Rabin and his government. When a poster depicting Rabin in a Nazi uniform was raised at a rally, Benjamin Netanyahu who was in attendance said nothing.[42] But neither was Labor unsullied. It too had contributed to the overheated atmosphere by characterizing anyone who objected to the peace process as a warmonger. It too had coined its own objectionable slogans, such as "Likud collaborates with Hamas."[43]

The assassination laid bare the crisis in Israel's soul and emphasized that the gulf between secular and religious Jews was fast becoming unbridgeable. Some spoke of the deed as the opening shot of civil war. On the one side stood a modern, assimilatory Israel, wanting to act with moderation and take advantage of growing world tolerance. On the other stood an insular religiosity rejecting the former and disbelieving the latter. Rabin's peace treaty not only attempted to end four decades of conflict but sought to normalize Israel's relationship with the world community, to put an end to the age-old notion that "Jews are people who dwell alone." Politically, intellectually, and theologically, the peace treaty and the assassination of its author revealed the depth of division within world Jewry.

American Jews hardly seemed to recognize the larger implications of the tragedy. The spectacle of Rabin's funeral, attended by most of the world leaders, with Bill Clinton barely holding back tears, seemed to evoke old patterns. Here was the old victimized Israel to which American Jews could relate with traditional emotionality. The practical and hardheaded Rabin, who had recently ordered the bombing of villages in Lebanon that harbored guerrilla bases, was immediately transformed into a sainted martyr for peace. American Jewish support for the peace process climbed ten percentage points, and charities reported substantial increases in donations.[44] Reports that there was some revelry and little mourning in Brooklyn and that funds were collected for the defense of Amir forced many American Jews to recognize the link between Orthodox militancy in America and Israel. Rabbi Norman Lamm, the president of Yeshiva University, the preeminent educational institution of modern Orthodoxy, spoke of "those raucous voices of vicious discord who declare that it is a mitzvah [good deed] to assassinate a Prime Minister of the state of Israel."[45] The Jewish press was filled with so much condemnation of the ultra-Orthodox for allegedly helping to create the atmosphere that encouraged the assassination that mainstream Orthodox leaders justifiably complained that the whole movement was being unfairly assaulted.

Despite the rank and file's obvious anger toward religious extremism, the American Jewish establishment strove to minimize the crisis. Rather than confront the gulf between the secular and the religious, they worked above all to present a picture of unity. Shortly after the funeral a huge rally was planned at Madison Square Garden to support the peace process. But fearing a lack of Orthodox support, the movement's organizers, who included the Conference of Presidents and National Jewish Community Relations Advisory Council, changed the theme to a memorial for Rabin and to the much less specific "support of the search for peace."[46] The result was a strange event in which the slain prime minister was eulogized but little was said about the peace treaty for which he had given his life. Only Leah Rabin, his widow, spoke explicitly about the conflicts leading to her husband's murder. In an effort to avoid offending the right wing, a video of Rabin's life omitted the famous handshake with Arafat that he probably considered his crowning achievement. Yet the unity that was expressed was an illusion, and the hope that all would find lessons in the assassination was equally groundless. Across the street from the rally ultra-Orthodox demonstrators carried signs proclaiming, "Peres is a traitor."[47]

| |8| |

"Who Is a Jew?"

The ultra-Orthodox protest at Rabin's memorial service in New York was just one small sign of the depth of American Jews' internal schism and of the continued erosion of restraints on criticism. It also emphasized the emergence of Orthodox power in a form increasingly disagreeable to most American Jews. The "Who is a Jew" controversy was also the result of conflict between Orthodox and secular Jews, in both Israel and the United States. Involving the most basic questions of Jewish identity, it encompassed nothing less than the character of the Jewish state and its relationship with American Jews. Should Israel evolve into a liberal, pluralistic society, accepting American Jews as valued partners or into an exclusivist, theocratic state deriding Jewish Americans as inauthentic Jews unable to contribute to Israel or Judaism?

The "Who is a Jew" controversy is the most bitter and protracted of all the conflicts between American Jews and Israel. It is also the most illuminating, since it encapsulates much of Israel's political and cultural history and presents in starkest relief many of the issues underlying the relationship with the Diaspora. The implications of the conflict reach beyond Israel's relationship with American Jews, vital in itself, to the very meaning of Zionism and its history. How has Israel, a nation founded by secular Zionists to in part supersede traditional religion, come to be increasingly influenced by the very forces it had hoped to replace? This extraordinarily intense controversy (and its implications for Israel's future) is rooted in the complex relationship between Zionism, religion, and the Jewish state.

The emergence of a viable Zionist movement in the 1890s inspired a variety of responses from the Orthodox, ranging from utter rejection to political alliance. In the pre-state era, Zionists' general contempt for religion as well as the detestation of most Orthodox for Zionism's secular definition of Judaism ensured a generally tumultuous relationship between them. After the birth of Israel, David Ben Gurion achieved an uneasy modus vivendi between the secular majority and the Orthodox minority by giving the latter control over religion and by eschewing a written constitution that would have defined the nature of the state.

Throughout the history of Israel, the determination of Jewish identity has been a principal battleground in the contest for dominance between the Orthodox and the secular. As the Orthodox became more powerful, particularly after 1967, they redefined their relationship with the state and increasingly sought to determine its domestic and foreign policy. The question of who is a Jew became both symbol and substance of this struggle. To understand the contemporary crisis, one must examine how it reflects and amplifies conflicts dating back to the early days of Zionism.

Most of Israel's founders were antireligious socialists who blamed Judaism for many of the negative traits they associated with Diaspora civilization. As Nachman Syrkin, one of the patriarchs of Jewish socialism, wrote, "The Zionism of the masses will not march arm and arm with sanctimonious religion, crowned by the traditions of the past. . . . Quite the contrary, the masses will draw from Zionism the strength to free themselves from the chains of spiritual folly, in order to rid itself [*sic*] of the useless bonds of religious Judaism."[1] Self-assured and intolerant, these Zionists had little doubt that their secular nationalism would create a new state, a new culture, and a new Jew. Ideologically contemptuous of spirituality, they considered religion and its practitioners to be the product of an earlier age, outworn, irrelevant, and doomed to disappear in the new Zionist era of progress.

The vast majority of the Orthodox repaid Zionist contempt with implacable hatred. The Zionists had committed the unpardonable sin of seeking redemption in the Holy Land without waiting for the Messiah. Even more detestable was Zionist irreligion and their attempt to transform the basis of Jewish identity from divine law to human culture, language, and national feeling. An anti-Zionist manifesto, written by the Lubavitch Rebbe and published in 1900, expressed the views of most of the Eastern European Orthodox leadership. The Rebbe stated that the sole desire and inclination of the Zionist is "to cast off the yoke of the Torah and *mitzvot* [commandments] and hold only to nationalism, which will be their Judaism."[2] An even greater threat than socialism or assimilation, Zionism alone strove not to eliminate Jewish distinctiveness but to redefine it. In 1899 the great Rabbi Hayim Soloveichik wrote, "The people in Israel should take care not to join a venture that threatens their souls, to destroy religion, and is a stumbling block to the House of Israel."[3]

After World War I, as the Zionists began mass immigration to Palestine and looked forward to the prospect of a Jewish state, religious Jews developed a variety of responses to the movement. Most extreme in their rejection were the Naturei Karta, a group founded in Jerusalem in 1935. It has about ten thousand adherents in Israel today and perhaps double that number in the United States. For its members, Zionism is the essence of evil, inspired by Satan to tempt the unwary from the path of righteousness. The creation of the State of Israel by human initiative is the ultimate abomination. As one of the movement's principal theoreticians wrote recently, "The Zionists transgress and violate [all the teachings] of the Torah but that is not Zionism, there were sinners in this world before Zionism came along. Zionism is one thing and one thing only the state; the State of Israel is the great defilement and the principal heresy that the Zionists have introduced."[4] Nevertheless, many of sect's members have chosen to live in Israel because they feel closer to God there, can keep more religious commandments, and want to be on hand to welcome the Messiah. But no contact is permitted with the state, which is seen as illegitimate, impure, and absolutely corrupting. Even the Six-Day War, which many Israelis felt to be a miracle of biblical proportions, they considered evil's last stand to tempt the righteous into contact with the abomination of the state.

The Haredim, or ultra-Orthodox, are slightly more accepting. They recognize the State of Israel but consider it no different from any other state in the pre-messianic era. Despite settling in massive numbers in Israel after World War II, they steadfastly maintain that "the Jewish people is still in exile, until the arrival of the redeemer, even when it is in Eretz Israel; this is neither redemption nor the beginning of the redemption."[5] As they established themselves in Israel, as well as in Brooklyn, the ultra-Orthodox were desperate to rebuild their shattered communities and chose through their Agudas party to cooperate with the government to promote their own interests. In return for their political support they were given a monopoly over religious affairs, an independent educational system, and development funds, which they used to re-create the life of an eighteenth-century Polish shtetl. The reception of such benefits has not given rise to a reciprocal sense of obligation. The Haredim refuse to sing the Israeli national anthem, do not observe political holidays, don't fly the Israeli flag, and refuse to serve in the army. By choice they have isolated themselves from modernity, the state, and the majority of the Jewish people.[6]

The religious Zionists display an attitude toward the state and the enterprise it represents that is diametrically opposed to that of the Haredim. Originally a small minority within Orthodox society, they somewhat naively considered Zionism to be purely political, aimed solely at improving the worldly condition of the Jewish people.[7] As such it had nothing to do with the Messiah. As Rabbi Isaac Reines, one of religious Zionism's founders, wrote, "Zionist ideology is devoid of any trace of the idea of redemption. Their sole intention is to improve Israel's situation, to raise their stature and accustom them to a life of happiness. Clearly, action in the present day does not trespass upon utopian hopes for the Time to Come."[8] From the pre-state era to 1967 the religious Zionists maintained a constant if loose alliance with the Labor Party. But even in the pre-state era an explicitly messianic version of religious Zionism appeared in the writings of Abraham Isaac Kook, the chief rabbi under the British administration. Kook also legitimized cooperation with the Zionists but in a way that, far from denying Zionism's connection with the Messiah, put messianic redemption at the very center of the movement. Creatively combining Jewish mysticism and German philosophy, Kook maintained that the Zionists, although personally antireligious, were nevertheless God's instrument in a divine plan of redemption. "There are people who do not have the slightest idea what an important role they play in the scheme of Divine Providence. They are called but do not know who is calling them. . . But this terrible concealment will end with a great disclosure of lasting import."[9] Whatever their conscious motives, by settling the land the Zionists were preparing the way for the Messiah. A complex and multilevel intellectual whose metaphysical acceptance of Zionist unbelief did not prevent him from attacking it in the everyday world, Kook was considered one of the great Jewish minds of his era. But while his philosophical system generated intense debate among talmudists and secular intellectuals, during his life he had few followers. Only when his abstract philosophy was converted to a concrete program by his son after the 1967 war would it utterly transform religious Zionism.

* * *

With the founding of Israel in 1948 prophecy gave way to politics. The establishment of a legal relationship between religion and state would shape the new nation. At issue was nothing less than the meaning of the Jewish state.[10] Fearful that an explicit definition of the relationship between religion and state would be terribly divisive, Ben-Gurion fudged and compromised. He created an ad hoc system of relations that laid the groundwork for contemporary religious conflict. In 1947, seeking Jewish unity before a UN commission charged with determining the fate of Palestine, the future prime minister assured Orthodox non-opposition by promising them control over religion in the future state. The religious authorities would be responsible for registering births and deaths and have exclusive control over marriage. Saturday would be the official day of rest, kosher food would be provided at state institutions, and a modified religious calendar would be instituted. Ben-Gurion also agreed to fund Jewish education for those who desired it and later gave four hundred Yeshiva students exemption from military service.

Ben-Gurion's concessions did not, as some historians maintain, reflect a debt he felt to Orthodoxy for keeping Jewish identity alive so that it could be rescued by Zionism. More likely, Ben-Gurion, a consummate politician, felt that he could co-opt the Orthodox into supporting Labor in future political coalitions. Alternatively, his concessions may have come from an arrogant dismissal of the potentialities of the Orthodox population that he was convinced would soon disappear. Indeed, he considered the Orthodox Mea She'arim neighborhood to be a kind of cultural preserve where modern Israelis could view the quaint and soon-to-be-extinct customs of their ancestors. Since the forces of religion were waning, it was similarly imprudent to push for a constitution that would evoke deep conflict and divert the nation from its more important priorities, such as immigrant absorption and the creation of an alliance with the United States.[11]

Since there was no agreement among Israelis as to the religious meaning of the state, Ben-Gurion's initial arrangements became a kind of shaky status quo that served as a baseline for conflicts between the secular and the Orthodox. A continuing source of dispute was the definition of Jewish identity. The first measure passed by the Israeli parliament was the Law of Return, which gave any Jew the right to become an Israeli citizen. The law, however, gave no definition of Jewishness. In its early days the state employed the secular definition that a Jew was anyone who claimed to be so.[12] In 1956, responding to religious agitation, Ben-Gurion affirmed that the halachic (religious) definition—that a Jew was one who either was born of a Jewish mother or had converted—would be used. But this did not end the matter, as a number of famous court cases refined the terms of conflict. In 1966 the Supreme Court heard the case of Oswald Rufeisen, a Polish Jew who had converted to Catholicism. As Brother Daniel he demanded Israeli citizenship under the Law of Return so that he could join the Carmelite Order in Haifa. The court rejected a strictly halachic definition of Jewishness—Brother Daniel had a Jewish mother, and Jewish religious law assumes that even an apostate can be saved—when it held that, by converting, Rufeissen had abandoned Jewish history and destiny. He was therefore not a Jew "as understood by ordinary Jews."[13] While the Orthodox welcomed this decision, an even more divisive case demonstrated that the court's refusal to be bound by Jewish law could cut both ways. Benjamin Shalit, a secular Israeli who had married a non-Jewish woman, petitioned the court to permit the registration of his children as Jews, stating in essence that Jewish ethnicity was separate from religion. In 1970 the court agreed, maintaining that the children were being brought up as Jews and were part of the Jewish destiny.

The decision unleashed a public outcry that threatened to topple the Labor government, which finally agreed to legislate a definition of Jewishness agreeable to the Orthodox. After much parliamentary wrangling a new section was added to the Law of Return in 1970, defining a Jew as "a person who was born of a Jewish mother or who has been converted to Judaism and who is not a member of another religion." Left open was the question of what should be the nature of any such conversion.[14] Hence, any conversion under Conservative or Reform auspices was simply to be rejected.

Over the years the Knesset repeatedly refused to add the stipulation that conversion be according to halacha. An ad hoc compromise evolved. Conversions within Israel had to be conducted by the Orthodox, but conversions conducted outside Israel by Reform and Conservative rabbis would be recognized as valid by Israel's Orthodox authorities. This state of affairs was confirmed by the Israeli Supreme Court in 1989. The issue was not so much who is a Jew or who is a convert but what kind of rabbi can produce a Jewish convert.

This modus vivendi sufficed for nearly two decades, during which Israel's underlying political and religious atmosphere underwent radical change. The ultra-Orthodox, the religious Zionists, and even mainstream secular Zionism evolved in ways that Ben-Gurion could not have imagined. While mainstream Labor Zionism became ideologically and politically weaker, both the Haredim and religious Zionists experienced a revival in vitality, self-image, and power. The unexpected result was that by the mid-1990s the ultra-Orthodox sought to take control of much of Israel's domestic policy while religious Zionists sought to determine much of Israel's foreign policy.

The ultra-Orthodox, so complacently dismissed by Ben-Gurion, simply refused to die out. Their state-sponsored yeshivas and high birth rate produced a demographic revival such that they could claim that there are now more students studying Talmud in Israel than at any time in all of Eastern Europe. Moreover, the tendency of the new generation of modern Israeli Orthodox to join their more uncompromising brethren has also augmented their ranks. Even more important has been the arrival of the Sephardic (Jews of Middle Eastern origin) ultra-Orthodox, who soon joined the political coalitions of their Ashkenazic (Jews of European origin) compatriots. The emergence of the Shas party (Sephardic Torah Guardians), articulating the spiritual and material needs of the Morrocan Haredim, demonstrated the empowerment of the Sephardim. The Shas party, which had no hesitation in taking part in politics, has greatly increased the power of the Haredim in the Knesset.

Ultra-Orthodox empowerment produced a great change in attitude toward politics and the state. In Israel's early days the Haredim, somewhat apologetically, took part in the government as a kind of rear guard action. As one of its representatives wrote, "We are weak. Laws that will injure our innermost being will make our situation tragic and unbearable, we must therefore maintain our guard and repulse attacks against us from within the government."[15] As demographic and secular trends and Israel's coalition political system transformed the Orthodox from a beleaguered minority to a powerful political force, their conception of their role in Israeli society has similarly evolved. In the past two decades, beginning with their support for the Begin government, the ultra-Orthodox have greatly increased their participation in the debates concerning the evolution of the Jewish state. They have been particularly concerned not only with increasing their share of government funding, which has grown exponentially, but with rescuing the rest of Israeli society from secularism by attempting to use state power to coerce religious practice. The attempt to close main arteries on the Sabbath, the campaign against permissive advertising on Jerusalem's streets, and the desire to prohibit the farming of pigs were all manifestations of the new ultra-Orthodox power and activism. Their recent ability to gain the chairmanship of major Knesset committees and in effect to become cabinet members has even led some of their number to question whether they are becoming too accustomed to and too comfortable with the political system, which ideologically they abhor. But the fact remains that, whether by desire or circumstance, the Haredim have reached the center of power.

* * *

The evolution of religious Zionism has been even more unexpected and radical, with extremely unsettling implications for most American Jews. From the pre-state era until 1967 the religious Zionists had allied with the Labor Party. Relatively dovish on foreign policy, right after the 1967 war the religious Zionists had even advocated giving up the West Bank. But religious Zionism was affected by the outcome of the war to an even greater degree than was the rest of Israel. By most accounts the unification of Jerusalem, the liberation of the Western Wall, and the conquest of biblical Hebron, Judea, and Samaria struck a religious chord even in many of the most devoted secularists. If these seemingly miraculous events affected even the secular, the religious were even more profoundly moved by the seeming immanence of the Divine presence. Religious Zionists now embraced the messianic philosophy of Abraham Isaac Kook, especially as elaborated and converted into a program of coherent political action by his son, Zvi Yehudah Kook. Whereas the elder Kook had perceived the Zionist enterprise as part of a generalized cosmic process, his son viewed contemporary Israeli history as the unfolding of a specific divine plan of redemption. "The Master of the Universe has His own political agenda according to which politics here below are conducted."[16] Thus, the founding of Israel, the 1967 war, the reunification of Jerusalem, the conquest of Judea and Samaria are all small steps in the redemption process. After the conquest of the Western Wall in 1967 he declared, "We hereby inform the people of Israel and the entire world that under heavenly command we have just returned home in the elevations of holiness and our holy city. We shall never move out of here."[17] In particular the younger Kook saw the liberation of land, now considered to be holy in itself, as a direct link in the coming of the Messiah. "The conquest and settlement of the land . . . is dictated by divine politics, and no earthly politics can supersede it."[18]

After 1967 religious Zionism was dominated by this messianism, which prohibited self-questioning, moderation, compromise, or retreat. The state and its institutions, particularly the military, were revered as the instruments of the Messiah and increasingly perceived as holy. As Yehuda Zvi himself said, "The state of Israel is divine. Not only can/must there be no retreat from a single kilometer of the land of Israel God forbid, but on the contrary we shall conquer and liberate more and more."[19] The religious Zionists no longer saw themselves as a minority or marginalized group fated forever to play second fiddle to the secular Zionists. On the contrary, animated by their new and specific religious vision, they aimed to do nothing less than to take control over much of Israel's foreign policy.

After the shock of the 1973 war, traditional Labor Zionism was blamed for the near defeat and in any case experienced a psychological malaise and a decrease in energy and morale. The religious Zionists moved into the ideological power vacuum by creating Gush Emunim (The Front of the Faithful) to build illegal settlements on the West Bank. Taking possession of the land would bring the Messiah closer and prevent any territorial compromise with the Palestinians. The new movement appealed to religious youth who had long felt denigrated by secular Zionism. Now they could be at the very center of the Zionist enterprise.

Their first settlement was founded in Hebron, chosen for its religious associations and because it was the site of an Arab massacre of Jews in 1929. It was also one of the principal Palestinian population centers on the West Bank. Allowed to remain by a weak Labor government, the Front grew into a mass movement, establishing scores of settlements throughout the occupied territories. Its uncompromising messianism dovetailed with the secularly based hard-line policies of Menachem Begin's Revisionists who, after three decades in the political wilderness, took control of the government in 1977. Dependent on religious support in 1977, Begin brought the Orthodox into the government in 1981. He created a coalition of religious Zionists, revisionists, and ordinary nonideological Israelis who, as settlers on the West Bank, could aspire to a quality of residential housing unattainable in Israel proper.

As religious Zionists helped transform Israel's foreign policy, their political stance became more and more radical. Their religious authorities drew the innovative halachic conclusion that the retention of land takes precedence even over the saving of human lives. The plot of a fringe group to bring on the messianic era by blowing up the mosques on the Temple Mount demonstrated how dangerous its extremists had become. Even within the center of ultra-Orthodoxy there was an increasing tendency to denounce debate, pluralism, and democracy.

The emergence of the religious parties as a decisive force in the 1988 parliamentary elections propelled the "Who is a Jew" question onto the center stage of Israeli-Diaspora relations. Voter disillusionment with the Labor Party, dating from the 1973 war, and with Likud, stemming from the debacle of the Lebanon invasion of 1982, had led to increased support for both single-issue parties and for the religious bloc. The shock of the Intifada had reinforced the distrust of secular politicians and produced a Knesset in which neither Labor nor Likud controlled more than one-third of the seats.

Lacking parliamentary majorities, neither large party was anxious to revive the coalition with each other that for the past years had produced the misnamed national unity government in which it seemed that the only thing the two could agree upon was their mutual detestation of the arrangement. As Yitzhak Shamir and Yitzhak Rabin desperately sought to put together governments without the other, the religious parties, who now controlled 18 of the 120 Knesset seats felt that their time had come. In coalition negotiations with both Labor and Likud they allegedly asked for control of the ministries of absorption, immigration, education, religion, and welfare, as well as greatly increased subsidies for their educational and welfare institutions. Topping off their demands was a requirement that any new government must pledge to pass legislation assuring that within Israel only conversions made by the Orthodox would be recognized as valid. The Orthodox further stipulated that such promises had to be made in writing. In mid-November it appeared that Shamir would agree to those demands and put together a coalition with the religious parties.

Within Israel there was much grumbling about religious blackmail. Ninety retired generals presented Shamir with a petition objecting to his governing with parties who encouraged draft evasion. But the real explosion came from America and made the reaction to the Pollard affair and even the Intifada seem like a friendly spat. The announcement of the proposed coalition coincided with the fifty-seventh annual meeting of the General Assembly of the Council of Jewish Federations, and discussion of the "Who is a Jew"question dominated the meetings. The council sent an emergency mission to Israel to explain why American Jews considered the proposed changes so damaging. What followed was a bonanza for El Al. During November and December almost every Jewish organization sent representatives to Jerusalem to voice their extreme displeasure with the Orthodox initiative.[20] Over two thousand Jewish leaders met with Prime Minister Shamir, with Rabin, with members of the Knesset, and with representatives of the religious establishment—indeed, with almost any Israeli who would listen to their almost frenzied expostulations. The office of Israel's president was innundated with letters of protest, phone calls, and telegrams from enraged American Jews.

On its face the American Jewish reaction seemed overblown. After all, the legal technicalities directly affected no more than the half dozen Jews per year converted by the non-Orthodox who chose to settle in Israel. But American Jews correctly grasped the symbolic nature of the legislation. In stating that Conservative and Reform conversions were invalid, the Orthodox were telling 85 percent of all American Jewry that they were second-class or partial Jews. An exclusivist religious conception of identity threatened the ethnic ties by which most American Jews related to Israel. This hit at the heart of American Jewish leaders' personal and institutional connection to Israel from which they derived great status and which had so benefited the Jewish state. For the rank and file it called into question the ties to Israel than that had become for so many the center of Jewish identity. It was also the kind of nonsecurity issue about which almost all American Jews could feel comfortable voicing public criticism. In this sense rage over the conversion law may have to some degree been a transference of the unexpressed anger that many American Jews had felt since Israel's invasion of Lebanon in 1982. As Martin Stein, the chairman of United Jewish Appeal (UJA), told Israeli television somewhat anachronistically, "Diaspora Jews do not presume to dictate to Israel on defense or other matters since they are not directly affected by them but the proposed legislation would disenfranchise us."[21] Closer to home, both the Boston and Atlanta Jewish Federations decided to withhold funds earmarked for Israel as long as the proposed religious legislation was pending.

* * *

Within Israel both Left and Right were chagrined by the American re-action. Shamir's official spokesman conceded that "I was surprised that so many [American Jews] took it as a personal matter. There is much we don't understand about American Jews." Teddy Kollek, longtime Labor mayor of Jerusalem and American icon, said he had never seen American Jews so offended by an Israeli action.[22]

When, in late December, Shamir abandoned the religious parties to forge yet another power-sharing coalition with Labor, American Jews were ecstatic. They were convinced that their intervention against the conversion legislation had forced Likud to abandon the religious par-ties. Harry Wall, the Anti-Defamation League's representative in Is-rael, crowed, "This is a watershed in the relationship between Ameri-can Jews and Israel."[23] In truth, more was at work. Shamir may have used the threat of allying with the "black hats" to pressure Labor into joining a Likud-led coalition. In addition, the recent decision of the American government to open a dialogue with the PLO required the establishment of a broadly based Israeli government to resist the diplo-matic pressure that would inevitably result. The Bush administration's recognition of the PLO also made the maintenance of a good relation-ship with American Jews all the more important. Whatever Shamir's motivation, the mass mobilization of American Jews had undoubtedly played an important part in determining Israeli domestic policy. The "Who is a Jew" question was again put on the back burner, but the Or-thodox in Israel and the Reform and Conservatives in America now understood the stakes involved.

When the "Who is a Jew" issue surfaced again in the mid-1990s, the Orthodox had become even more powerful and the non-Orthodox more aggressive. In 1995 the Central Conference of American Rabbis and the American Reform Zionist Organization (ARZA), two of the largest reform organizations in America, embarked on "Operation Equality," a two-year campaign designed to end the unequal treatment of the non-Orthodox in Israel by lobbying for legislation to give Israe-lis the option to have civil or non-Orthodox weddings. This was a logi-cal issue for the Reform movement to use to build an alliance with na-tive Israelis. The Orthodox monopoly over marriage was preventing thousands of halachicly "impure" Russian immigrants from marrying, and no less than 20 percent of the Israelis chose to marry abroad rather than under Orthodox auspices. But it was the small Israeli Conservative movement that reanimated the conflict over nonrecognition. In 1995 the Conservatives went before the Israeli Supreme Court to force the interior ministry to register as Jews thirteen adopted children who had been converted in Israel by a Conservative rabbi. By ruling that Orthodox conversion was not necessary for recognition as Jews the court opened the door, however slightly, to a potentially greater official role for the non-Orthodox in Israel.

The swelling Russian immigration had given greater urgency to that ruling. Since 1988 over 700,000 Russian immigrants had settled in Israel. It was estimated that between 150,000 and 200,000 were not considered Jewish by Orthodox law. To own property, to be able to marry, or to have a Jewish burial such immigrants would have to convert under Orthodox auspices. But the Orthodox limited the number of converts to less than four hundred per year out of ten thousand applications submitted. In a country where over 80 percent of the population is secular it seemed unfair to compel recent immigrants to adhere to a stricter standard of Judaism than the rest of the nation. The Supreme Court's recognition of non-Orthodox conversion within Israel would do much to alleviate these problems. The Orthodox were about as likely to accept baptism as changes in the religious status quo. Considering the Reform movement as Godless, as responsible for confusing Jewish identity in its 1993 decision to recognize patrilinial descent, and as leading Diaspora Jewry into an assimilatory oblivion, the Orthodox saw any concession as religiously unacceptable.

At least equally important, the Supreme Court decision threatened the Orthodox monopoly over religion. The Orthodox were, however, in an unprecedented position to defend their interests. The twenty-three seats that the religious parties had gained in the May 1996 elections were a third of Benjamin Netanyahu's coalition—without them he could not retain power. As both sides girded for battle, the Union of Orthodox Rabbis, representing 5 percent of the Jewish population in America and Canada, declared that "the reform and conservative are not Judaism at all" and urged both to "abandon their erroneous ways." The motivation for this pronouncement, which was repudiated by most American Orthodox, was eminently clear: "We're formulating a halachic ruling that will give the parliament in Israel very strong and irrefutable arguments against the reform and conservative efforts."[24] Israel's Orthodox hardly needed help. On April 1, 1997, the ultrareligious Shas

Party introduced legislation stating that the "conversion of persons in Israel will be conducted according to the law of the Torah" and could only be carried out by the Orthodox rabbinate. Moving from the high road of ideology to the low road of patronage, the measure also sought to bar the non-Orthodox from the local religious councils, which allocate money to religious establishments. The bill, which had to be approved three times to become law, passed its first reading 51–32 with 7 abstentions. In another indication of the power of the Orthodox and of the willingness of both major parties to defer to them, three of the four candidates for Labor Party leadership absented themselves from the vote for fear of alienating those whom they might need in future coalitions.[25]

The proposed law changed little, since non-Orthodox conversion outside of Israel, the validity of which had been confirmed by the Supreme Court in 1989, would still be acccepted by the government. It would, however, legally enshrine the existing discrimination. American Jews, having become accustomed to confronting Israel on the Pollard affair, the Intifada, and the 1988 version of the "Who is a Jew?" controversy, were determined to push the issue. Rabbi Eric Yoffee, the president of the Union of American Hebrew Congregations, an organization representing nine hundred Reform synagogues stated, "If Reform rabbis in Israel are not rabbis and their conversions are not conversions that means our Judaism is not Judaism, and that we are second class Jews."[26] Ironically, the controversy arose just as the Central Conference of American Rabbis, completing eight years of deliberations, celebrated the one-hundredth anniversary of Zionism by introducing a new platform, which made support of Israel a specific religious obligation. But the new platform criticized both religious Zionism and the ultra-Orthodox by stating that "the sanctity of Jewish life takes precedence over the sanctity of Jewish land" and that "the Jewish people will be best served when *Medinat Yisrael* [the State of Israel] is constituted as a pluralistic Democratic society."[27]

On the Conservative side, the Rabbinic Assembly resolved, "We are outraged at the latest attempt to deny full religious rights to the largest segment of world Jewry—an act that denies the pluralistic nature of Judaism and betrays the inclusive vision of Zionism."[28] Rabbi Ismar Schorch, chancellor of the Jewish Theological Seminary, sent a letter to Conservative rabbis and major Jewish organizations demanding that the Orthodox rabbinate of Israel be disbanded and that donations to groups that oppose the recognition of the non-Orthodox be ended. He characterized the system of the chief rabbinate and its courts as "without a scintilla of moral worth."[29]

This was merely the tip of the iceberg. American Jews refused to accept Benjamin Netanyahu's assertion that "the law changes nothing essential and real in our relationship with the Jewish communities in the world." By being so rigid the Orthodox rabbinate created an issue that the non-Orthodox could use to mobilize support both within and outside the Jewish state. From pulpits all over America, Reform and Conservative rabbis decried the bill as a symbol of Orthodox religious tyranny. For many American Jews the issue was, as New Israel Fund director David Arnow put it, "How can the Jewish State of all places deny Jews religious freedom? The irony became too unbearable."[30] The Reform and Conservative movements called on their 1800 member congregations to boycott any member of the Knesset who did not oppose the bill.

The confrontation left Netanyahu caught in the middle. On the one hand, many Orthodox sincerely believed that what the Americans called religious pluralism would result in religious anarchy. As one Orthodox Knesset member said, "[The Conservative and Reform movements] are going to turn the most sacred thing to the Jewish people, the basis of our existence into a laughingstock." More crucially for the prime minister, the coalition agreement stipulated that the government would work to ensure that "the Conversion Law be changed so that conversions to Judaism in Israel will be recognized only if approved by the Chief Rabbinate."[31] If Netanyahu did not support the new law, it would most likely bring down his government. On the other hand, to support it would precipitate an all-out war with American Jews. Desperately searching for a way out, Netanyahu created a seven-member committee to seek a compromise. Chaired by Finance Minister Yaakov Ne'eman, himself Orthodox, the committee included one representative each from the Reform and Conservative movements. It would present its findings by August 15. In the meantime the Orthodox would suspend their legislative efforts while the non-Orthodox would refrain from asking the Supreme Court to enforce its decision.[32]

Throughout the summer of 1997 the conflict grew more bitter at all levels. While Orthodox, Conservative, and Reform leaders continued their wars of words, followers turned to action. In June, Conservative and Reform leaders protested outside the prime minister's office carrying baskets filled with petitions from American Jews. On the holiday of

Shavuot a group of Reform and Conservative Jews worshipping at the Western Wall were attacked by Haredim enraged at the sight of men and women praying together. The Haredim revealed their collective demonology by calling the worshipers "Nazis," "Christians," "whores," and "goyim." Escaping worshipers were reputedly pelted with excrement from the windows of a nearby yeshiva.[33] The deputy mayor of Jerusalem justified the attack by stating that the very presence of Conservative Jews, "who symbolize the destruction of the Jewish people," was itself a "provocation." On Tisha B'av the non-Orthodox again attempted to hold a religious service at the Western Wall and were expelled by police acting on orders from the Holy Sites Authority.

American Jews now engaged in what only could be called a mass revolt against Israel. Accustomed to being denigrated by Israel's Orthodox, now they felt the power of the state itself was being turned against them. The Jewish media, from national publications to the smallest local journal, bristled with indignant editorials and opinion pieces that ranged from the high road ("Judaism belongs not to the rabbis in Israel but to the Jews of the world.")[34] to the low ("as a throwback to the sthetl, Israel will be of no consequence for the majority of the Jews in the diaspora"). Lay leaders, Jewish commentators, and rabbis urged a redirection of contributions away from the Federations, with their close ties to the Israeli government, to alternative charities, particularly those that promoted pluralism. During the High Holidays of 1997 many Reform and Conservative Rabbis used their sermons to ask their congregants to donate to funds and projects controlled by the non-Orthodox in Israel.[35] The New Israel Fund reported a 25 percent increase in contributions. In Northern California the East Bay Federation shifted funds to encourage pluralism.[36] Nationally, many Jews refrained from their customary donations, as much as $20 million being withheld or diverted to other causes.[37] Moreover, an increasing number of donors insisted on tying their contributions to specific Israeli institutions. Hoping to head off further revolt, the UJA quickly pledged $10 million per year to the cause of religious pluralism.[38]

A small number of Reform Jews even attempted to lobby Congress to pressure Israel on the issue of pluralism, thereby demonstrating that immoderate actions were not restricted to the other side. In November, Prime Minister Netanyahu addressed the national convention of Jewish federations in Indianapolis, where he was received coldly by the assembled delegates, traditionally a bastion of reflexive support. Many in the assembly wore buttons with the slogan "Don't write off four million Jews." The prime minister's speech, in which he declared that no power on earth can rob any Jew of his or her identity; every Jew is a legitimate Jew, did little to assuage their resentment. By contrast, Labor leader Ehud Barak's condemnation of the conversion law met with sustained applause. It was Yacov Ne'eman, however, who was embraced by the gathering as the man who could end the crisis and avert a split of historical proportions. But even Ne'eman's expressed optimism was received skeptically by those who wondered why it was not reflected in the Haredi community.[39]

* * *

Most secular Israelis, if not indifferent, were mystified by the outrage of their American cousins. Influenced by classical Zionist ideology, which dismissed the Reform and Conservative movements as assimilationist manifestations of the Diaspora mentality, the vast majority of Israelis knew little of these movements, even though they had been making slight inroads into Israeli society. The Israeli Conservative movement (Masorti), which encourages adherence to religious law without coercion, claims twenty thousand members. The Reform (Progressive) movement, which keeps kosher and rejects American Reform's recognition of patrilineal descent, claims half as many. Both groups maintain educational systems, youth movements, and seminaries that reach many times their official membership. The failure of the non-Orthodox Jewish streams to become much more than fringe movements in Israel is attributable in part to the fact that they are foreign implants that reflect American conditions. It is often argued that American Jews join a Reform synagogue not so much as a religious act but as a proclamation of ethnic identification. Whatever problems Israel has, a lack of ethnic identity is hardly one of them. Rather, Israelis tend to see religion as an all-or-nothing proposition. Even the most secular view Orthodoxy as the only legitimate form of Judaism. As the common joke goes, "The shul I don't attend is Orthodox." In such an environment the innovations of the Conservative and Reform movements simply don't resonate. The notion of religious pluralism, so dear to the hearts of Americans, evokes little response among Israelis. The Labor Party has been hardly less opportunistic than the Likud in its attempts to form coalitions with the ultra-Orthodox. For the 80 percent of the population that is secular, the overriding religious issue is the inordinate power of the Orthodox over their lives and the desire of the nonreligious to erect secular alternatives. Rabbi Gordon Tucker, one of the leaders of the Masorti movement notes, "How can you have so many marriages taking place outside the state? It doesn't happen in the worst tyrannies."[40] Thus, the original Reform strategy of using the Orthodox monopoly over marriage as the issue upon which to fight for recognition would probably have gained them many more secular allies.

Reform and Conservative leaders in both Israel and America are convinced that the Orthodox establishment has stifled their movements' growth in the Jewish state. While undoubtedly so, the image of both as foreign implants and Reform's historical indifference to Zionism have been equally important factors inhibiting their growth. Now their leaders feel that both movements have the potential to play a crucial role in meeting Israel's spiritual needs. They maintain that Israel is becoming less and less religious, at least in part because Orthodox fanaticism is giving Judaism a bad name. Israeli opinion polls do show that many secular Israelis detest the ultra-Orthodox for draft dodging, for alleged corruption, and for their control over marriage and divorce. In some surveys the Haredim are disliked more than the Palestinians.[41] A recent letter to the *Jerusalem Post* vehemently articulated the hatreds and fears of much of the secular population:

Disconnected from the world, educated to despise Zionism and the state, sinking into condescending ignorance and obediently serving their religious leaders, this gargantuan, unenlightened force goes on amassing political and public power. No longer satisfied with the crumbs a corrupt secular government has used to bribe them, they sense their time has come, and have gone from the defensive to the attack—"converting" secular Israelis to Judaism, imposing their lifestyle on the system as a whole.[42]

In this context, to be secular is not necessarily to be antireligious in the American sense. Fully 90 percent of Jewish Israelis circumcise their sons, and 80 percent bar-mitzvah them. But since Labor Zionism ceded religion to the Orthodox, many Israelis turned off by Orthodoxy have had no alternative but to opt out of religion entirely. The result has been the creation of a new generation largely ignorant not just of religion but also of Jewish history and culture. By providing a religious alternative to Orthodoxy, the Conservative and Reform movements seek to arrest collective Jewish assimilation in Israel. It is probably not coincidental that the movements have experienced their greatest growth in their education systems, as increasing numbers of Israeli parents seek to provide their children with a Jewish, if non-Orthodox, religious and cultural context. The Orthodox themselves have begun to take note of the threat, however small. On major holidays they take out ads in Israeli papers warning potential worshipers that they can not fulfill holy commandments in non-Orthodox synagogues.[43]

In October the Ne'eman Committee's recommendations for a compromise were leaked to the press. A centralized conversion institute would be established, directed by a seven-member executive composed of representatives of all three movements that would determine procedures and curriculum. The graduates of this institute would then be converted by a special rabbinic court composed entirely of the Orthodox. In addition the committee proposed that Reform and Conservative rabbis perform marriages under the supervision of the chief rabbinate. The plan assured that conversions would be halachicly pure by maintaining the Orthodox monopoly over the process of conversion while giving the non-Orthodox a morsel of recognition. Even before the compromise was officially made public, the chief rabbinic council rejected it, ridiculing the Reform and Conservative movements as "clowns," "non-Jews," and even "members of a movement that was responsible for the Holocaust."[44] Taking their cue, the religious parties were equally condemnatory. The chairman of Shas called the proposals "horrific."

The Reform and Conservative leaders now felt that they had been duped into deferring their legal challenges and that "this whole process was nothing but a tactic to buy time."[45] Stressing that "we were unable to find a single major official within the rabbinate willing to work in keeping with the outline of the nearly completed Ne'eman agreement," the Reform and Conservative representatives threatened to withdraw from the committee and reinstitute their case before the Supreme Court. Only after a meeting with President Ezer Weizman, attended also by an official of the chief rabbinate, albeit in an "unofficial capacity," did they agree to keep the litigation on hold and to prolong the committee's deliberations for another three months.[46]

* * *

In America the revolt intensified. Israel's ambassador to Washington, Eliahu Ben-Elissar, declared that "Jewish organization leaders have warned us clearly that this will lead to the worst crisis ever between

American Jews and Israel."[47] Moreover, he received an "unequivocal warning" from AIPAC that passage of the bill would harm Israel's "unique" political standing in the United States.[48] The truth of these warnings soon became apparent. As the conflict between American Jews and the Israeli government became more public and more bitter, the Clinton administration began to apply heavy pressure on Prime Minister Netanyahu to speed Israeli troop withdrawals from the West Bank. On December 1, the Conference of Presidents, one of Israel's strongest supporters, met to prepare a response to the pressure. But finding no consensus among its member organizations, it chose not to defend Israel but to remain silent. When the prime minister visited the United States in January 1998, he sought political support from the Christian Right and did not meet with Reform Jews.

After nearly fifty meetings, during which they heard the testimony of eighty witnesses and deliberated for over 150 hours, the Ne'eman committee presented its findings in mid-January. The most significant changes from the proposal leaked three months earlier was that the Reform and Conservative groups agreed to cease performing their own conversions in Israel independent of the conversion institute. They also agreed that the marriage issue would be subject to later negotiations. Both represented substantial concessions. But the major Haredi and national religious party rabbis immediately rejected the proposed agreement in the strongest possible terms. A letter signed by four of Israel's most prominent rabbis forbids (Orthodox) Jews "to negotiate with destroyers of religion who falsify the Torah and bring about the assimilation and destruction of Jewry in the Diaspora."[49]

In officially rejecting the compromise, the chief rabbinate demonstrated that it took a backseat to none in the expression of invective. Refusing to call the non-Orthodox by name, the rabbis referred to "those who do not believe in Torah from the heavens, who seek to undermine the foundations of the Jewish faith." Furthermore, "the sages of Israel forbade any cooperation with them or their ways. We cannot consider establishing a joint institute with them."[50] That the rabbinate naturally accepted the other major provision of the Ne'eman compromise—the creation of special rabbinic courts that would maintain their monopoly over conversion—prompted Ne'eman and the government to put a positive spin on the rejection. Splitting hairs with the skill of the most accomplished talmudist, Ne'eman argued that the Orthodox rejection of the conversion institute was not crucial since the rabbinate would judge candidates for conversion on their individual merits regardless of how or where they were prepared. He called for his committee's proposals to be implemented.[51] Prime Minister Netanyahu went even further. Explicitly ignoring their rejection of the conversion institute and dismissing their insulting language as expected background noise, he hailed the Orthodox response "as promoting a real consensus among the Jewish people and the state of Israel." Indeed, the Ne'eman recommendations were widely supported in Israeli opinion polls, were endorsed by the cabinet, and gained the support of two-thirds of the Knesset in a nonbinding vote. But all such support was negated by the simple fact that the Orthodox establishment had undercut the compromise by refusing to accord the other streams even the smallest shred of recognition. As the president of Israel's Conservative movement noted, "The government is trying to present it as if the committee's proposals were accepted. Nothing could be further from the truth. The *chutzpa*."[52]

Spin doctoring and wishful thinking aside, the true situation was shown a few days later. During a symposium called to explain each side's position, the Reform and Conservative representatives were not permitted to sit at the dais until the Orthodox representative left. They were livid over the continuous litany of Orthodox insult and the rejection of the conversion institute despite the many compromises they had made. The Orthodox had "declared war on the Jewish people."[53] Therefore the non-Orthodox would renew their Supreme Court case to force recognition.

The reaction of American Jews was virtually apoplectic. Jewish Theological Seminary chancellor Rabbi Ismar Schorsch again called for dismantling the chief rabbinate, whose actions "threaten to sunder the fabric of Jewish unity so vital to the cohesion and survival of the state."[54] The American Jewish press used terms like "irretrievable break" and "religious civil war" to describe the relationship between Israel and the non-Orthodox Diaspora. In February, when Prime Minister Netanyahu spoke to the annual convention of the Rabbinical Assembly (the national board of American Conservative rabbis), which was meeting in Jerusalem, the audience was hostile due to his glossing over the fact that the Orthodox had sabotaged the Ne'eman proposals.[55]

But Netanyahu bravely soldiered on. In late April the conversion institute was called into being despite the fact that the Orthodox had neither given the recognition upon which the compromise was based nor any assurance that they would recognize its graduates. The Reform and

Conservative movements officially reinstituted their case, upon which the Supreme Court would begin deliberations in early June. In response the government reintroduced a new conversion bill embodying the conversion institute of the Ne'eman Committee. But since the bill was neither the product of compromise nor of mutual recognition and maintained the Orthodox monopoly over religion, Reform head rabbi Eric Yoffe called it "the conversion law under another name."[56]

In early June, 170 American Reform rabbis arrived in Jerusalem and immediately proceeded to the Western Wall to pray. This time they were given sufficient police protection and carried out their service without incident. But when the group met with Prime Minister Netanyahu, he angered them by implying that they carry out quickie conversions rather than the year or more of study and community involvement that they in fact require. In America the rhetoric was escalating. A national meeting of Reform rabbis declared that passage of the bill "would devestate the Israel Diaspora relationship and cause severe and deleterious consequences in the political, philanthropic, and religious realms." Another commentator was more direct. The passage of such legislation would "abruptly end the centrality of Israel for American Jews."[57] Indeed, the rhetoric of both sides has grave implications for the much larger issue of Jewish unity. In an interview a prominent Jewish professional spoke of his "visceral detestation" at the sight of the ultra-Orthodox. If his feelings are even moderately representative of liberal Jews, the real war may be lost no matter which side wins the specific battles.

| |9| |

An Ambivalent Anniversary

In both the Jewish and Western traditions, the passage of fifty years is marked by celebration. Biblical law mandates a jubilee year during which property reverts to its original owners, slaves are freed, and debts are forgiven. After this period of repose, communal life is renewed on a new basis of equality. In the Western tradition an individual's fiftieth birthday is ideally a time of maturity and of the secure identity of a person at the height of his or her power.

As it approached its fiftieth birthday, Israel surely had much to celebrate. In the half century of its existence, Israel had progressed in countless ways far beyond the most optimistic dreams of the early Zionists. The state's Jewish population had increased from 860,000 to almost 5 million. From a military that in 1948 mounted sewer pipes on trucks to foster the illusion that it possessed artillery, Israel has become an atomic power and a regional superpower. Once known only for its oranges, Israel is now a major player is the cyber world of high technology and possesses a per capita income comparable to that of Western Europe.

Yet Israel's fiftieth anniversary was marked by neither unfettered celebration nor repose. The question of land ownership and control that had bedeviled the state for the entire half century of its existence continued to cause deep divisions, not only between Israel and the Arab world but within Israeli society. At a time when Israel's physical security and economic welfare have reached unprecedented levels, its fiftieth birthday was marred by a national identity crisis and political, social, and religious divisions that increasingly threatened the fabric of society. The bitterness and controversy surrounding the actual anniversary celebration reflected these divisions.

American Jews were similarly ambivalent. Great pride in Israel's achievements vied with fears about the peace process and with an increasing alienation brought on by Orthodox influence in the Netanyahu government. The anniversary manifested the growing division within American Jewry and between Israel and American Jews. During this jubilee year, American Jews' journey from from conformity to independence culminated in much of the community siding with their president against an Israeli prime minister.

American Jews were especially unhappy that Prime Minister Benjamin Netanyahu's negative attitude toward the Oslo Accords had resulted in the greatest conflict between Israel and the United States since the fight over loan guarantees a decade earlier. Elected in May 1996 in the shadow of Yitzhak Rabin's assassination, Netanyahu had defeated Shimon Peres by appealing to Israeli uneasiness over the Oslo Accords. He demanded "a secure peace" and criticized Yasir Arafat's failure both to change the PLO charter (which called for the destruction of Israel) and to control terrorism. He also attacked Peres's willingness to ignore Arafat's apparent inability to live up to the Oslo Accords.[1] Netanyahu's campaign rhetoric included the 'three no's—no to any compromise on Jewish rule over Jerusalem, no to a Palestinian State, and no to any surrender of the Golan Heights. Unlike Peres, who envisioned Israel as an integral part of "a new Middle East," Netanyahu still saw Israel as a bulwark of Western values in a hostile, alien world.

The requirements of the Oslo Accords that Israel give up most of Hebron and conduct three major "redeployments" in the West Bank were hardly congenial to the new prime minister, who had compared the peace agreement to the Munich Pact. After forming his cabinet, Netanyahu had wasted little time in demonstrating a new Israeli firmness toward the Oslo agreement and the Palestinians. In early August the cabinet voted unanimously to overturn the Labor government's policy of freezing settlement growth except in parts of the West Bank near Jerusalem. The Palestinians regarded this as "a real threat to the peace process and to the possibility of compromise between Israel and the Palestinians."[2] Indeed, the new prime minister did fail to resume the final phase of the peace talks that Peres had begun in May.

The new government soon extended its muscular stance toward the administration of Jerusalem. In late September the government opened the eastern end of a long disputed archaeological tunnel running from the Western Wall along the base of the Temple Mount, creating a new exit in the Muslim quarter. The 534-yard tunnel, which retraced an ancient road discovered in 1987, opens onto subterranean caverns, displaying spectacular artifacts from earlier eras of Jerusalem's history, and the ensuing tourism would increase traffic from seventy thousand to four hundred thousand annually. But the real point of the tunnel's opening was to assert Jewish political and practical control over all of Jerusalem—despite the fact that issues relating to the Holy City were to be negotiated as part of the Oslo agreement's final status talks. As Jerusalem's mayor, Ehud Olmert, stated, "We will not agree that everything that happens in Jerusalem is subject of negotiation because we are the sovereign of the city."[3] When Palestinian rioting greeted the tunnel's opening, the prime minister, sensing that the United States would not pressure Israel during a presidential election year, rebuffed Clinton's request to close the tunnel. The violence escalated to gun battles between Israeli forces and Palestinian police that left seventy dead. That the Palestinians had been given their weapons under the Oslo Accord made matters worse.

The mutual trust between Israelis and Palestinians so laboriously built up during the previous three years evaporated. Palestinians were increasingly convinced that Netanyahu would not carry out the Oslo Accords; Israelis were just as convinced that Arafat would not clamp down on terrorism. Even the conclusion of an agreement in mid-January, providing for an Israeli withdrawal from Hebron, did little to restore mutual trust. The evacuation (stipulated in the Oslo agreement), which left 20 percent of the city under Israeli control, was undertaken by Netanyahu grudgingly and as a result of American pressure. In return for Arafat's promise to fight terrorism and change the PLO charter, Netanyahu committed Israel to further West Bank deployments. Any goodwill generated by this agreement was dissipated soon thereafter. The prime minister, bowing to the contrary pressure of his own political party, announced that Israel would build 6,500 units of housing at Har Homa in Arab East Jerusalem. Arafat responded by suspending the negotiations that had been restarted after Israel's withdrawal. As U.S. ambassador Martin Indyk noted on May 18, "the core bargain of Oslo has broken down."[4]

By this time Prime Minister Netanyahu's relations with American Jews were in a similar state of deterioration. Following his election, despite having had a two-to-one preference for Peres, American Jews had been willing to give the new prime minister the benefit of the doubt. On his first trip to America as prime minister he attempted to reach out to all American Jews, stating that a new task of Zionism was to assure

Jewish identity in America and proposing a summer airlift for American Jewish youth. At a speech to Congress in which he proposed a cut in aid to Israel and Israeli concessions to the Palestinians on the basis of true reciprocity, he received four standing ovations. In New York, Netanyahu was received somewhat skeptically by the Jewish establishment and treated like a returning son by the rank and file. By the time he left America, 62 percent of American Jews had a favorable impression of him. One reason for this support was that the prime minister's view of the Middle East and of Israel's place in it was in accord with American Jews' traditional anxieties and with their own notion of Jews as victims. Netanyahu's siege mentality and his courting of American Jews were in direct contrast to the years of the Labor Party's "we don't need you." Barely noticed by the mainstream during this honeymoon period was that Netanyahu, in deference to his ultra-Orthodox supporters, made a special trip to Queens to visit the grave of the Lubavitcher Rebbe, Menachem Schneerson.

It was Netanyahu's Orthodox supporters who helped precipitate the greatest rift in the relationship between Israel and American Jews. Comprising about a third of his governing coalition, they sought to use their pivotal position to pass legislation requiring the government to recognize only conversions made under Orthodox auspices. Perceiving their own streams of Judaism to be denigrated and delegitimized, American Jews, 87 percent of whom are non-Orthodox, can only be described as going crazy with anger. Having become accustomed to confronting Israel on the issues of Lebanon, Pollard, and the Intifada, they engaged in the mass revolt against the Israeli government described in chapter 7. As the summer of 1997 moved on, the conflict grew ever more bitter, and American Jews' detestation of Netanyahu's courting of the Orthodox reinforced their suspicions about his commitment to the peace process, which at times he seemed to deliberately stall.[5] There was even a growing debate in the liberal Jewish press as to whether the prime minister was evil or merely incompetent.

In August one hundred prominent Jews took out an advertisement in the *New York Times* to express support for Secretary of State Madeleine Albright, who had advocated a greater U.S. mediating role in the peace process. Entitled "Thank You, Secretary of State Albright," the ad was signed by two of American Jewry's largest organizations—the Reform Union of American Hebrew Congregations and the United Synagogue of Conservative Judaism. Other signers included former leaders of mainstream Jewish organizations, such as the Conference of Presidents, the American Israel Political Action Committee (AIPAC), and the United Jewish Appeal. When Secretary of State Albright traveled in September to the Middle East to demand a Palestinian crackdown on terrorism and Israeli cessation of provocative unilateral acts that jeopardize the peace process, she had the enthusiastic support of mainstream Jewish leaders. Both publicly and in private conversation, they asked the administration to use its influence with Israel to discourage one-sided actions that damaged the climate for peace. That American Jews should be asking the administration for help in influencing Israel indicated both their level of frustration and their alienation from the policies of Netanyahu. It also demonstrated how independent they had become from the former object of their devotion. J. J. Goldberg, a prominent observer of American Jewry, stated, "What we are seeing is a much greater willingness of mainstream Jews to distance themselves from Israeli policy."[6] Since the mass of American Jews were alienated by the conversion crisis and ambivalent about Netanhayu's attitude toward Oslo, the prime minister bypassed them by calling upon AIPAC and the Conference of Presidents to counter American pressure on Israel. Both responded that American pressure should be put upon the Palestinians, not upon the Jewish state. But Robert K. Lifton, past chairman of the American Jewish Congress, told Secretary of State Albright that "a large segment of the Jewish community . . . would support pushing the parties to agreement and if that involved pushing Israel that's okay."[7]

As the jubilee year dawned, relations between the Netanyahu government and American Jews failed to improve. The prime minister's failed attempts to reach a compromise on the conversion law elicited new levels of vituperation. The inability of all parties to advance the peace process led to increasing bitterness between the United States and Israel. When Netanhayu visited the United States in late January, he met with Christian Evangelical leaders just before a session with the president. The prime minister's action demonstrated not only insensitivity to Clinton, who was a prime enemy of right-wing Christian leaders but also to indignant American Jews who opposed the right-wing domestic agenda and were suspicious of their attitude toward Jews despite their support of Israel. Abe Foxman, head of the Anti-Defamation League, echoed the sentiments of most when he characterized the meeting as "curious and inappropriate."[8]

In the growing tug-of-war between Clinton and Netanyahu both sides courted American Jews. The prime minister sent his advisor, David Bar Ilan, on a special mission to America to gain the support of Congress and American Jews. As the United States prepared to present a comprehensive plan to Israel and the Palestinians, calling for an Israeli withdrawal from 13 percent of the West Bank, Netanyahu tried to use Congress and Jewish leaders to derail it. In a sign of the renewed importance of the American Jewish community, Secretary of State Albright called American Jewish leaders to tell them "we are in trouble with the peace process and need your support." She pointedly objected to the notion that the United States was shoving a settlement down Israel's throat. The presumed target of her anger was AIPAC head Howard Kohr, who had criticized the State Department for "their idea of promulgating a so called American plan and then using pressure tactics to try to force Israel into accepting it."9 American Jews were caught in the middle, but their rage over the "Who is a Jew" crisis and their genuine uneasiness with Netanhayu prevented the kind of unity that had usually followed world condemnation of Israel. AIPAC and the Conference of Presidents allegedly refused three direct appeals from Netanhayu to issue clear-cut statements supporting the prime minister in his opposition to the US plan as undermining Israel's security.10

AIPAC did initiate a lobbying campaign against the peace plan that led to a bitter and public split within the American Jewish establishment. In response to AIPAC's pressure, eighty-one senators wrote to the president, siding with Israel against the American peace plan. Almost two hundred members of the House signed a similar letter. But the other Jewish political powerhouse, the Conference of Presidents, refused to endorse the senators' letter and accused AIPAC of creating an unnecessary sense of crisis and of failing to consult adequately with other Jewish organizations. The conference simply thanked the senators and sent its own letter to Clinton supporting the administration's assertive and central role in the peace process. A third letter, written by the dovish Israel Policy Forum and sponsored by Connecticut representative Sam Gejdenson, praising Clinton's efforts was signed by thirty-one house members, including fifteen of the twenty-four Jewish congressmen.11 Instead of the communal unity that had for so long been a source of pride and power, the major Jewish organizations had to endure the embarrassment of a headline in the *New York Times*— "Jewish Groups Go to Washington Squabbling among Themselves."12

When a motion to condemn Clinton by the Conference of Presidents failed by a large margin, it became apparent that criticism by Congress of the presidential pressure on Israel was harsher and more pronounced than that of the Jewish mainstream.

As American pressure on Netanhayu intensified, some American Jews moved to defend the prime minister. In May, on the eve of a visit to the United States, Netanyahu rejected an ultimatum that Israel withdraw from 13 percent of the West Bank. The ultimatum elicited a new letter from the Conference of Presidents to President Clinton. While acknowledging a wide range of opinions within the American Jewish community, it stated that "among the issues on which there is clear consensus is that the government of Israel alone must make the difficult determination affecting Israel's security." The administration was put on the defensive. Albright emphasized that "security has no expiration date," and Assistant Secretary of State Martin Indyk noted that "Clinton did not get his reputation as the most pro Israel president for nothing."[13] But with regard to American Jews at least, the prime minister overplayed his hand. In June he announced a plan to expand Jerusalem beyond its current borders and increase its territory by half. Its purpose was to strengthen the Jewish hold on the capital, link it to outlying settlements, and expand the city's tax base. Previous patterns reasserted themselves as the United States called the plan provocative and many American Jews were again worried that Netanhayu appeared to be deliberately sabotaging the Oslo peace process.

The peace conference convened by President Clinton at Wye plantation in late October 1998 emphasized the importance and independence of American Jewry. Seeking to demonstrate presidential effectiveness in the midst of the Lewinsky scandal, Clinton spent an enormous amount of time in convincing Israelis and Palestinians to move on to this next phase of the Oslo Accords. Initially, Netanyahu refused to accept the phased 13 percent Israeli withdrawal from the West Bank in return for specific Palestinian actions to fight terrorism and threatened to leave the conference. He then called the Conference of Presidents, asking for its support of his proposed departure. When the conference refused, the prime minister reluctantly signed the agreement.[14] The action of the Jewish umbrella group merely reflected the feelings of most American Jews. In a poll taken slightly later, 64 percent of them felt that "the Palestinians should have their own country."[15] In the struggle between Netanyahu and Clinton over the peace plan the

American Jewish community had again become principal players. But to the dismay of Israel, their potential political power was dissipated by division. If anything, given the mistrust of Netanyahu's diplomacy and religious policies, the preponderance of American Jewish influence seemed to be on the side of the president.

As the struggles over the peace accord continued and as the "Who is a Jew" controversy roiled, Israel celebrated its fiftieth birthday. Objectively, there was a great deal to celebrate. In a half century, Israel had produced a vibrant democracy, a flourishing economy, and a rich culture while successfully defending itself against the continuous threat of annihilation. But rather than a celebration of Israel's achievements, the state's fiftieth anniversary served as a kind of Rorschach test of the upheavals within the collective psyches of Israeli and American Jews. The attitude surrounding the jubilee year and its commemorative events reflected the turmoil in both Israel and the United States as the nature of official celebrations became part of the continuing struggle between the various political and religious factions in both countries.

In Israel the government-sponsored celebration, planned by Likud, was criticized as too right-wing for failing to make any mention of the peace pact. Israeli peace groups had to go to court to even be included in the jubilee program. Initially, the official ceremony even failed to mention Yitzhak Rabin's assassination, an omission rectified only by a huge public outcry. With the celebration's agenda so politicized, issues of content and interpretation were even more controversial. A segment of a commemorative series shown on Israeli television that reassessed official Zionist history by conceding that the Palestinians had been dispossessed elicited a firestorm of criticism and death threats to its producer. The breadth and depth of controversy belied the celebration's slogan, "Together with Pride—Together with Love," which, given the fissures in Israeli society was dismissed by many as more than faintly ridiculous.

The day of the anniversary itself was no more a celebration of togetherness than the events surrounding its planning. To the outrage of many, the government kicked off the festivities with a $150,000 party marking the thirtieth anniversary of the Jewish resettlement of Hebron that symbolized both Israel's desire for "biblical borders" and her aggressive stance toward the Palestinians. Outside the Hebron settlement, protesting peace activists clashed with police. Both the Left and the Right used the anniversary to make political points. Reform and

Conservative Jews prayed at or at least near the Western Wall. At Har Homa, advocates of Jewish development laid a symbolic cornerstone while opponents jeered from below the hilltop. The main celebration, a three-hour outdoor gala at which Vice President Gore was the guest of honor was, unsurprisingly, not able to escape controversy. Entitled "Jubilee Bells" and tracing Israel's history through song and dance, one segment featured the Bat Sheva Dance Company, who on stage removed some articles of clothing. When the ultra-Orthodox objected—even though they had no intention of celebrating the anniversary—the dancers withdrew from the production. In another segment devoted to the conclusion of the Oslo agreement, Yasir Arafat was not shown.

Given the divisions within American Jewry as well as its deepening gulf with Israel, it was hardly surprising that the American celebration of the anniversary was also controversial. An ambitious plan by some of Prime Minister Netanyahu's wealthiest American supporters to sponsor "a monster gala" to be televised worldwide foundered over lack of funds, charges of corruption, and the Israelis' determination not to let their anniversary be Americanized.

The most probing of the commemorative events was to be an examination of the vital issues confronting the Jewish state planned by the Smithsonian Institution. Entitled "Yesterday's Dreams, Today's Realities," it was cosponsored by the New Israel Fund (NIF), a left-liberal fund-raising organization devoted to the encouragement of pluralism in Israel, Jewish-Arab reconciliation, and civil rights. The anniversary program, developed by the NIF, was billed as a look "at the difficult challenges that Israel must face if it is to fulfill its founders' vision as a nation based on the concepts of freedom, justice and peace." The proposed speakers were generally critical of Likud and Netanyahu and included Thomas Friedman of the *New York Times*, Professor Ehud Sprinzak of Hebrew University, and Azmi Bishara, an Arab member of the Knesset. Their topics did not focus on Israel's achievements but sought to illuminate her contemporary problems. Among the proposed titles were "Peace: The Price of Occupation," "Full and Equal Citizenship? The Place of Israel's Palestinian Citizens," and "The End of the Zionist Dream. The Rise of Post Zionism." Such a program would help familiarize Americans with the vital issues that were the subjects of routine debate among the Israeli public. The Israeli embassy declared it had no problem with the subject matter.

But no matter how sophisticated the program, there was little question of its left-wing and anti-Netanyahu bias. The Smithsonian soon found itself under attack from both right-wing and mainstream critics for observing the anniversary in an inappropriate manner and for letting an organization with an avowed political agenda "hijack" its program. What made the museum especially vulnerable was its status as a publicly funded and theoretically nonpartisan forum. Americans for a Safe Israel, a small but well-financed rightist organization, led the charge. Evidently operating on the assumption that the best offense is outrageous hyperbole, the group stated that the Smithsonian's program "would be an analogous to celebrating a U.S. Centennial by inviting [Louis] Farrakhan, David Duke, the Branch Davidians and other extremist critics of American society to be spokesmen."[16]

The campaign was taken up by the *New York Post*, the *Washington Times*, the Zionist Organization of America, and more important, Congressman Michael Forbes (R, N.Y.), a member of the House Appropriation Committee, which approves 70 percent of the Smithsonian budget. Forbes, particularly objecting to the presence of Pulitzer Prize–winner Thomas Friedman, maintained that "he had heaped unjust and insulting criticism on Israel's leaders." In response the NIF expanded the speakers list to include well-known members of Likud, Zalman Shoval and Ze'ev Begin.

The broadening of the roster of speakers was insufficient to satisfy the program's critics, which now included such mainstream organizations as B'nai B'rith International and the Anti-Defamation League. ADL head Abe Foxman, by no means a conservative, characterized the program as "a shopping bag of flaws and anxieties. . . . While I do not expect the Smithsonian to have a birthday party, there was very little they were celebrating."[17] The ADL proposed joining the NIF as a cosponsor to revamp the program. But when Forbes threatened a congressional investigation, the Smithsonian, still reeling from the controversy over the *Enola Gay* exhibit (which critics said was too sympathetic to Japan), decided it didn't want any partners. Its secretary, Michael Heyman, jettisoned the NIF as a sponsor and wrote to Forbes that the museum itself was developing "a fair and appropriate program."

The Smithsonian was now assailed by critics on the Left who accused it of caving in to political censors and of abandoning serious inquiry. The executive director of the NIF, Norman Rosenberg, decried the capitulation to "right-wing extremists who wished to stifle any open commentary about Israel."[18] Anthony Lewis, in a *New York Times* op-ed column, branded the attacks on the Smithsonian and the NIF as "Jewish McCarthyism." In general this second wave of Smithsonian critics maintained that open discussion of Israel's problems in any forum offered the only hope of solving them.

In mid-October, four months after Israel's actual anniversary, the Smithsonian announced its revised celebratory plans. Instead of a program spread over several weeks as originally envisaged, the revamped commemoration would be sponsored solely by the museum and be restricted to one day. Entitled "Israel at 50: Looking Back/Looking Ahead," it was studiously mainstream. Moderated by presidential advisor David Gergen, the program boasted a distinguished but mostly noncontroversial list of participants, including Zalman Shoval, the Israeli ambassador; noted historian Howard M. Sachar; and Rabbi Norman Lamm, president of Yeshiva University. Slightly less establishment speakers were Shibley Telhami, a professor at the University of Maryland, and *New York Times* columnist Thomas Friedman, the only speaker from the original group. As a museum spokesman commented, "We wanted to make sure we were focusing on the achievements in the first 50 years."[19]

The whole controversy left neither side untarnished. By endorsing a program that was ideologically and politically unbalanced, the Smithsonian should have realized the minefield it had entered. As the museum's director of communications conceded, "We were naïve to think to think we could go forward with just one group and pull together a program as complicated as this."[20] But criticism of the museum and of the NIF was often hysterical and simply inaccurate. Ironically, the Smithsonian affair was the only anniversary-related event that generated national publicity and debate.

The problems of the Smithsonian should have reassured the heads of other institutions of their wisdom in mounting nonpolitical celebrations of Israel's anniversary. Throughout the United States, commemorations appeared to be studiously bland, noncontroversial, and notably lacking in introspection. The first one took place in Philadelphia, where 2,500 invited guests affirmed their Jewish connections by dining on artichoke hearts with kasha and potato pancakes with sour cream and caviar, then attending a concert performed by the Philadelphia Orchestra and the Israel Philharmonic. In Washington and New York the main event was the screening of the Academy Award–winning documentary

The Long Way Home, which depicts the flight of Holocaust victims from Europe to Israel. Other events included exhibits of manuscripts relating to Zion, the work of Israeli silversmiths, an exhibit recounting President Truman's recognition of Israel, and even performances of the works of George Gershwin, whose connection to the Jewish state was tenuous at best.

While the rank and file celebrated innocuously if at all, many American Jewish intellectuals expressed darker thoughts about Israel's anniversary. As the day of celebration drew near, the Jewish press and American Jewish journalists produced a seemingly endless stream of articles that were less celebrations of the Jewish state than sober assessments or even lamentations about Israel's current situation. Deemphasizing Israel's truly incredible achievements, American Jewish journalists highlighted Israel as a nation in multiple crises; the titles included "A Victim of Its Own Success? Internal Debate Saps Israel's Vitality,"[21] "Israel Diaspora Unity Withering as State Turns 50,"[22] and "Picnics and a Quarrel Mark Israel's 50th Anniversary."[23] These journalists underscored the conflict between young and old, Orthodox and secular, Sephardic and Ashkenazic, as well as the growing gulf between Israeli and Diaspora Jews. Another major theme was that in the face of such crises Israel was no longer blessed with giants like Ben-Gurion, Eban, and Meir but with Benjamin Netanyahu, the vacillating master of the sound bite. What was missing from most accounts was anything more than a perfunctory appreciation of Israel's very real achievements. Instead, each author stressed whatever perceived cultural, political, or religious shortcoming was most relevant to his or her worldview.

This emphasis on the negative was in part the result of the historically bred Jewish tendency to perceive the worst in any situation. Even one hundred years of American prosperity has failed to remove the disaster psychology that makes Jews suspicious of the reality of good fortune and uncomfortable with its acknowledgment. The negativism also reflected, somewhat contradictorily, the tendency to take Israel's success for granted as the wonder at Jewish power has faded over the generations. But most specifically, the use of the anniversary to highlight Israel's faults was the result of widespread alienation from the foreign and domestic policies of the Netanyahu government, particularly his perceived undermining of the Oslo Accords and his support of Orthodox exclusivity. A columnist in the *Jewish Ledger of Northern California* wrote of "a feeling of rejection, of having too little in common with a country whose orthodox rabbis and their political parties can impose their beliefs by enacting them into Civil Law with the help of non-religious parties that lack the courage to challenge them."[24] Few were so Grinch-like as *Tikkun*, which sanctimoniously proclaimed that "if American Jews turn away from Judaism today Israel has played no small part in the process."[25] But most of the articles, even as they acknowledged Israel's virtues, tended to expend their emotional energy on a detailed recitation of her faults. Glen Frankel's *Washington Post* article began by noting that Israel "has never been more prosperous or more secure but at the same time more divided or uncertain about its fate." Frankel perceptively detailed many of Israel's current problems: the decline of Zionist ideals, the domination of the Orthodox over religious life, Benjamin Netanyahu's slow suffocation of the peace process. He quoted *Ha'aretz*'s description of the prime minister, "not as a leader with authority, but as a barrel reverberating with the collection of pressures put on him."[26] As a kind of apotheosis, Frankel devoted a full paragraph to a recent scandal surrounding a Russian immigrant soldier killed near the Lebanese border. After his heroic death it was revealed that his family lived in abject poverty and that, since the Orthodox rabbinate would not allow him to be buried as a Jew, his father had sent his body back to Russia. While every criticism in Frankel's story was justified, he made little effort to present the positives that he had conceded in his introduction.

It is tempting to see this widespread criticism as marking a new phase in the political maturity of American Jewry. No longer tied to the notion of Israel's perfection or needing such an illusion to buttress their own sense of Jewishness, American Jews are now able to perceive Israel, warts and all, and are able to offer the positive and constructive criticism it needs. But while the widespread excoriation of Netanyahu's policies had much validity, the emotionality and one-sidedness of the treatment of Israel as a whole seemed to indicate that American Jews were responding with the spleen of lovers betrayed. While this did not render their criticism any less appropriate, it called into question whether American Jews have totally reached the political maturity that many like to think they have achieved. Delineating Israel's very real faults is not terribly difficult. Placing these faults (and virtues) in a historical and cultural context is a much more sophisticated exercise that still eludes many of Israel's critics and supporters. The very important issues engaged by the "Post-Zionism" debate in Israel (see chapter 10) have barely entered American Jewish consciousness. A recent tour by Zeev Sternhell, a prominent "post-Zionist," was staged as a series of debates with a conservative Israeli historian, as if "post-Zionism" by itself was too shocking to present to American Jewish audiences. Whether the source of American Jews' criticism is emotional or objective, its volume and variety reveals the increasing distance between Israel and her most important supporters in the world.

Two recent developments demonstrate the degree to which American Jewish unity on Israel has given way to extreme diversity and the level of bitterness that has resulted. Amazingly, in October 1999 it was revealed that the United Jewish Communities, the new entity formed by the merger of the United Jewish Appeal, the Council of Jewish Federations, and the United Israel Appeal, had planned to confer upon Yasir Arafat its prestigious Isaiah Award. Previous recipients have been Yitzhak Rabin, Bill Clinton, and Nelson Mandela. Upon learning of these plans of its junior executives, senior leadership quashed the award, maintaining that "inappropriate and unauthorized steps were taken."[27] Executives within American Jews' principal philanthropic and social organization had desired to outpace Israel by honoring a man whom many still considered to be the devil.

Disagreement within the Jewish community has become so commonplace and criticism so vituperative that the mainstream has found it necessary to define legitimate dissent. An advertisement taken out by eleven Jewish foundations, which ran in thirty-five Jewish newspapers in the United States and Canada, read, "A diversity of views is a sign of healthy debate. Sensationalism and slander are not." Moreover, each of the eleven organizations signed a pledge that when they consider the awarding of grants, any institution whose representatives have engaged in irresponsible rhetoric will be viewed "with disfavor."[28] In a community so bitterly divided among itself and from Israel that even elementary civility has been lost, only one thing is certain. Barring a crisis of survival, American Jewish unity concerning Israel is unlikely to be seen again.

| | 10 | |

The Hidden Crisis

For quite a while we have followed a series of crises and explained their implications for the relationship between American Jews and Israel. The invasion of Lebanon, the Pollard affair, the Intifada, and the "Who is a Jew" controversy impelled American Jews' evolution from an enforced unity on Israel to a new regime of diversity and critical scrutiny. But in the end the story is about more than the growth of American Jewish dissent. The ending of American Jews' critical silence can't help but reflect the transformation of Israeli and American Jews. Over the past fifty years both have evolved in ways that have confounded the expectations of the other and rendered both Zionist and Diaspora stereotypes increasingly irrelevant.

Ironically, all the recent tumult masks a decline in the importance of Israel to American Jews. Despite the volume, intensity, and diversity of debate concerning Israel, fewer and fewer American Jews may be listening or caring. As Rabbi Gordon Tucker, the spiritual leader of the 840-family Temple Israel in White Plains, New York, has noted, "My own experience and it's shared by nearly all of my colleagues, is that there is much less interest in Israel."[1] Opinion polls, changes in synagogue programming, and tourism demographics all suggest the diminishing connection of American Jews to the Jewish state. The changing scope and substance of charitable contributions, long the glue that has held the whole relationship together, foretell a new relationship between Israel and American Jews. These changes are in part the product of forces external to Israel and American Jews—from the disunity of the Arab world to the breakup of the Soviet Union. But to an even greater degree, they reflect the internal evolution of Israel and of American Jews and the relationship between them.

Two decades of opinion polls conducted by sociologist Steven Cohen for the American Jewish Committee (AJC) highlight the diminishing role of Israel in American Jewish consciousness. The days when a vast majority of American Jews felt that "if Israel were to disappear it would be one of the greatest tragedies of my life" have been replaced by feelings much more diffuse and less intense. Recent studies show a smaller percentage of American Jews who "very strongly or strongly support Israel." Even more distressing, growing indifference is most pronounced among the young. Cohen has found that for every ten-year drop in age there is a 5 percent decline in support for Israel. The 1990 Council of Jewish Federation Population Study reveals that 31 percent of American Jews between the ages of eighteen and twenty-four reported no emotional attachment to Israel at all.[2] As one Jewish professional observed, "The annual campaigns are being supported by older Jews for whom Israel holds a special place but not by the next generation of givers. Israel is often not even on the map."[3] A 1998 poll conducted by the *Los Angeles Times* and the Israeli newspaper *Yediot Aharonot* found that only 58 percent of American Jews felt close to Israel, a 17 percent decline within a decade, with an even greater fall in support among younger Jews.

American Jewish travel to Israel indicates a similar decline in commitment. Fifteen years ago, 60 percent of all travel to the Jewish state was Jewish; now the percentage is between 30 and 40.[4] While this indicates the growth of non-Jewish travel, Jewish travel has simply not kept pace. Part of this may be due to an exaggerated fear of terrorism. In 1990, Israelis were angered when many American Jews, fearing a possible Gulf War as well as terrorism brought by the Intifada, cancelled trips to Israel. Even more telling, these cancellations were made not only by ordinary tourists but by Federation donors, Federation conventions, and trips. In the past three years, only one in eight Jews who have traveled abroad has chosen to visit Israel. In all, only about a third of American Jews have ever visited the Jewish state, and within this group the Orthodox are highly overrepresented. While they compose 7 percent of the American Jewish population, 84 percent of the Orthodox have visited Israel. The relative indifference of the rest of the community is clear—only 34 percent of American Jews feel that a visit to Israel is important for maintaining Jewish identity.[5] In November 1999 a Reform rabbi lamented to me that out of his congregation of 375 families he was able to interest only 4 in a trip he is leading to Israel and that the source of that interest is Israeli biblical associations, not the modern state.

Charitable contributions to the Jewish state reflect the same dynamic. While the superficialities of "checkbook Zionism" have long been lamented, it has been charity campaigns that have traditionally mobilized American Jews and provided the basic framework for their relationship with Israel. As Irving Bernstein, an executive vice president of the United Jewish Appeal (UJA) noted, "At one time we used the campaigns to raise money. Now we use the campaigns to raise Jews."[6] For many, contributing to Israel has become their sole affirmation of Jewish identity and their last institutional tie to the Jewish community.

Collections for the UJA and Jewish Federation of North America Campaign, the two traditional umbrella organizations that heavily emphasize Israel in their fund-raising, have declined. In 1990, the combined amount collected from the annual fund drive and from special appeals—primarily Operation Exodus to rescue Russian Jews—peaked at $1.2 billion. Since then, annual revenues have diminished by about $400 million, much of this decline reflecting the end of Operation Exodus. But annual giving as of 1995, when adjusted for inflation, is also significantly below amounts collected a decade earlier.[7] While this may reflect to some degree the introduction of new charitable instruments outside the annual campaign, such as endowments and funds under Jewish Federation auspices, the fact remains that in the last two decades the number of donors contributing to UJA/Federation campaigns has fallen by two hundred thousand.

American Jews' changing priorities are evident in their distribution of the money raised. A decade ago, about 70 percent of all Federation funds was earmarked for Israel. Now the proportion is between 35 percent and 40 percent, with an increasing percentage devoted to domestic needs. The Jewish press is filled with articles such as "The Pipeline of Money Has Sprung a Serious Leak"[8] or "Synagogues Cutting Israel Bond Drives?"[9] Some of this diminution of funds to Israel is the result of the changing demographics that have affected Jewish giving in general. The oldest population, that segment of American Jewry most dedicated to Israel and Jewish charitable giving, is dying out. The replacement of Jewish entrepreneurs by an increasingly salaried and professional population has reduced the potential pool of very large givers who normally account for the bulk of any campaign's contributions. The growing population of doctors and professionals has less inclination and fewer means to give.

Assimilation has also resulted in the exponential growth of Jewish support of non-Jewish causes. Twenty years ago, one-half of American Jews gave to non-Jewish charities. Now two-thirds give to non-Jewish charities, and many of those give little or nothing to Jewish ones.[10] In recent years, Jews have been assiduously courted as directors for charitable boards on which their membership would have previously been unthinkable. Jews now direct the affairs of operas, ballets, libraries, and universities whose boards had long been the province of the Protestant social elite.

The average American Jew has also become less enamored of the AJC/Federation umbrella charities. Some commentators blame the bloated Federation bureaucracy and the politicization, inefficiency, and even the corruption of the Jewish agency, which distributes Federation funds in Israel. Rather than fund charitable causes within Israel on their merits, the quasi-governmental Jewish Agency has long been criticized for being composed of political appointees who see the money collected from American Jews as one gigantic pork barrel. But since most potential givers are unaware of these problems, the roots of decreased giving reach much deeper. The new generation did not grow up as Zionists and take the existence of Israel for granted. The old catastrophic appeals to donors no longer suffice, and American Jews' recent political skepticism toward Israeli policies has naturally extended into the philanthropic realm. Many donors no longer simply give and trust the Federation to do what is best. An increasing number stipulate how and where their funds should be employed. As a result of changing demographics, the more secure position of Israel, and increasing assimilation, the kind of reflexive giving to UJA/Federation that sustained Israel for two generations is seriously weakening. Only 11 percent of Jewish baby boomers give to Federation or UJA.[11] As Richard Perlstein, the head of UJA/Federation has noted, "We have to make ourselves more relevant or there won't be any such organization as the UJA in the next century."[12]

Establishment jeremiads aside, the general picture of American Jewish giving to Israel is by no means bleak. Giving outside the traditional avenue of UJA/Federation has grown rapidly in the past two decades. Hundreds of Israeli political, social, educational, and cultural institutions have established fund-raising arms in the United States. Charities on the right, such as the Yesha Fund for West Bank Settlers, and those on the left, such as Americans for Peace Now, present American Jews with unprecedented individual choices. There are charities for educational institutions, such as the Weitzman Institute and Technion; for cultural institutions, such as Yad Va'Shem; and for innumerable smaller organizations. There is even a fund started by a kibbutz north of Eilat that encourages American Jews to "adopt," name, and visit their milk cows. This diversity is a natural reflection of the fragmentation of Israeli politics. Just as the overarching traditional Zionism—so long articulated by UJA/Federation—has been replaced by a seemingly infinite range of ideology and opinion, American Jews have increasingly expressed their philanthropic independence. Charities outside the traditional UJA/Federation framework now send to Israel more than double the amount of funds of the old umbrella organizations.[13]

Changing patterns of charitable contributions also reflect the growing political polarization of the American Jewish community. In 1992, after Prime Minister Yitzhak Rabin reduced government funds to settlements on the West Bank and Gaza, settlers set up a fund-raising mechanism in the United States. They urged American Jews to supplement their donations to UJA or even shift them entirely. According to their umbrella organization, Yesha, the response of individuals, particularly within the Orthodox community, has been "off the charts." Some synagogues have shifted their fund-raising drives from UJA to settler-based charities. Other congregations have "adopted" individual West Bank settlements to which they contribute and regularly visit. Even more worrisome for the establishment is the fact that in 1995 the Jewish Federation of Middlesex, New Jersey, announced that it would bypass the Jewish Agency and give its funds directly to Jewish settlements in the territories.[14] This was particularly significant because until then, as a point of policy, no Federation money had ever been expended beyond Israel's pre-1967 borders.

The growth of what might be called charities of the Left has been encouraged by American Jewish disillusionment with government policy in the territories, by the peace process, and by the "Who is a Jew" controversy. The most prominent of the liberal newcomers is the New Israel Fund. It was founded in 1979 to strengthen Israel's democracy by assisting organizations fighting for social change. Starting with eighty donors who contributed $80,000, by 1983, it had ten thousand with a collection of $9.4 million.[15] While this is a drop in the bucket compared to the umbrella organizations, the New Israel Fund has grown rapidly, especially after the fight over the conversion bill. The loss of faith in the general charities and the new individuality of those who do give has been noted and studied by Gary Tobin, who found general increases in targeted giving to social causes, especially after the peace treaty.[16] In response the Federations have had to accede to donors' desires to set up specific funds and programs of tied giving, which had long been anathema to the charity establishment. Such tied giving has also been increased by the "Who is a Jew" controversy, as large numbers of American Jews insist that their money not be used to support ultra-Orthodox establishments.

The politicization of charity has been extended to the peace process. Thomas Friedman, long a prominent dove, has used his column in the *New York Times* to urge American Jews to give only to organizations that support "tolerance, pluralism, democracy [and] the Oslo Peace."[17] As settlers and doves compete for dollars, traditional patterns of giving have been further fragmented. This individualization of charity, while attractive to the new generation of donors, also indicates the lack of a compelling philanthropic vision. Barring a military or economic crisis in Israel, the campaign to settle Russian Jews may have been the last cause to unify and mobilize most of world Jewry. A study made for the UJA by Gary Tobin states that the organization must not use the old ideologies but must concentrate on multiple themes that resonate with baby boomers. "The crisis orientation needs to be supplanted with projects that promote Jewish culture and identity in Israel, help American Jews build their own identity through connections to Israel and assist Jews in need everywhere."[18] Tobin's view has received reinforcement from some Israelis. In 1994, Deputy Foreign Minister Yossi Beilen, speaking to the Women's International Zionist Organization, shocked his audience by telling them that their charity might be better spent on Jewish education at home. "If our economic situation is better than in many of your countries how can we go on asking for charity?" Articulating decades of resentment at Israel's being treated as a poor relation, he went on, "You want me to be the beggar and say we need the money for the poor people. Israel is a rich country I'm sorry to tell you."[19] While Beilen's remarks were dubbed "moronic" by Yitzhak Rabin, who feared not only for American Jewish donations but for the $3 billion that Israel receives from the United States annually, they provided further insight into the changing relationship between the two communities. Similar statements have been made by Avram Burg, head of the Jewish Agency, and by author A. B. Yehoshua, who blatantly told American Jews, "We don't need you."[20]

After the Oslo Agreement, Federation fund-raisers tried new campaigns such as "Keeping the Promise for Peace" and the "Promised Land Never Looked So Promising." As American Jews became somewhat disillusioned with the peace process, the Federation shifted its emphasis to the establishment of Israel's economic independence. Israel's universities in particular now appeal to American Jews to finance the higher and technical education that will enable the Jewish state to maintain its economic boom and reach the ranks of a First World economy. Technion and the Weitzman Institute have been particularly successful with such appeals. To a people conditioned by five thousand years of history to expect disaster, the effectiveness of such positive appeals in the long run remains to be seen.

In 1998 the Council of Jewish Federations and the UJA announced that they would combine forces. In June the two moved to occupy one office complex, preparing the way for a full merger within the year. Since the UJA raises money in concert with two hundred local federations and the Council of Jewish Federations is an umbrella organization providing training and other services to those same federations, there was a good deal of duplication of personnel and services.[21] Undoubtedly, the merger will reduce costs. Yet to be addressed is the obligation of local federations to contribute to national and international needs, most notably, to Israel through the Jewish Agency. Unless a new synergy of vision can reanimate the umbrella organizations, the move may be simply like the combination of Packard and Studebaker—a merger on the way to oblivion.

* * *

The general decline in the intensity and focus of the American Jewish relationship with Israel may be inevitable. The generation that experienced the Holocaust and the birth of Israel is dying, and emotions, even of unparalleled horror and boundless ecstasy, lose potency over generations. Other demographic trends—the tremendous increase in intermarriage, the decline in Jewish education and the falling rate of religious observance—have all diminished the importance of Israel to the younger generation while simultaneously rendering a connection to the Jewish state ever more important as a focus of Jewish identity.

Changes in Israel's demography have similarly fostered a sense of separation. In its first decades of existence, Israel was populated predominantly by an Ashkenazic majority who enjoyed near-absolute domination of society, politics, and culture. The European Jews who ruled Israel often had close family connections with American Jews and at the very least had ancestors from the same towns and villages. Most Israeli leaders, such as the Polish David Ben-Gurion and the American-born Golda Meir, were products of the same cultural and intellectual backgrounds as their American Jewish cousins. They shared a common set of references—the liberal ideas of the Labor Party—and were united through the common experience of living through the Holocaust. The influx of Sephardic Jews and the growth of the native-born Israeli population has left European Jews a minority of the population. Native Israelis, even of European origin, have little in common with Diaspora Jews. Their experiences and frames of reference are often dissimilar, and there is a world of difference between living as a minority and having one's own country. The Sephardic Jews, whose origins and sensibilities are Middle Eastern and who are becoming increasingly empowered in Israeli society have even less in common with the mass of American Jews. As bonds of family and shared cultural experience no longer assert much mutual attraction between Israeli and American Jews, the person-to-person contacts between the Israeli and the American communities, except among the Orthodox, appear to be quite tenuous. As a highly placed Jewish professional told me, "When I go to Israel, I still have a sense of kinship, but Israelis increasingly seem like citizens of another country and another society. I see them as people that I care about, but that sense of *mishpocha* is fading, even for Jews like me who know about these things."[22]

One might have expected communal bonds to compensate for the weakening of the personal ties between American Jews and Israelis, but the emotional ties that bind the two communities together are, at the very least, in the process of great transition. In a sense, Israel and Zionism have become prisoners of their own success. Since its foundation, American Jews' relationship to Israel has been largely defined by the devotion to Israel's great tasks—the building of the state, the greening of the desert, the provision of a haven for millions of immigrants, and the defense of a weak and vulnerable state against an implacable and potentially overwhelming foe. The support of these objectives became the principal task of American Jews, whose efforts during the first four decades of the state's existence played a major role in Israel's success.

Israel's and Zionism's great tasks have been largely achieved. A viable Jewish state exists. That such a state should have a rich culture is impressive but hardly unexpected given the history of Jewish cultural achievements. Perhaps even more impressive, given Israel's continual state of siege, is the strength of her democratic values and her rich and vibrant, if contentious, political culture. Economically, the bloom of the desert has been followed by the boom of industry. In the last three decades, Israel has evolved from a poor Third World country into a nascent industrial powerhouse. The conquests of the 1967 war produced a new consumer base, a cheap source of labor, and a construction boom on the West Bank. The breakup of the Soviet Union greatly stimulated the Israeli economy. The influx of well-educated Soviet immigrants provided a large supply of skilled experts for the expanding computer and electronic industry and caused another construction boom. The Soviet Union's fall also broke down the Arab boycott and made possible an exponential increase in Israeli exports to the former Soviet republics.

By many economic measures, Israel is now approaching First World status. Its per capita income of $20,000 per year exceeds that of Greece and Spain, and Israel has been added to the list of industrial nations by the International Monetary Fund. Israel's recent rate of growth is among the highest in the world. Over sixty Israeli companies are listed on the New York Stock Exchange, and Israel produces more scientific papers per capita than any other country.[23] On the negative side the Jewish state has now passed Hong Kong as having the most crowded roads in the world. Apartments in Tel Aviv sell for millions, and the consumer goods and lifestyle on Dizengoff Street resemble a Mediterranean southern California. American consumer icons, from Charmin to the latest Gillette razors, from CD players to Nike and Adidas, are eagerly consumed by Israel's ever more prosperous population. Megamalls abound, and the English word *shopping* has entered the language. A new fashion that harks back to America's own consumerist 1950s is the holding of Tupperware parties.

The new consumerism does not mean that Israel's economic problems have been solved. Wealth is not evenly distributed, and poverty and unemployment persist, particularly among the Sephardic population. Life for most new immigrants is often grim. But the Israel about which my 1950s generation learned pioneering songs exalting the tasks of finding water, planting trees, and picking apples is but a memory for the older generation. As far as I know, no one has been able to inspire today's American Jews with songs of one's *avodah* (sacred labor) of designing cell phones or programming computers. The formerly inspirational task of development is saddled with new ambiguities. The press is filled with accounts of the problems of pollution, of Americanization, and of the moral dilemmas brought on by Israel's conversion to a consumer society. While American Jews may see the emergence of these disturbingly familiar problems as a sign of Israel's economic arrival, the task of development no longer strikes a great emotional chord.

The support of immigrants is similarly losing its ability to inspire. The Sephardic immigrants of the 1950s, whose absorption into Israeli society was a focus of American Jewish philanthropy, have become more and more part of the country's political and social establishment. The rescue of Ethiopian Jews has long been accomplished. Even the massive campaign to free Soviet Jews and bring them to Israel, so long a principal preoccupation of American Jews, has just about come to an end. But even Operation Exodus caused bitter disputes between Israeli and American Jews over the desirability of allowing Russian immigrants to choose to come to America rather than Israel. When in 1985 the World Zionist Organization attempted to compel Russian Jews to go to Israel by cutting off the American option, American Jews reacted with indignation. Over the years the difference in perspective has remained. In a split, which strikes at the very heart of Zionism, a portion of Operation Exodus is now used to help settle Jews in New York. In 1997 a Federation advertisement that would have been unthinkable years ago appeared in the *New York Times*. It stated: "Let's help settle Russian Jews in Israel and New York."

Of all areas of American Jewish concern the greatest has been Israel's defense and security. It is there that realities and perceptions have perhaps undergone their greatest transformation. While a secure and lasting peace has not yet come about, Israel is obviously no longer the nation that Abba Eban described to the UN as "embattled, blockaded, and besieged and fighting a battle for its security anew with every approaching nightfall and every rising dawn."[24] Five wars, immeasurable heroism and sacrifice, and a constant vigilance has produced a state that, while vulnerable to terrorism, is no longer existentially in danger. Israel is the only nuclear power in the Middle East and possesses the region's strongest and best-equipped army. The breakup of the Soviet Union has deprived Israel's Arab enemies of their principal ally and arms supplier and has left America, Israel's patron, as the only remaining superpower.

These changes have reduced the sense of urgency for many American Jews, whose forty years of political and financial support for Israel was mobilized with the message that the Apocalypse was just around the corner. The difference between the 1967 and 1973 wars of survival and Israel's invasion of Lebanon in 1982 (which the state initiated for political reasons) illustrates the change in Israel's security. The result of Israel's military victories—the conquest of the West Bank and Gaza and the inheriting of one million hostile Palestinians—has transformed the perceptions of peace and security issues from the one-dimensional world idealized in the movie *Exodus* to the political complexities and moral ambiguities of a military occupation. The great heroic days have passed. Fractious normalcy has replaced the emotional high points of the founding of the state, the Six-Day War, and the Entebbe raid. The crises noted in earlier chapters, such as the invasion of Lebanon, the Intifada, and even the "Who is a Jew" crisis, stem directly or indirectly from the state's new sense of security. While these events evoked in many American Jews a strong opposition, they have also led to a tuning out and growing indifference on the part of others, for whom Israel's needs appear less evident and the purity of her cause less strong. These findings were articulated by a forty-year-old Reform rabbi who leads a congregation in Westchester County, New York. "I feel a sense of responsibility, and yet I don't understand what that responsibility is. I no longer feel I'm responsible for Israel's security, so I'm trying to figure out what that relationship is. Until I do, I don't really have much [concerning Israel] to bring to the congregation, but that is what I'm working on."[25]

The weakening of these community ties would be less serious if in the previous four decades a real cultural bond had been built between Israel and American Jews. Ahad Ha'am's notion that a Jewish state would serve as a spiritual center for a revived Judaism in the Diaspora has remained much more hope than reality. Most non-Orthodox American Jews know no Hebrew, and it is rare to find an American Jew who can discuss Israeli politics beyond what is found in local Jewish newspapers. Almost no one has any acquaintance with what is happening in Israeli literature, cinema, or theatre. As Arthur Hertzberg has written, "Israel's culture remains a mystery except perhaps to Israelis."[26]

The cultural bonds that had existed between the two communities are similarly in peril. The secular, humanistic Zionism with which American Jews so identified has become passé. The liberal politics of

Ben-Gurion and Eban are threatened by a religious nationalism and territorial expansionism that inspires few American Jews but the ultra-Orthodox. Lacking a sense of common purpose, American Jews have begun to focus more on their own internal problems.

The recent perception that the American Jewish community may be in deep trouble has redirected inward much of the emotion that American Jews previously lavished on the Jewish state. The transformation of Israeli identity as a result of recent worldly success is but a pale reflection of a much more powerful process that has occurred in the psyche of American Jews. The great paradox of American Jewish life is that the better American Jews do in the public arena, the more imperiled their interior life—as Jews—becomes. America had been good to the Jews beyond their wildest immigrant dreams. Its streets have not only been paved with gold but with power, accomplishment, and an infinity of options. That American Jews have arrived is hardly news. The "community" boasts six senators, fifteen congressmen, and the chairman of the Federal Reserve Board. When President Clinton appointed the most recent Supreme Court Justices, their Jewishness was so accepted that it was barely mentioned at the time. Of *Fortune* magazine's wealthiest individuals, no less than one-third are Jewish. Jews occupy 40 percent of the college professorships in America.

Jews no longer need to assimilate but are increasingly assimilated to. In one university a dean bought a copy of Leo Rosten's *The Joy of Yiddish* so that he could schmooze with his faculty. My hometown of Scarsdale, New York, is a microcosm of social and cultural change. As late as World War II it was a WASP enclave that excluded Jews—an old joke defined idleness as a kosher butcher in Scarsdale. Now the town not only has a kosher butcher but two bagel bakeries, three synagogues, and a Jewish mayor. Scarsdale's Jews now exert a cultural influence far beyond mere acceptance. For decades, Gentile teenagers have been attending the bar mitzvahs and bat mitzvahs that have long been a social as well as a religious rite of passage. In a reversal of the usual pattern, some Gentile parents have begun to hold lavish confirmation parties for their children, held at the same places as bar mitzvahs and supplied by the same caterers.

Until recently, the public and private gains of American Jews had resulted in an uncharacteristic optimism concerning the American Jewish future. The well-received *A Certain People* by Charles Silberman[27] actually presented a positive assessment of Jewish prospects in America.

Not only were American Jews the most successful Diaspora community in history, they were undergoing a transformation in Jewish consciousness and a meaningful spiritual revival. The uncharacteristic Jewish optimism, born of prosperity, security, and influence, did not last long. The 1990 Council of Jewish Federations' Population Study devastated the optimists and confirmed the worst fears of the most strident pessimists. It found that despite or, more precisely, because of American Jews' worldly success, the problem of American Jewish identity was much more serious than anyone had realized. The survey found a 52 percent rate of intermarriage with rates approaching 80 percent in some areas outside New York City. Twenty-five years earlier the rate had been 9 percent. Even more troubling was that only about one-quarter of the children of these marriages were being raised as Jews. Other recent findings were equally worrisome for those who were concerned with Jewish spiritual life and identity. Most Jews are not members of synagogues, and most spend less than three days per year at religious services. Most have not been to Israel and feel that a fuller Jewish life can be lived in the United States than in the Jewish state. The American Jewish birthrate, 1.6 per thousand, is considerably less than that needed merely for replacement. It is therefore not surprising that, although in 1960 the Jewish community constituted 3.3 percent of the American population, it has declined now to 2.1 percent.[28]

The Council of Jewish Federations' Population Study has provoked a crisis of confidence among American Jews. Jewish pundits have now noticed that religious revival movements are restricted to less that 10 percent of the American Jewish population and that the transformation of spirit taking place often had less and less Jewish content. In our age of "do your own thing," Judaism is increasingly being transformed from a collective experience to an individual one. One noted scholar speaks of a trend toward religious minimalism and fragmentation.[29] To many, what seemed at first to be American Judaism's revival is now perceived as its potential dissolution.

The new challenge for American Jews is not how to support an increasingly secure Israel but formulating a Jewish response to America's open society. How is one to give meaning and emotional resonance to a non-Orthodox Jewish life in the Diaspora? In November 1992 the Council of Jewish Federations took as its task the reinvigoration of Jewish identity by focusing on the traditions of Judaism. As its president, Shoshana Carden, told its annual convention, "We have proven we can speak collectively with success on issues of international concern. . . . Today we are going to change our focus, to the issue of Jewish identity."[30] To demonstrate this new resolve, delegates broke into small groups to study Torah. To further emphasize the point, the text of study was the chapter in Deuteronomy in which the Jewish people receive the Torah at Sinai.[31]

Symbolism aside, the problem of massive Jewish ignorance of Judaism has hardly diminished. In 1997 the AJC, with great fanfare, announced the publication of a new book directed at Jewish professionals and the general public, *Understanding Jewish History: Texts and Commentaries.* Authored by Steven Bayme, the AJC director of communal affairs, the book is an elementary primer of the Jewish knowledge that two generations ago was much more widespread. In a masterpiece of diplomatic understatement the author notes in the introduction that "this book assumes that most American Jews have attained a relatively high level of secular education but only rarely have applied the same level of rigor and expertise to the study of the Jewish experience."[32] Rarely indeed. Taking nothing for granted, Bayme begins by noting that the Hebrew Bible is divided into three components and goes on to present a perceptive but necessarily superficial overview of Jewish religion, history, and culture from Genesis to the present. The author, whose long experience as a college and adult education teacher has presumably given him a sense of what students will accept, has produced a work that is long on commentary but short on text. For example, Genesis is quoted in three pages and all the prophets in about ten. In contrast to the usual practice, the commentary precedes the text reflecting the author's view that "I don't think anyone is going to grow poor underestimating the sophistication of the [Jewish] reading audience." The author cogently maintains that a more sophisticated approach risks alienating the audience at which the book is aimed. Yet he notes that "the feedback I've gotten within this building [AJC headquarters] was that the book was too hard."[33] If the non-Orthodox leadership of American Jewry, presumably the most committed elements of the community, must be educated at such a level, it is reasonable to assume that the average American Jew is even more ignorant of Jewish religion and culture. Nor does mass ignorance stop at Jewish religious and cultural knowledge. In 1995, according to an AJC poll, less than half of American Jews knew that Shimon Peres and Benjamin Netanyahu were members of different political parties.

As American Jews recognize what many consider to be the shallowness of their religious commitment, some have begun to feel that forty years of obsession with Israel has prevented them from laying the religious and spiritual groundwork for the next generation. In a larger sense, there is the growing realization among many Jewish professionals that American Jews' legitimate concern with Israel has served as an excuse for their failing to ask the most basic of questions: What does it mean to be Jewish amidst the wealth, freedom, and secularity of American society?

"Jewish continuity," an unfortunate term that perhaps unintentionally implies satisfaction with the status quo rather than evolution and growth, has become the new watchword for many communal leaders, and its promotion is a priority at least equal to that of support for Israel. Any number of "solutions" have been proposed, including expanded day schools, adult education, and all sorts of outreach programs to the uncommitted, the indifferent, and the intermarried. Discussions of the problems of Jewish education and the chronic shortage of qualified teachers have filled the pages of both specialized and popular Jewish journals.

Old habits die hard. While there has been increasing emphasis on day schooling, camping, youth activities, and family education, many still look to Israel as a panacea for the problem of Jewish continuity. Rightly focusing on the drop in the commitment of young people, in 1994 billionaire Charles Bronfman donated $6 million to sponsor a program that would give fifty thousand American Jewish teenagers per year the opportunity to spend a summer in Israel. The assumption was that the Israeli atmosphere would somehow convert indifferent teens into believing and committed Jews. Whatever the hoped-for result, the program did not meet recruitment expectations. Fear of riots, terrorism, and perhaps changes in priorities have obviously taken their toll.

More recent efforts to entice Jewish college students to visit Israel have been far more successful. A less ambitious program, funded by Bronfman, money manager Michael Steinhardt, and the State of Israel, seeks to offer young Jews six thousand free trips to Israel during winter break, with two thirds of the places reserved for Americans. Marketed by a million-dollar campaign on radio and in campus newspapers, Birthright Israel has had many more applications than places. On most of the participating college campuses, lotteries were held to determine the participants.

Birthright Israel's first trips took place during the winter break of 1999–2000. In addition to the usual touring, students met their Israeli counterparts and took part in dialogues concerning their relationship to Israel, Judaism, and Jewish history. Early anecdotal evidence concerning the effects of the first trips is encouraging. Many students stayed beyond the subsidized ten days and have already made arrangements to return in the summer to study language or Torah. A group of returnees at Boston University now regularly attends Sabbath services. These initial results support the contention of Birthright's founders that a trip to Israel will stimulate more lasting aspects of Jewish identity. As one Birthright group leader, who is also an Orthodox rabbi and Hillel director, noted, "I'm thrilled with the results now but let's see what happens in a month or two."[34]

The program's long-term prospects present a similar mixture of optimism and uncertainty. Even the nine thousand applicants who so oversubscribed the initial trips represent only a small fraction of the fifty thousand that Birthright hopes to send to Israel annually. And even Birthright's founders concede that there is no guarantee that a short free trip to Israel will change the long-term Jewish priorities of participants. Notwithstanding the unproven results of these high-profile initiatives, the use of Israel as a prop to American Jewish identity has now been legitimized within the highest circles of Israel itself. In 1995, shortly before his assassination, Prime Minister Yitzhak Rabin explicitly stated that the new task of Zionism was to assure Jewish continuity in Diaspora.

Israel's new commitment to Jewish continuity in the Diaspora, while laudable and perhaps long overdue, is somewhat problematic. On the one hand the experience of a half century has shown that relying on the vicarious experience of Israel cannot by itself induce a genuine Jewish identity. Israel has never penetrated into the consciousness of most American Jews much beyond the public sphere of charitable giving and political support. Against the hopes of early Zionists, it has failed to excite their spiritual imagination. From the Israeli point of view, Zionism's "new task" is equally problematic. That Israel's government, which ideologically has always looked forward to the total ingathering of Jews and the end of the Diaspora, should now devote its efforts to propping up a Jewish existence it has long considered inauthentic and even shameful represents nothing less than an ideological revolution. That the Jewish state recognizes its interest and obligation to help assure

Jewish continuity in the Diaspora represents a commendable attempt to make Zionism relevant to contemporary problems. But it also indicates the magnitude of Israel's own ideological transformation. What American Jews often fail to recognize is that Israel's people and society are in the midst of a crisis of identity, hardly less severe than that of their American cousins. For American Jews to look to Israel for spiritual guidance is not to gaze at a fixed beacon but at a quickly changing kaleidoscope. The potential spiritual guide is itself increasingly rudderless. Put less charitably, Israel's own spiritual problems are such that were it to offer guidance to American Jews it might be a classic case of the blind leading the blind.

Israel's near fulfillment of the basic tasks of defense, state building, and development have led to an examination of the contemporary meaning of the state and of Zionism. Existential security has encouraged many Israelis to ask hitherto buried questions about their own identity. As the previous chapter has shown, one result of the end of Israel's continual state of crisis has been the emergence of open, bitter, and continuous conflict between the secular and religious populations. Even as it battles the religious Right, an even greater change is occurring within the secular majority that comprises some 80 percent of Israel's population. The old Zionist truths and assumptions about the nature of the state and the individual's relationship to it are being subjected to widespread scrutiny. A small but significant number of Israelis, particularly among the elite, have begun to question not only the Zionist view of history but the political foundations upon which the whole national enterprise has been built. For large numbers of Israelis, a new sense of social flexibility, political skepticism, and personal liberation has taken hold. These phenomena have been collectively referred to by Israeli commentators as post-Zionism.

In its most common form, post-Zionism refers to the diminishing hold Zionist ideology has on the hearts and minds of Israelis. As early as 1972, prominent journalist and author Amos Elon had spoken in *The Israelis* of "the post-Zionist generation."[35] In recent years, the popular skepticism has expanded from a distrust of ideology to a lessening of commitment to the demands of the state itself. Traditional Zionism in whatever form—socialist, religious, or nationalist—always exalted the group at the expense of the individual. The imperatives of building a religious community, a socialist society, or the nation meant that to acknowledge, much less satisfy, personal aspirations and needs was discouraged as at least slightly subversive. The kibbutz, with its communal wages, group meals, and even common child rearing, became the symbol of Israel's elevation of collective over individual identity. Amos Oz, one of Israel's most prominent contemporary writers, speaks of how he was alienated and suffocated by the kibbutz's suppression of individuality. "They had contempt for everything I was. Contempt for emotions other than patriotism. Contempt for literature other than [the nationalist poet Nathan] Alterman. Contempt for values other than courage and stoutheartedness. Contempt for law other than the law of 'strength makes the man.'"[36] Oz's objections notwithstanding, the overwhelming tasks of the young state made necessary the emphasis on state power and the articulation of collective goals. The national spirit that stemmed from them was indispensable to Israel's establishment and success.

Israel's growing security and recent prosperity have made the demands of the state less imperative and less heeded. Old-line Zionists lament the weakening of the spirit of self-sacrifice, while liberals rejoice in what political scientist Yaron Ezrahi has termed "the counter revolution of the individual."[37] This counterrevolution takes several forms. The perception of the Israeli Defense Forces (IDF) as the embodiment of national virtue has suffered severe blows as it became not simply the instrument of national defense but also an army of occupation. The treatment of Arabs in the occupied territories, the invasion of Lebanon, and the Intifada have led to protests in the army, refusal to serve in the territories, and increasing draft evasion. This growth of what some would term individual morality and others would call the waning of the old idealism has led to a new attitude toward the IDF. The proportion of the national budget devoted to defense has fallen from 25 percent to 19 percent. Service in the army is no longer a preferred career as young people are attracted to business or technology. Israelis in ever greater numbers are also seeking to avoid the reserve duty in the IDF to which they are subject until the age of fifty. Perhaps most indicative of the changing perception of the army and of the collective goals it represents is that failure to serve in the IDF is no longer a death sentence to career advancement.[38] Collective goals are also under fire in the educational system. The traditional nature walks and strenuous group hikes that were long ago made a part of all school curricula to encourage a tie to the land and promote group cohesion among classmates are being criticized by parents as too dangerous.

Post-Zionism may be most influential in its economic dimensions. The traditional state ownership and social welfare system are being replaced by private and effective entrepreneurial capitalism. The kibbutz movement is almost dead and those that survive often do so by entering the world of capitalist entrepreneurial activity. Many kibbutzim still battle against religion, not from the old socialist perspective but by the establishment of mass discount outlets that do most of their business on the Sabbath. The new ethos of accumulation, of taking foreign vacations and driving fancy cars, is as far from the old kibbutz ethic as one could imagine. Like America in the 1950s, Israel appears to be compensating for its much longer sacrifices of war with a frenzied consumerism. One of my neighbors, about to leave for Israel, indignantly told me, "Ten years ago when I visited my *mishpochah* [relatives] they were delighted with the used clothing I brought. Now they send me lists of all the latest designer fashions they want and they warn me not to bring irregulars since the kids won't wear them." As Israelis embrace the good life, the would-be spiritual center is being overwhelmed by the material center. The culture of Judaism and Zionism is being supplanted by the culture of narcissism.

Above all, post-Zionism represents the desire for normalcy—for a middle-class life untroubled by the vicissitudes of economic crises and by the constant demands of military necessity. A half century of military call-ups, eternal vigilance against terrorism, and material sacrifice cannot help but wear down even the most committed of patriots. The election of Yitzhak Rabin in 1992 reflected the desire of many Israelis to escape the burden of being "a people who dwell alone" and to live a more normal existence.

Post-Zionism's desire for normalcy has led to a critical examination of the official history of the state and in its most extreme form to a questioning of the state's very desirability. On the one hand, a new generation of post-Zionist historians are scrutinizing the whole received corpus of Israel's history, from the founding of the state to the origin of the refugee problem to the Entebbe raid. Some of the myths they have called into question include the notion that the early pioneers did not come to exploit the Arabs, that in 1948 only the Jews favored partition, and that the refugee problem was created because the Palestinians were told by their leaders to flee their homes. The most radical post-Zionist historians perceive Zionism and the foundation of the state not so much as an attempt to save and transform the Jewish people as an imperialist plot against the Arabs. There is much to be said for revising the one-dimensional pieties of much of Israel's official history, and the excesses of some post-Zionist historians may be a reaction to that piety.

Post-Zionist historians' response to the persistent failure of the intellectual establishment to examine the underside of Israeli history has provoked a furious debate in the intellectual and popular press. Critics accuse the new historians of ignoring the context of Israeli history, of illegitimately projecting Israel's present feeling of security onto a much more vulnerable past and of contaminating their historical judgment with ideology. The fury of such critics is exemplified by novelist Aaron Megged, whose article "The Israeli Instinct for Self Destruction" was one of the first to take on the new historians. Megged denounces the Israeli intellectuals who, "with great pleasure, demonstrate that our defensive wars were actually wars whose purpose was to destroy the other and attribute to the Israeli soldier, whom we know very well as our flesh and blood, the countenance of the Kluges S. S."[39] The fact that a meaningful portion of Israel's intellectual elite can write and accept historical accounts that bear more than a passing resemblance to the works of Israel's enemies demonstrates both the fraying of Israel's ideological bedrock and the maturing of Israeli intellectual life.

In pursuit of normality and desiring to better fit into the Middle East, some post-Zionists hope to convert Israel into a pluralistic state of all its citizens by deemphasizing or even eliminating its Jewish components—thereby fulfilling Ahad Haam's prediction that Herzl's movement would ultimately produce a state of Jews but not a Jewish state. Their advocacy of an Israeli as opposed to a Jewish society entails an increasing distance and alienation from the Diaspora. Post-Zionist pluralism has made some limited institutional headway. The new code of ethics for the IDF does not mention the Jewish people, Jewish culture, or the land of Israel. The Rabin government also sought to change Israel's educational system by emphasizing "the language, culture, and unique heritage of the various population groups in the country" at the expense of "Jewish culture" and "loyalty to the Jewish people."[40] Rabin's immediate successor, Shimon Peres, shares at least a part of this vision. In *The New Middle East*, he expresses the hope that Jewish and Arab individual identities will eventually fuse into one Middle Eastern identity.[41]

As the Israeli public responds strongly to the siren songs of consumerism and normalcy, there is an increasing temptation to jettison five thousand years of history and culture in an effort to be like everyone else. Israeli society has become more and more secular, and the problem of group acculturation is now almost as much a concern in Israel as is individual assimilation in the Diaspora. Political commentators, particularly on the right, paint dire portraits of a future Israel devoid of Jewishness and lacking the identity and sense of national purpose necessary to sustain herself. But despite its current fashion among the intellectual elites, post-Zionism is only one of many conceptions competing in Israel's ideological marketplace. This fact is itself crucial for American Jews. Buffeted by post-Zionism on the left, by religious messianism on the right, and by a relentless consumerism in the center, the old unified Israel from which American Jews for so long sought guidance no longer exists.

Israel's religious and political divisions are so strong that the old joke that the way for the Arabs to triumph is to make peace, sit back, and let Israeli society destroy itself no longer appears so humorous. The ultra-Orthodox anathematize secular Jews as abandoners of God and agents of Western corruption who delay the coming of the Messiah. Secular Jews at times fear the "black hats" as a greater threat to their existence than the Arabs. As both sides harden their positions, their inability to reach any national consensus cripples the political process and diminishes the possibility of concluding a lasting peace. In this context Israel has ceased to be the spiritual inspiration for American Jews. On the contrary, the American Jewish community, despite its own problems of present identity and future continuity, possesses a tradition of pluralism and tolerance that can itself be an important source of inspiration to the Jewish state.

The old Zionist dogma that contrasts an independent, self-assured Israel with a supine American Diaspora living in someone else's society and unable to make cultural or spiritual contributions to Jewish life was always hopelessly inaccurate. Even Israelis are beginning to recognize that American Jews have provided their own alternative solution to the Jewish problem. By any standard—freedom, equality, social status, and political influence—American Jews are justified in conceiving American society to be theirs as much as anyone's. Indeed, given that considerations of race are outpacing ethnicity as a vital determinant in American society, Jews are increasingly perceived as members of the dominant majority.[42] The rate of intermarriage, so shocking in other contexts, indicates the extent to which American Jews have been successful in their struggle to achieve a normal life. It hardly needs to be said that the contemporary problems of American Jewry stem not from unfulfillment but from the very magnitude of their victory.

American Jews and Israelis have sought their respective solutions to the Jewish problem by embracing different aspects of the American and French Revolutions. By seeking their collective salvation in nationalism, the Zionists created a society whose emphasis was on collective values and the primacy of the group. By putting their trust in the liberal individualism of the American Revolution, American Jews produced a culture extolling individualism and freedom of choice. This difference in social vision and political sensibility does much to explain the chasm between American and Israeli Jews. But these very differences also provide a means for bridging the gap between the two peoples.

Building upon nationalist and to a lesser degree socialist ideology, Israeli articulation of collective goals and values provided the élan, the energy, and the self-sacrificing cohesiveness that made the establishment of the state possible. Once the state was in place, Jewish identity became a matter of law, of citizenship in a Hebrew-speaking nation whose rhythms followed the Jewish calendar. Orthodox Judaism was thrust upon Israeli Jews as the recognized state religion and was considered even by the majority that rejected it to be the only valid expression of the Jewish faith. For most Israeli Jews, religion, tied to the state, is an all-or-nothing proposition. Israel's emphasis on collective goals has also left little room for individualism, and the overiding task of state building and defense equally devalued dissent. Notions of tolerance, pluralism, and respect for one's opponents come hard in a society that historically has had to devote so much of its political and psychological energy to collective goals. The assassination of Yitzhak Rabin was the most spectacular and appalling instance of the intolerance and conflict that affect every level of Israeli society. Despite American Jews' perception of Israel to be a miniature version of America, the democratic virtues of tolerance, pluralism, and respect for others are in short supply in Israeli political culture.

It is by developing precisely the political and social characteristics that Israelis seem to lack that American Jews built their Zion in America. As Israel built its political culture upon nationalism, American Jews constructed theirs upon the quintessentially American revolutionary notion of liberalism. Even American Judaism, reflecting its Protestant counterpart, is the product of individual conscience and freedom of choice. As American Jews followed their individual moral and spiritual visions, the traditional branches of American Judaism have been augmented by scores of gradations, combinations, and variations—all of which purport to be authentic expressions of Judaism. So diverse has this "pick and choose" Judaism become that some have seen it as less an expression of religious vitality than a dilution of the meaning of Judaism. A further variation, even less tied to tradition, is the replacement of Judaism by Jewishness—the desire that somehow the Jews survive as Jews unencumbered by the requirements of religion.

Israelis have little understanding of American Jews' problems or empathy with the society from which they spring. American Jews, reared in liberal individualism, cannot understand the mentality of those who seek to impose their views on others. This gulf in political sensibility and vision has always existed, but Israel's achievement of physical security has now led to its public expression. The "Who is a Jew" crisis revealed the dimensions of the rift between the two peoples, not only in the Orthodox rejection of American Jewry but in the failure of most Israelis to empathize or even care about the agony of their Conservative and Reform cousins.

To state that the only way to bridge the gulf is to cultivate a mutual respect and recognition of one another's strengths and problems sounds like the kind of bland palliative that one hears at innumerable organizational gatherings. But in fact, American Jews and Israelis share common concerns, and each can help the other solve its problems. Both peoples' common heritage is threatened by the secularization of society. As Israelis embrace the good life, they have been almost as prone to discard Jewish learning and culture as their Diaspora cousins. At his father's funeral, Yitzhak Rabin's son had difficulty in pronouncing the Aramaic-based Mourners' Kaddish (prayer for the departed). Over the years there have been a number of official commissions that have viewed with alarm this decline in religious and cultural literacy among the non-Orthodox, who comprise 80 percent of Israel's population. While in a Jewish state this loss doesn't portend annihilatory consequences, as in the Diaspora, many Israelis worry that their descendants will be "Jewish Goyim," Jews by birth but totally assimilated to European culture. Since many Israelis' disenchantment with Judaism stems from their rejection of state-supported Orthodoxy, American Jews can provide the inspiration for an Israeli Judaism, not buttressed by law but arising from the consciences of its practitioners. Even if the

American Conservative and Reform movements don't provide the precise model, the notion of a nonhomogeneous Judaism of individual conscience may help provide a solution to the collective assimilation in Israel that rivals American Jews' individual assimilation.

American Jews' tradition of tolerance, liberalism, and pluralism can also have a positive effect on Israeli society. Israelis have shown a willingness to engage in some of the less savory aspects of American politics. Their use of American political advisors converted the 1999 election campaign into a series of sound bites. In time, Israel may accept more of the political culture upon which American elections are based. While American political virtues can't be transferred like a coat of paint, American Jews can help transform the Jewish state by supporting that substantial portion of Israel's population that believes the growth of pluralism and tolerance to be vital to Israel's survival as a democratic society. To maintain an Israel whose institutions and policies can command their enthusiastic support, the mass of American Jews must become as mobilized and involved in Israel's affairs as are their Orthodox and ultra-Orthodox compatriots. Indeed, the first message delivered to American Jews by Ehud Barak after his election as prime minister in May 1999 was that they should put "all of their retroactive differences aside"[43] to support the peace process.

In seeking a return to the days when there was a single homogeneous relationship between American Jews and Israel, the prime minister is engaging in wishful thinking. Over the past quarter century the one overarching relationship between the two has become many, as political and religious factions in both countries have established individual relationships with their overseas counterparts. I believe that within this new atmosphere of diversity the mass of American Jews must assert their values independent of Israeli direction. American Jews have transformed themselves from an inert, well-meaning mass whose reflexive support could be manipulated by Israeli governments to a new position of assertiveness within world Jewish affairs. Now, by demanding and exercising a partnership with the Jewish state, they can help determine Israel's future as well as their own.

The last fifty years have demonstrated that liberalism alone cannot sustain the American Jewish identity and that American Jews' identification with Israel, however naïve or superficial, has been a principal , if insufficient, bulwark against assimilation. If, with neither a bang nor a whimper but with a gradual silent alienation American Jews loosen

their ties to Israel, the Jewish state will be the poorer, not only financially and diplomatically but also culturally and spiritually. It is unfortunate that American Jews' retreat from their role as principal fund-
raisers and advocates occurs at a time when Israel needs such support
more than ever. Any peace settlement will cost untold billions in foreign aid, both to ensure Israel's security and to mollify other signatories
to a comprehensive peace. Moreover, these demands will occur just as
other American ethnic groups are claiming an increasing share of foreign aid priorities and resources. A less obvious loss to Israel from
American Jews' alienation would be the diminishing zeal with which
they will provide the Jewish state with, if not a model, at least an example of a conscience-based modern Judaism and of a liberal, pluralistic
society. Yet the potential loss to American Jews is even greater. If they
continue to distance themselves from Israel, they will then have lost
one of their last supports of communal identity. While their love affair
with Israel has never guaranteed a viable Jewish identity, it has at least
prevented the decline in Jewish identification from becoming a total
surrender and has kept alive that sense of communal obligation indispensable for the well-being of both Israeli and American Jews. Barring
a mass spiritual revival, American Jews' further rejection of a sense of
peoplehood with Israelis would render all the more plausible the jeremiads of those who predict the ultimate demise of the non-Orthodox
Jewish community in America. American Jews' love affair with Israel
will then have been just one more way station on the road to complete
assimilation.

Epilogue

The traumatic events of the first autumn of the twenty-first century have, at least in the short run, ushered in yet another pattern in American Jewish/Israeli relations. At a July conference convened at Camp David to reach a final peace agreement, Ehud Barak went much further than ever before in attempting to solve one of the conflict's most intractable issues by offering the Palestinians autonomy in East Jerusalem and religious control of portions of the Temple Mount. But when Yassir Arafat, unwilling or unable to take the final steps toward peace, refused to budge from his maximalist demands or even offer counter proposals, the conference ended in failure.

The outbreak of sustained Palestinian rioting in response to opposition leader Ariel Sharon's visit to the Muslim holy places reignited familiar patterns of violence at a time when real peace had seemed so tantalizingly close. Arafat did nothing to restrain the rioters, who now reinforced their rock throwing with gunfire, often from weapons given to the Palestinian police at an earlier phase of the peace accords. Scores of Palestinians were killed by Israeli police as the disturbances spread over the West Bank, Gaza, and within Israel itself. In Nablus a mob destroyed a Jewish shrine known as the Tomb of Joseph. In an incident that quickly became emblematic of Palestinian hatred and of the utter breakdown of the peace process, two Israeli reservists who had made a wrong turn in Ramallah were stabbed and beaten to death by a Palestinian mob, which then mutilated and burned their bodies. The hopeful symbolism of the clasped hands of Rabin and Arafat, however tentative, was supplanted by its polar opposite—a picture of the bloody hands of one of the lynch mob, who had raised them triumphantly for his compatriots' approval. Ehud Barak, who had been willing to make far greater concessions in the cause of peace than any of his predecessors, now ordered Israeli helicopter gunships to shell selected targets in the West Bank and Gaza. In the twinkling of an eye, Israel had moved from the brink of peace to the brink of all-out war.

The unexpectedness and severity of the crisis stunned American Jews. When the United Nations, aided by a U.S. abstention, condemned Israel for using "excessive force" against the rioters, American Jews rallied to her support. Moreover, attacks on Jews in America and throughout the world further increased their identification with Israel. American Jews now mobilized with what had become a new unity of purpose. In New York, a "rally for solidarity," organized by the UJA, the Conference of Presidents, and the United Jewish Community, covered six city blocks and was merely the largest of scores of similar gatherings throughout the United States. Besides condemnation of Arafat and the UN, a common theme was that anti-Israel violence had been extended to all Jews. Shortly thereafter much of the leadership of the principal American Jewish organizations traveled to Israel on a "solidarity mission."

The breakdown of the peace process may have been even more influential in producing this new consensus, as leading Jewish advocates of negotiations were among the first to condemn the Palestinians. Menachem Rosensaft, who had been among the first Jewish leaders to meet formally with Arafat in 1988, criticized him for failing to halt the rioting, while Alexander Schindler maintained that the PLO Chairman had been waiting for an excuse to restart the violence. Tom Friedman, long one of American Jewry's most influential doves, characterized the crisis as "Arafat's War," brought on by the PLO Chairman's refusal to make peace. The strong support of Israel's harsh response to the rioting from all sides of the political spectrum reflected the disillusionment of liberal American Jews who had invested so much emotion in Arafat and the peace process.

The severity of the conflict and the unprecedented level of violence between Jewish and Arab Israelis have rendered the struggle for peace ever longer and more difficult but more necessary than ever. Ehud Barak's announcement of an indefinite "time out" to the peace process and of a plan to physically separate Israelis and Palestinians has initiated a new and ominous phase of the Middle East conflict. If, as Israel struggles to redefine its relationship to the Palestinians, the feeling of crisis abates, American Jewish solidarity will similarly diminish. But even if increasing threats to Israel re-create, in the long term, the traditional alliance between the two communities, there is no going back to the old system of American Jewish dependence and obedience. For on issues of security, as in all areas of mutual concern between American Jews and Israel, American Jews' attitudes and conduct will continue to be the product of the independent judgment that has matured so greatly in the last quarter century.

Notes

Introduction (pp. xiii–xxii)

1. *New York Times,* June 19, 1982.
2. *The Economist,* November 27, 1997.
3. Daniel Elazar, *Community and Polity* (Philadelphia and Jerusalem: Jewish Publication Society, 5755/1995), p. 107.
4. See Jonathan Woocher, *Sacred Survival: The Civil Religion of American Jews* (Bloomington, Ind.: University of Indiana Press, 1986) .
5. *New York Times,* October 13, 1994.

1. Zionist Ideology, American Reality (pp. 1–21)

1. Moses Hess, *Rome and Jerusalem* (New York: Bloch, 1958).
2. Mitchell Cohen, *Zion and State* (Oxford: Oxford University Press, 1987), p. 60.
3. Esco Foundation, *Palestine* (New Haven: Yale University Press, 1997), p. 15.
4. Leo Pinsker, "Auto-Emancipation," *The Zionist Idea,* ed. Arthur Hertzberg (New York: Atheneum, 1971), pp. 183–84.
5. Alex Bein, *Theodor Herzl: A Biography* (Philadelphia: Jewish Publication Society, 1956), pp. 115–16.
6. Theodor Herzl, "The Jewish State," *The Zionist Idea,* p. 209.
7. Ibid., 220.
8. Ibid.
9. Ibid., 225–26.
10. Walter Laqueur, *A History of Zionism* (New York: MJF Books, 1972), p. 106.
11. Max Nordau, "Speech to the First Zionist Congress," *The Zionist Idea,* p. 239.
12. Ibid.
13. Jacob Klatzkin, "Boundaries," *The Zionist Idea,* pp. 322–23.
14. Ibid., p. 325. For a discussion of the persistence of rejection of the Diaspora in the post-state era, see Eliezer Schweid, "The Rejection of the Diaspora in Zionist Thought: Two Approaches," *Studies in Zionism* 5 (spring, 1984); reprinted in Jehuda Reinharz and Anita Shapira, eds., *Essential Papers in Zionism* (New York: New York University Press, 1996), pp.133–60.
15. Ahad Ha'am, "The Jewish State and the Jewish Problem," *The Zionist Idea,* p. 267.
16. Paul Mendes-Flohr and Jehuda Reinharz, eds., *The Jew in the Modern World: A Documentary History* (Oxford: Oxford University Press, 1995), p. 469.

17. The order is reproduced in Anita Lebeson, _Pilgrim People_ (New York: Harper, 1950), pp. 289–90.

18. Leonard Dinnerstein, _Anti-Semitism in America_ (Oxford: Oxford University Press, 1994), pp. 14–34.

19. See Marc Lee Raphael, _Jews and Judaism in the United States_ (New York: Behrman, 1983), p. 251.

20. Laqueur, _History of Zionism_, p. 402.

21. Arthur A. Goren, "Between Ideal and Reality: Abba Hillel Silver's Zionist Vision" in _Abba Hillel Silver and American Zionism_, ed. Mark A. Raider, Jonathan D. Sarna, and Ronald W. Zweig (London: Frank Cass, 1997), pp. 73–74. Also Evyatar Friesel, "The Meaning of Zionism and Its Influence Among the American Jewish Religious Movements" in _Zionism and Religion_, ed. Shmuel Almog, Jehuda Reinharz, and Anita Shapira (Hanover, N.H.: University Press of New England, 1998), pp. 176–81.

22. Richard Gottheil, "The Aims of Zionism," _The Zionist Idea_, p. 499.

23. Oscar Janowsky, _The American Jew: A Reappraisal_ (Philadelphia: Jewish Publication Society, 1964), p. 305.

24. Arthur Hertzberg, _The Jews in America_ (New York: Simon and Schuster, 1989), p. 217.

25. Evyatar Friesel, Allon Gal, Henry Feingold, and Melvin Urofsky, "The Influence of Zionism on the American Jewish Community: An Assessment by Israeli and American Historians," _American Jewish History_ 75 (December 1985): 160.

26. Mark A. Raider, _The Emergence of American Zionism_ (New York, New York University Press, 1998), p. 29.

27. Yonatan Shapiro, _Leadership of the American Zionist Organization_ (Urbana: University of Illinois Press, 1972), p. 136.

28. Melvin Urofsky, _American Zionism from Herzl to the Holocaust_ (Garden City, N.Y.: Anchor, 1975), p. 322.

29. Shapiro, _Leadership_, p. 126.

30. Laqueur, _History of Zionism_, p. 549.

31. Ibid.

32. Shapiro, _Leadership_, pp. 167–75.

33. Urofsky, _American Zionism_, p. 420.

34. Menahem Kaufman, "American Zionism and U.S. Neutrality from 1939 to Pearl Harbor," _Studies in Zionism_ 9 (spring 1988): 23–24.

35. Paul R. Mendes-Flohr and Jehuda Reinharz, _The Jew in the Modern World_, pp. 470–71.

36. American Zionist Council, _False Witness_ (New York, 1955), p. 8.

37. Samuel Halperin, _The Political World of American Zionism_ (Detroit: Wayne State University Press, 1961), p. 327.

38 Menahem Kaufman, _An Ambiguous Partnership_ (Detroit: Wayne State University Press, 1991), p. 201.

39. Urofsky, _American Zionism_, p. 125.

40. Arthur Goren, "A Golden Decade for American Jews," _Studies in Contemporary Jewry_ 8, ed. Jonathan Frankel, Peter Medding, and Ezra Mendelsohn (1992): 3–20.

41. _Truman Memoirs_, quoted in John Snetsinger, _Truman, the Jewish Vote and the Creation of Israel_ (Stanford, Calif.: Hoover Institution Press, 1974), p. 67.

42. Urofsky, _American Zionism_, p. 147.

43. Kaufman, _Ambiguous Partnership_, p. 273.

44. Michael A. Meyer, "Abba Hillel Silver as Zionist within the Camp of Reform Judaism," _Abba Hillel Silver and American Zionism_, p. 29.

2. The Making of the American Jewish Consensus (pp. 22–41)

1. Jonathan Woocher, *Sacred Survival*, p. 51.
2. Naomi Cohen, *Not Free to Desist* (Philadelphia: Jewish Publication Society, 1972), p. 94.
3. Ibid., p. 9.
4. Melvin Urofsky, *We Are One* (Garden City, N.Y.: Anchor, 1978), p. 261. Also Gideon Shimoni, "Reformulation of Zionist Ideology since the Establishment of the State of Israel, " *Studies in Contemporary Jewry* 11 (1995): pp. 12–15.
5. Calvin Goldschedier, "American Aliya: Sociological and Demographic Perspectives," in *The Jew in American Society*, ed. Marshall Sklare (New York: Behrman, 1974), p. 353.
6. Urofsky, *We Are One*, p. 314.
7. Naomi Cohen, *American Jews and the Zionist Idea* (Hoboken, N.J.: KTAV, 1975), p. 112.
8. Paul Breines, *Tough Jews* (New York: Basic Books, 1990), p. 55.
9. Quoted in Steven Whitfield, "Value Added: Jews in Postwar American Culture," *Studies in Contemporary Jewry*, p. 77.
10. *New York Times*, December 16, 1960.
11. *Time*, December 19, 1960.
12. Urofsky, *We Are One*, p. 373.
13. Marshall Sklare, *Jewish Identity on the Suburban Frontier* (New York: Basic Books, 1967), p. 228.
14. Urofsky, *We Are One*, p. 356.
15. *Life*, June 23, 1967, p. 22.
16. Cohen, *American Jews*, p. 141.
17. Woocher, *Sacred Survival*, chap. 3.
18. Eugene Borowitz, in Histadrut Symposium, *The Impact of Israel on American Jewry* (New York, 1969).
19. See, for example, *New York Review of Books*, December 12, 1974, p. 21.
20. Norman Podhoretz, "The Abandonment of Israel," *Commentary*, July 1976.
21. "Breira Statement of Purpose," quoted in Rael Jean Isaac, *Breira: Counsel for Judaism* (New York, 1977), p. 2.
22. *New York Times*, December 16, 1976.
23. Ibid., December 30, 1976.
24. Alexander Cockburn and James Ridgeway, "Doves, the Diaspora, and the Future of Israel, " *Village Voice*, March 7, 1977.
25. David Charles, "Breira: Alternative of Surrender," *American Zionist*, November 1976, p. 12.
26. *American Zionist*, November 1976, p. 16.
27. Rael Jean Isaac, *Breira: Counsel for Judaism*, p. 3.
28. Ibid., p. 27.
29. Jacques Schwartz, "Why Our Doves Are Pigeons," *American Zionist*, September 1976.
30. Charles, "Breira: Alternative of Surrender."
31. Joseph Shattan, "Why Breira," *Commentary*, April 1, 1977.
32. Cockburn and Ridgeway, "Doves," p. 26.
33. *New York Times*, May 6, 1977.
34. Cockburn and Ridgeway, "Doves," p. 26.
35. Alan Mintz, "The People's Choice: A Demurral on Breira," *Response*, fall 1977, pp. 108–18.

36. Ibid.

37. *American Zionist*, November 1976, p. 16.

3. The World Turned Upside Down (pp. 42–60)

1. William Quandt, *Camp David: Peacemaking and Politics* (Washington, D.C.: Brookings Institution, 1986), pp. 148, 173.

2. Camp David Agreement, September 17, 1978, quoted in Itamar Rabinovich and Jehuda Reinharz, *Israel in the Middle East* (Oxford: Oxford University Press, 1984), p. 330–36.

3. Quandt, *Camp David*, pp. 154–6, 168.

4. Walter Laqueur, "The View from Tel Aviv," *Commentary*, July 1978, p. 33.

5. Leonard Fine, "Skeptics, Cynics, and Rational Debate," *Moment*, June 1978.

6. Ibid.

7. See *Sh'ma*, May 26, 1978.

8. *New York Times*, July 10, 1978.

9. Ibid.

10. For the text of this portion of the agreement, see Rabinovich and Reinharz, *Israel in the Middle East*, p. 331.

11. Quandt, *Camp David*, p. 244.

12. Ibid.

13. *New Republic*, April 7, 1979, p. 8.

14. Murray Friedman, "Black Anti-Semitism on the Rise," *Commentary*, October 1978.

15. Amos Perlmutter, "The Courtship of Iraq," *New Republic*, May 3, 1980.

16. Irving Greenberg, "Cossacks and Peace, Another View," *Sh'ma*, February 8, 1980.

17. *New York Times*, July 2, 1980.

18. Jewish Telegraphic Agency, July 3, 1980.

19. Ibid.

20. Ibid., August 21, 1980.

21. *New York Times*, November 30, 1980.

22. Jewish Telegraphic Agency, March 20, 1980.

23. "Reagan's Desert Mirage," *New Republic*, November 18, 1981, pp. 5–6.

24. Presidential news conference, October 1, 1981.

25. *The Jewish Press*, July 17, 1981.

26. Leonard Fine, "The New Anti-Semitism," *Moment*, December 1981.

27. Murray Friedman, "AWACS and the Jewish Community," *Commentary*, April 1982.

28. *Near East Report*, November 20, 1981, p. 212.

29. *Jerusalem Post*, July 24, 1981; *Washington Post*, July 23, 1981.

30. "A Roadblock to Peace," *Newsweek*, September 14, 1981, p. 38.

31. Ibid.

32. *Jerusalem Post*, January 20, 1981.

33. Ibid.

34. *New York Times*, June 30, 1981.

35. *Washington Post*, November 15, 1981.

36. Jewish Telegraphic Agency, December 26, 1981.

4. The Invasion of Lebanon (pp. 61–75)

1. Itamar Rabinovich, *The War for Lebanon, 1970–1983* (Ithaca, N.Y.: Cornell University Press, 1984), pp. 118–19.

2. Ze'ev Shiff and Ehud Yaari, *Israel's Lebanon War* (New York: Simon and Schuster, 1984), p. 69.

3. For a fuller discussion of Israeli strategy, see Yair Evron, *War and Intervention in Lebanon* (Baltimore: Johns Hopkins University Press, 1987), chap. 4.

4. See *Ha'aretz*, June 21, July 28, 1982.

5. Charles Winslow, *Lebanon, War and Politics in a Fragmented Society* (London: Routledge, 1996), p. 232.

6. Schiff and Yaari, *Israel's Lebanon War*, pp. 58–59.

7. *Washington Post*, June 11, 1982.

8. Ibid., June 17, 1982.

9. *Newsweek*, June 28, 1982.

10. *Baltimore Sun*, June 28, 1982: *Washington Post*, July 18, 1982.

11. Schiff and Yaari, *Israel's Lebanon War*, p. 74–76; Rabinovich, *War for Lebanon*, p. 126.

12. *Washington Post*, July 12, 1982.

13. Ibid.

14. *Los Angeles Times*, June 18, 1982.

15. *New York Times*, July 15, 1982.

16. Ibid., June 19, 1982.

17. Ibid.

18. *Village Voice*, June 29, 1982.

19. *Jerusalem Post*, July 28, 1982.

20. *New York Times*, September 27, 1982.

21. *Jerusalem Post*, July 4, 1982.

22. *Jewish Week*, September 10, 1982.

23. *Jerusalem Post*, September 14, 1982.

24. *New York Times*, July 4, 1982.

25. Ibid., June 30, 1982.

26. *Los Angeles Times*, July 3, 1982; *Jerusalem Post*, July 16, 1982.

27. *New York Times*, September 7, 1982.

28. Ibid.

29. Rabinovich, *War for Lebanon*, pp.138–39.

30. *Kahan Report*, p. xii.

31. Evron, *War and Intervention*, p.152.

32. Schiff and Yaari, *Israel's Lebanon War*, p.182.

33. *New York Times*, September 23, 1982.

34. *Washington Post*, September 30, 1982.

35. Edgar O'Ballance, *Civil War in Lebanon* (New York: St. Martins, 1998), p. 119.

36. Schiff and Yaari, *Israel's Lebanon War*, p. 261–62; *Kahan Report*, pp. 22–24.

37. *Washington Post*, September 23, 1982.

38. Schiff and Yaari, *Israel's Lebanon War*, p.261.

39. *New York Times*, September 22, 1982.

40. Ibid., September 26, 1982.

41. Ibid., September 23, 1982.

42. Quoted in *New York Times*, September 23, 1982.

43. *Jerusalem Post*, September 26, 1982.
44. *New Statesman*, June 25, 1982.
45. *Philadelphia Inquirer*, September 23, 1982.
46. *New York Times*, September 21, 1982.
47. *Washington Post*, September 21, 1982.
48. *Philadelphia Inquirer*, September 21, 1982.
49. Jewish Telegraphic Agency, October 25, 1982.
50. *New York Times*, September 23, 1982.
51. Ibid., September 26, 1982.
52. Ibid., September 24, 1982.
53. *New Republic*, October 11, 1982.
54. *Newsweek*, October 4, 1982.
55. *Jerusalem Post*, October 27, 1982.
56. *New York Times*, September 25, 1982.
57. *Chicago Tribune*, September 17, 1982.
58. *Chicago Tribune*, October 29, 1982.
59. Jewish Telegraphic Agency, December 17, 1982.
60. *Commentary*, September 1982, pp. 121–31.
61. Jewish Telegraphic Agency, December 6, 1982.
62. Kahan Report, p. 63.

5. The Pollard Affair (pp. 76–92)

1. Wolf Blitzer, *Territory of Lies* (New York: Harper and Row, 1989), p. 164. Also Dan Raviv and Yossi Melman, *Every Spy a Prince* (Boston: Houghton Mifflin, 1990), pp. 301–23.
2. Jewish Telegraphic Agency, March 3, 1987.
3. Hillel Halkin, *Letters to an American Friend: A Zionist Polemic* (Philadelphia: Jewish Publication Society, 1977), p. 72.
4. Ehud Sprinzak, "Illegalism in Israeli Political Culture: Thoughts and Historical Footnotes to the Pollard Affair and the Shin Bet Cover-up," *Jerusalem Quarterly* 47 (summer 1998): 86–89.
5. Raviv and Melman, *Every Spy a Prince*, p. 318.
6. Editorial, *New York Times*, March 6, 1981.
7. Editorial, *Boston Globe*, March 9, 1987.
8. *New York Times*, March 9, 1987.
9. *Washington Post*, March 8, 1987.
10. Jewish Telegraphic Agency, March 12, 1987.
11. *Jerusalem Post*, March 18, 1987.
12. Ibid.
13. *Washington Post*, March 14, 1987.
14. Ibid., March 4, 1987.
15. *Jerusalem Post*, March 10, 1987.
16. *New York Times*, April 16, 1987.
17. *Washington Post*, March 18, 1987.
18. *New York Times*, March 24, 1987.
19. *Jerusalem Post*, March 17, 1987.
20. Blitzer, *Territory of Lies*, pp. 285–86.
21. David Biale, "J'Accuse: American Jews and L'Affaire Pollard," *Tikkun* 22.(2). Also Burton Levine, "Justice for the Pollards," *Present Tense*, January/February 1989.
22. William Mehlman and A. S. Epstein, "An Ugly Distortion of Justice," *Jerusalem*

Post, June 9, 1987. Also Avi Weiss, "Justice, Not Vengeance," *Jerusalem Post*, August 20, 1993.

23. Even the generally sympathetic Wolf Blitzer notes that "not all the documents he collected were essential to Israeli security." Blitzer, *Territory of Lies*, p. 316.

24. Steven Cohen, *After the Gulf War: American Jews' Attitudes toward Israel* (New York: American Jewish Committee, October, 1991), p. 59.

25. Edward Langer and David Wolfe, "Pollard: An American-Israeli Patriot," *Jerusalem Post*, January 30, 1991. Also William Northrop, "The Ghost of Israel's Sealed Rooms," *New Dimensions*, June 1992.

26. *New York Times*, March 21, 1992.

27. *Jerusalem Post*, October 15, 1992.

28. *New York Times*, October 25, 1992.

29. "A Spy Seeks Clemency," *ABA Journal*, December 1993.

30. *Jerusalem Post*, October 25, 1992.

31. Ibid., February 18, 1993.

32. Ibid.

33. Ibid., March 4, 1993.

34. Thomas Friedman, "Clinton Is Asked by Rabin to Cut Spys and Term," *New York Times*, November 11, 1993.

35. *New York Times*, November 30, 1993.

36. "Will Clinton Blunder into Pardoning Convicted Spy?" *Human Events*, December 31, 1993.

37. Interview by author, May 30, 1999.

38. "Pollard Passed over Costly Document," *Time*, December 13, 1993.

39. *Jerusalem Post*, December 8, 1993.

40. *New York Times*, January 2, 1994.

41. *Jerusalem Post*, March 25, 1994.

42. *New York Jewish Week*, July 14, 1995.

43. Ibid., April 7, 1995.

44. John Loftus, "Will Disclosures Help Unlock Jonathan Pollard's Cell?" *Miami Herald*, April 23, 1995. Also Sidney Zion, "The Case for the Spy Who Should Be Free," *New York Daily News*, June 2, 1995.

45. Milton Viorst, *International Herald Tribune*, June 6, 1995. Also Editorial, *Chicago Tribune*, December 11, 1995, and Si Frumkin, "A Naval Story with Heart," *Jerusalem Post*, January 30, 1996.

46. *Baltimore Sun*, December 30, 1993.

47. Mrs. Emile Schindler, December 20, 1994, <http://www.interlog.com /~abrooke/jp/1994/122094.htm>.

48. Blitzer, *Territory of Lies*, p. 295.

49. *Jerusalem Post*, January 20, 1993.

50. Elyakim Rubenstein, "The Right Thing," *Jerusalem Post*, January 7, 1994.

51. *Jerusalem Post*, October 22, 1995.

52. *New York Times*, March 31, 1995.

53. *Jerusalem Post*, October 22, 1995.

54. *Maariv*, October 25, 1995.

55. Conference of Presidents, letter to Clinton, November 5, 1995.

56. *Maariv*, January 12, 1996.

57. *Maariv*, May 13, 1996.

58. *Maariv Political Supplement*, July 12, 1996.

59. *Washington Jewish Week*, January 2, 1997.

60. Jack Wertheimer, October 13, 1997, <http://www.interlog.com/~abrooke /jp/1997/101397.htm>.

61. Jonathan Pollard to Rabbi Avi Weiss, November 4, 1997. Also Edward Alexander, "Why Pollard Is Suing the American Jewish Leadership," *New Jersey Jewish News*, November 13, 1997.

62. Jewish Telegraphic Agency February 10, 1998; *New Jersey Jewish Times.*

63. Conference of American Rabbis, news release, March 11, 1998.

64. Interview by author, May 30, 1999.

65. Associated Press, May 11, 1998.

66. *Ha'aretz*, October 25, 1998.

67. *New York Times*, November 11, 1998.

68. Reuters, December 10, 1988; *Washington Post*, December 12, 1988.

69. Press release, letter to President Clinton, January 11, 1997.

70. *Connecticut Jewish Ledger*, February 5, 1999.

71. *New York Times*, November 14, 1998; CBS News, December 13, 1998.

72. *New York Times*, January 11, 1999.

73. *New Yorker*, January 18, 1999, p. 29.

74. Ibid., p. 30.

75. Jewish Telegraphic Agency, January 12, 1999.

6. The Intifada (pp. 93–115).

1. *Washington Post*, October 7, 1987.

2. Ibid., October 20, 1987.

3. Ibid., October 7, 1987.

4. Ibid., October 20, 1987.

5. Ibid., December 13, 1987.

6. Ibid., December 13, 1987.

7. Ze'ev Schiff and Ehud Yaari, *Intifada* (New York: Simon and Schuster, 1989), p. 80.

8. *Ha'aretz*, December 9, 1997.

9. *New York Times*, June 1, 1988.

10. Edgar O'Balance, *The Palestinian Intifada* (New York: St. Martins, 1998), p. 28.

11. *Washington Post*, December 23, 1987.

12. *New York Times*, January 13, 1988.

13. Ibid., January 11, 1988.

14. Ibid., January 13, 1988.

15. Ibid., January 22, 1988.

16. Ibid.

17. Ibid., March 13, 1988.

18. Ibid., January 22, 1988.

19. *Washington Post*, January 24, 1988.

20. *New York Times*, January 25, 1988.

21. *Washington Post*, February 14, 1988.

22. *New York Times*, January 25, 1988.

23. Ibid., January 26, 1988.

24. Ibid., January 25, 1988.

25. Ibid., January 22, 1988.

26. Ibid., February 14, 1988.

27. Ibid., February 10, 1988.

28. Ibid., March 1, 1988.

29. Ibid., March 2, 1988.

30. Charles Krauthammer, "No Exit," *New Republic*, March 14, 1988, p. 29.

31. *New York Times*, January 28, 1989.

32. *Commentary*, February 1988, p. 21.

33. See Leonard Fein, *Where Are We: The Inner Life of American Jews* (New York: Harper and Row, 1988); Michael Waltzer, "Liberalism and American Jews: Historical Affinities, Contemporary Necessities," *Studies in Contemporary Jewry* 11 (1995): pp. 3–10.

34. *New York Times*, March 6, 1988.

35. Ibid., March 15, 1988.

36. Ibid., April 1, 1988.

37. Ibid., April 23, 1988.

38. Ibid., April 18, 1988.

39. Ibid., May 16, 1988.

40. *New York Times Magazine*, May 8, 1988, p. 40.

41. Ibid., May 8, 1988, pp. 51–52.

42. *New York Times*, June 22, 1988.

43. Ibid., June 22, 1988.

44. Ibid., May 18, 1988.

45. Ibid., September 11, 1988.

46. Ibid., October 18, 1988.

47. Ibid., December 8, 1988.

48. Ibid., December 8, 1988.

49. Ibid., December 15, 1988.

50. Ibid., March 21, 1989.

51. Ibid., March 22, 1989.

52. Carolyn Toll Oppenheim, "Talking Peace," *Present Tense* (fall 1989): pp. 32–38.

53. *New York Times*, May 16 1989.

54. Ibid., May 24, 1989.

55. Ibid.

56. Ibid., June 9, 1989.

57. Ibid., July 23, 1999.

58. Ibid., October 19, 1989.

59. *Washington Post*, November 17, 1989.

60. Ibid.

61. *Jerusalem Post*, February 9, 1990.

62. *Washington Post*, December 19, 1989.

63. *Jerusalem Post*, May 17, 1990.

64. Ibid., July 6, 1990.

65. Ibid., July 17, 1990.

66. *New York Times*, October 16, 1990.

67. *Washington Post*, October 19, 1990.

68. Ibid., October 27, 1990.

69. *Jerusalem Post*, October 26, 1990.

70. Ibid., October 29, 1990.

71. "Dome of the Rocks," *The New Republic* (October 29, 1990): p. 8.

7. The Perils of Peace (pp. 116–133)

1. *New York Times*, January 14, 1990.

2. Ibid., June 26, 1991.

3. Ibid., September 14, 1991.

4. *Jerusalem Post*, September 13, 1991.
5. *Washington Post*, September 29, 1991.
6. *Jerusalem Post*, September 13, 1991.
7. *New York Times*, November 22, 1991.
8. *Jerusalem Post*, October 4, 1991.
9. *Washington Post*, November 21, 1991.
10. *Jerusalem Post*, October 7, 1991.
11. Ibid.
12. Ibid., February 20, 1992.
13. Ibid., August 21, 1992; *Washington Post*, November 1, 1992.
14. *Jerusalem Post*, August 22, 1992.
15. Yitzhak Rabin, *The Rabin Memoirs* (Boston: Little Brown, 1979), p. 229.
16. *Jerusalem Post*, August 21, 1992.
17. Ibid., July 22, 1993.
18. *New York Times*, February 1, 1994.
19. *Commentary* (April 1993): pp. 19–33.
20. *Jerusalem Post*, July 1 and 9, 1993.
21. Ibid., July 3, 1993.
22. Ibid., July 9, 1993.
23. *New York Times*, July 11, 1993.
24. Ibid., July 2, 1993.
25. *Jerusalem Post*, September 18 and 28, 1993.
26. Ibid., October 6, 1993.
27. Ibid., February 18, 1994.
28. *New York Times*, March 1, 1994.
29. *Jerusalem Post*, November 30, 1994.
30. Ibid., October 1, 1995; *New York Times*, September 30, 1995.
31. *New York Times*, September 3, 1994.
32. *Jerusalem Post*, September 2, 1994.
33. Interview by author, July 6, 1999.
34. *New York Times*, November 13, 1995.
35. *Jerusalem Post*, September 7, 1994.
36. Ibid., September 13, 1995.
37. *Washington Post*, May 26, 1996.
38. Ibid.
39. Amnon Bartur, "No Consensus on the Peace Process," *Midstream* (April 1994): pp. 14–15.
40. *Jerusalem Post*, May 23, 1995.
41. *New York Times*, September 22, 1995.
42. Hillel Halkin, "Israel and the Assassination: A Reckoning," *Commentary* (January 1996): p. 27.
43. *Jerusalem Post*, February 22, 1996.
44. *Washington Post*, December 11, 1995, May 20, 1996.
45. Ibid., December 10, 1995.
46. "The Civil War Has Begun," *Tikkun*, January-February 1996, pp 33–39.
47. *Jerusalem Post*, December 11, 1995.

8. Who Is a Jew? (pp. 134–155)

1. Ehud Luz, *Parallels Meet* (Philadelphia: Jewish Publication Society, 1988), p. 194.
2. Ibid., p.213.

3. Aviezer Ravitzky, *Messianism, Zionism and Jewish Religious Radicalism* (Chicago: University of Chicago Press, 1996), pp. 13–14.

4. Ibid., p. 68.

5. Ibid., p. 147.

6. For a sensitive depiction of Haredi society, see Samuel Heilman, *Defenders of the Faith* (New York: Schocken, 1992).

7. Luz, *Parallels Meet*, pp.235–36.

8. Ravitzky, *Messianism*, pp. 33–34.

9. Ibid., p. 111.

10. On the constitutional question, see Peter Medding, *The Founding of Israeli Democracy* (Oxford: Oxford University Press, 1990), pp. 37–42.

11. Edward Norden, "Who Is a Jew," *Commentary*, April 1989, p. 28.

12. Medding, *Founding of Israeli Democracy*, p. 74.

13. Asher Maoz, "Who Is a Jew," *Midstream*, June/July 1989, p. 12.

14. For a discussion of traditional views of the conversion process, see Lawrence H. Schiffman, *Who Was a Jew* (Hoboken, N.J.: KTAV, 1985), pp. 19–39.

15. Ravitzky, *Messianism*, p. 164.

16. Ibid., p. 131.

17. Ehud Sprinzak, *The Ascent of Israel's Radical Right* (New York, 1991), p. 44.

18. Ravitzky, *Messianism*, p. 131.

19. Ibid., p. 132.

20. *Washington Post*, November 29, 1988.

21. Jewish Telegraphic Agency, November 21, 1988.

22. *Washington Post*, November 29, 1988.

23. Ibid., November 30, 1988.

24. *New York Times*, April 1, 1997.

25. *Jerusalem Post*, April 2, 1997.

26. *New York Times*, April 11, 1997.

27. CCAR website <ccarnet.org/platforms/miami.html>.

28. *Jerusalem Post*, April 11, 1997.

29. Ibid., April 23, 1997.

30. Interview by author, August 9, 1999.

31. *Jerusalem Post*, October 15, 1997.

32. Ibid., June 23, 1997.

33. Ibid., May 21, 1997.

34. *Midstream*, August-September, 1997.

35. *Ha'aretz*, September 26, 1997.

36. *Jewish Bulletin of Northern California*, <www.shamash.org/jb/bk960524>.

37. *New York Times* November 12, 1997.

28. *Ha'aretz*, September 18, 1997.

39. Ibid., December 3, 1997.

40. Interview with author, August 8, 1999.

41. *Jerusalem Post*, April 11, 1997.

42. Letter to editor, *Jerusalem Post*, April 11, 1997.

43. Ina Friedman, "Judaism in Israel," *Moment* (February, 1993): p. 50.

44. *Ha'aretz*, October 28, 1997.

45. *Jerusalem Post*, October 15, 1997; *Ha'aretz*, October 14, 1997.

46. *Jerusalem Post*, October 29, 1997.

47. *Ha'aretz*, October 12, 1997.

48. *Jerusalem Post*, October 22, 1997.

49. Ibid., January 27, 1998.

50. Ibid., February 10, 1998.

51. *New York Times*, February 10, 1998.
52. *Jerusalem Post*, February 11, 1998.
53. Ibid., February 10, 1998.
54. *Newsday*, February 13, 1998.
55. *Jerusalem Post*, February 19, 1998.
56. *Ha'aretz*, June 9, 1998.
57. Jewish Telegraphic Agency, June 25, 1998.

9. An Ambivalent Anniversary (pp. 156–169)

1. Itamar Rabinovich, *Waging Peace* (New York, 1999), p. 90.
2. *Washington Post*, August 3, 1996.
3. Ibid., September 23, 1996.
4. American Jewish Committee, Middle East Briefing, June 3, 1997.
5. Rabinovich, *Waging Peace*, p. 10.
6. *Washington Post*, September 19, 1997.
7. Ibid.
8. Ibid., January 22, 1998.
9. Jewish Telegraphic Agency, March 30, 1998.
10. Ibid., March 31, 1998.
11. Ibid., April 7, 1998.
12. *New York Times*, April 7, 1998.
13. Jewish Telegraphic Agency, May 14, 1998.
14. *New York Times*, October 22, 1998.
15. Ibid., February 28, 1999.
16. Ibid., January 12, 1998.
17. *Jewish Bulletin of Northern California*, January 9, 1998.
18. *Washington Post*, January 7, 1998.
19. Ibid., October 6, 1998.
20. Ibid., January 7, 1998.
21. Glen Frankel, "A Victim of Its Own Success? Internal Debate Saps Israel's Vitality," *Washington Post*, May 8, 1998.
22. Douglas Bloomfield, "Israel, Diaspora Unity Withering as Jewish State Turns 50," *Jewish Bulletin of Northern California*, <http:www.shamash.org>.
23. Serge Schmemann, *New York Times*, May 1, 1998.
24. Bloomfield, "Israel, Diaspora Unity."
25. Michael Lerner, "Post Zionism; Restoring Compassion, Overcoming Chauvinism," *Tikkun* (April 1998): p. 33.
26. Frankel, "Victim of Its Own Success?"
27. Jewish Telegraphic Agency, October 26, 1999.
28. Ibid., November 27, 1999.

10. The Hidden Crisis (pp. 170–194)

1. Interview by author, August 8, 1999.
2. Steven Cohen, *AJC Annual Surveys of American Jewish Public Opinion* (New York).
3. *Jewish Bulletin of Northern California* <www.shamash org/jb/bk960524>.

4. *Ha'aretz,* January 14, 1998.

5. Ibid.

6. Melvin Urofsky, "American Jewish Leadership," *American Jewish History* 70 (June 1981): p .415.

7. Jack Wertheimer, "Politics and Jewish Giving," *Commentary,* December 1997.

8. *Jerusalem Post,* June 23, 1995.

9. *Jerusalem Post,* September 17, 1995.

10. Gerald Bubis, "Jewish Dollars Drying Up," *Moment* (December 1992): p. 31.

11. *Jerusalem Post,* April 7, 1996.

12. *Moment,* October, 1994, p. 38.

13. Jack Wertheimer, "Current Trends in American Jewish Philanthropy," *American Jewish Year Book 1997* (New York, 1997), p. 45.

14. *Jerusalem Post,* June 23, 1995.

15. *Jerusalem Post,* November 10, 1997.

16. Cynthia Mann, "The Rise of the New Israel Fund," *Moment* (October 1994): p. 38.

17. *New York Times,* October 9, 1997.

18. *Forward,* May 23, 1997

19. *Washington Post,* February 20, 1994.

20. *Jerusalem Post,* April 5, 1996.

21. JTA, <www.jtaorg./June 19/30>.

22. Interview by author, July 6, 1999.

23. Shimon Shure, "Jews, Judaism, Israel, and the Third Millenniun," *Midstream,* June/July 1997.

24. Abba Eban, *Washington Post,* February 7, 1993.

25. Interview by author, May 23, 1999.

26. Arthur Hertzberg, "One Hundred Years Later, A Jewish Writer's Time Has Come," *New York Times,* March 31, 1991.

27. Charles Silberman, *A Certain People: American Jews and Their Lives Today* (New York: Summit, 1985).

28. *New York Times,* June 8, 1997.

29. Jack Wertheimer, "Judaism without Limits, " *Commentary,* July, 1997, pp. 24–27.

30. *Jerusalem Post,* November 15, 1992.

31. Ibid.

32. Steven Bayme, *Understanding Jewish History: Texts and Commentaries* (Hoboken, N.J.: KTAV, 1997), p. xiii.

33. Interview by author, July 19, 1999.

34. *Jerusalem Post,* January 14, 2000.

35. Amos Elon, *The Israelis* (New York: Holt Rinehart and Winston, 1972): p. 204.

36. Amos Oz, quoted in Yoram Harzony, "The Zionist Idea and Its Enemies," *Commentary,* May 1996, p. 34.

37. Yaron Ezrahi, *Rubber Bullets* (New York: Farrar, Straus and Giroux, 1997), p. 294.

38. David Ben-Tal, "Army Fatigue," *Moment* (October 1995): pp. 35–40.

39. Quoted in Laurance J. Silberstein, *The Post Zionism Debates* (New York: Routledge, 1999), p. 115.

40. Yoram Harzony, "The Zionist Idea and Its Enemies," *Commentary,* May 1996, pp. 30–38.

41. Shimon Peres, *The New Middle East* (New York: Henry Holt, 1993), pp. 61–74.

42. Jonathan Sarna, "The Secret of Jewish Continuity," *Commentary*, October 1994, p. 56.

43. Jewish Telegraphic Agency, July 19, 1999.

Selected Sources

Given the multitude of works concerning Zionism, Israel, and American Jews, this essay makes no claim to be exhaustive. Instead, I will discuss works that I have found particularly valuable, stimulating, or provocative. Readers seeking a general scholarly bibliography should consult Jack Wertheimer, editor, *The Modern Jewish Experience* (1993). Divided into twenty-nine chapters of study, each covered by an expert in the field, it is a marvelous resource for further reading in Zionism, Israel, or American Jewry. The most complete bibliography of American Jewry is *Judaica Americana* (1995). General readers should consult the relevant sections of the very valuable *Schocken Guide to Jewish Books* (1993).

Any study of Zionism must begin with Arthur Hertzberg's *The Zionist Idea* (1971), an anthology of almost all varieties of Zionist thought, illuminated by a masterful introductory essay that places the movement within the context of both European and Jewish history. The best general history is Walter Laqueur's *History of Zionism* (1972), a great work of synthesis, well balanced and organized. Shlomo Avineri's *The Making of Modern Zionism: Intellectual Origins of the Jewish State* (1981) presents the movement through its principal thinkers, as a response not so much to physical threats to the Jews as to the challenge of emancipation and assimilation. Ben Halpern's *The Idea of the Jewish State* (1969) is a concise summary of the objectives and methods of Labor Zionism and the means by which it brought about the birth of Israel. The first half of Amos Elon's *The Israelis: Founders and Sons* (1972) provides an impressionistic but vivid portrayal of the world of early Zionism.

The struggles within the Zionist movement have received much scholarly attention. The pre-state ideological struggle between the Zionist Left and Right is depicted by Mitchell Cohen in *Zion in State* (1987). The contributors to *Zionism and Religion* (1998), edited by

Shmuel Almog, Jehuda Reinharz, and Anita Shapira, illuminate many facets of the complex relationship between Zionism and Judaism in both Europe and the United States. In *Parallels Meet: Religion and Nationalism in the Early Zionist Movement* (1988), Ehud Luz details the conflicts between religious and secular Zionists over the role of religion in public life. While concentrating on Eastern European Zionism, the work illuminates the roots of one of contemporary Israel's most pressing problems. For a well-written and stimulating modern restatement of the classic Zionist notion of "negation of the Diaspora," see Hillel Halkin's *Letters to an American Jewish Friend: A Zionist Polemic* (1977).

The best general history of Israel is Howard Morley Sachar's *History of Israel from the Rise of Zionism to Our Time* (1996). A model of scholarly synthesis, its treatment of the Arab-Israeli conflict and the evolution of Israeli society is especially effective. For Great Power conflict and diplomacy leading to the birth of the State of Israel, see Christopher Sykes's *Crossroads to Israel* (1973). Nadav Safran's *Israel: The Embattled Ally* (1981) provides a detailed historical, political, and diplomatic analysis of the state's first three decades. It closely examines the evolution of Israel's relationship with the United States. A sensitive and objective look at Israeli society is provided by the second half of Amos Elon's *The Israelis* (1972), which describes the conflict between the founding generation of Zionists and their offspring. While brilliant and incisive, the account gives short shrift to Israel's Sephardic Jews.

The revolution in Middle East politics represented by the Israeli-Egyptian Peace Accord is well presented by William Quandt in *Camp David: Peacemaking and Politics* (1986). He painstakingly traces the negotiation process and the role of personalities, giving much credit to President Carter.

The various crises in recent Israeli history have received more than their share of historical analysis. For the 1982 invasion of Lebanon, see *Israel's Lebanon War* (1984), written by Zeev Schiff and Ehud Yaari, two of Israel's most respected journalists. It blames the conflict on the Likud Party, particularly Defense Minister Ariel Sharon. Itamar Rabinovich's *The War for Lebanon: 1970–1983* (1985) is more balanced and untangles the political maze of the Israeli-Lebanese-Syrian relationship.

The Pollard affair has generated much heat but comparatively little analytical light. For a general overview of the development of Israel's

Secret Service, see Dan Raviv and Yossi Melman's *Every Spy a Prince* (1990), a breathless and anecdotal journalistic account. *Israel's Secret Wars: A History of Israel's Intelligence Services* (1991) by Ian Black and Benny Morris is more businesslike and objective. The only full-length account of the Pollard affair, Wolf Blitzer's *Territory of Lies* (1989), is overly long and sympathetic to Pollard but fair. Now seriously dated, it is still valuable for the questions it raises.

Zeev Schiff and Ehud Yaari's *Intifada: The Palestinian Uprising* (1990) is no less critical of Israeli government policy than is their work on Lebanon. The authors are particularly penetrating in their portrayal of the roots of the uprising and the behind-the-scenes reactions of Israelis and Palestinians. As is inevitable in an "instant book," the work is less effective on the Intifada's impact.

The emergence of Israel's political and religious right is the subject of a number of excellent works. In *The Rise of Israel's Radical Right* (1991), political scientist Ehud Sprinzak examines the political and cultural forces behind the ascendence of the extreme rightist politics, which he perceives as a threat to Israeli democracy. Aviezer Ravitzky brilliantly probes the nexus between religion and politics in *Messianism, Zionism, and Jewish Religious Radicalism* (1996). He explains the variety of Jewish religious reactions to Zionism and the state and analyzes the different Orthodox responses and modes of revival. This is an indispensable work. For a sensitive and sympathetic account of the ultra-Orthodox, see sociologist Samuel Heilman's *Defenders of the Faith* (1992). In a well-written, jargon-free account, Heilman reveals how the culture is maintained.

Israel's fifty-year effort to come to terms with its Arab neighbors and the Palestinians is perceptively analyzed by diplomat and scholar Itamar Rabinovich in *Waging Peace* (1999). Emphasizing the period since the 1991 Madrid peace conference, Rabinovich objectively presents all sides of the conflict. In *The Process* (1998), Uri Savir, Israel's chief negotiator at Oslo, provides intimate details of the talks that led to the Israeli-Palestinian peace treaty.

Laurence Silberstein provides a critical review of post-Zionist writing and critical responses to it in *The Post Zionism Debates: Knowledge and Power in Israeli Culture* (1999). The work illuminates a vital Israeli cultural trend yet unknown to most Americans. Major post-Zionist works include Avi Shlaim's *The Iron Wall: Israel and the Arab World since 1948* (1999) and Benny Morris's *Righteous Victims: A History of the*

Zionist-Arab Conflict (1999). Both seek to demythologize traditional Israeli history—Shlaim concentrating on military and political affairs and Morris on diplomatic history. Shlaim is more ideological and prone to make sweeping revisionist conclusions; Morris is more cautious in his evaluations. A post-Zionist analysis of contemporary Israeli society is Yaron Ezrahi's *Rubber Bullets* (1997). A political scientist at Hebrew University, Ezrahi uses the Israeli response to the Intifada to reflect on the clash between the old nationalist/collective ideal and the new liberal individualism. He has produced a nuanced though controversial cultural analysis.

The literature on American Jews contains some excellent general histories. The best, Howard Morley Sachar's *A History of the Jews in America* (1992) is extremely comprehensive, analytically brilliant, and a joy to read. The author's treatment of the relationship between America and Israel is especially enlightening. Henry Feingold's *Zion in America* (1981) places the Zionist movement within its American context. Edward Shapiro's *A Time for Healing* (1992) covers the post–World War II era and depicts the material and social success of American Jewry and the consequent threat to Jewish identity. For a more specialized study, see *The American Jewish Experience* (1997), edited by Jonathan Sarna, a series of essays by preeminent historians of American Jewry that also contains very useful bibliographies.

The best general history of American Zionism is Melvin Urofsky's *American Zionism from Herzl to the Holocaust* (1975), a massively researched volume that demonstrates how European Zionism was adapted to American conditions and how American Zionists attained political power. *We Are One* (1978) continues the history, presenting an equally impressive account of how Israel became the principal basis of American Jewish identity. Naomi Cohen's *American Jews and the Zionist Idea* (1975) explains how Zionism was adapted to American conditions and how it conflicted with the ideal of assimilation. A more specialized treatment of the same theme is provided by Menahem Kaufman's *An Ambiguous Partnership* (1991). Although short on general historical context, the work describes how American non-Zionists were brought on board to support a Jewish state. On Abba Hillel Silver, see Mark Raider, Jonathan Sarna, and Ronald Zweig, editors, *Rabbi Abba Hillel Silver and Zionism* (1997), a work largely based on newly opened archival material. The contributors illuminate the many phases of Silver's public personality, including his relations with Zionist leaders, with the

World Zionist Organization, the Jewish state, and the American Jewish community. Leonard Dinnerstein's *Anti-Semitism in America* (1994) is the definitive treatment of a phenomenon, the strength of which helped determine the appeal of Zionism to American Jews.

The organization and development of the American Jewish community is examined by pioneering sociologist Marshall Sklare, editor, and contributors in *The Jew in American Society* (1974) and *The Jewish Community in America* (1974). Both volumes chronicle the success of American Jewry and the growth of what today would be called the "problem of Jewish continuity." Daniel Elazar's *Community and Polity* (1976) details the history, organization, and functioning of organized American Jewry as well as the emergence of devotion to Israel as its major organizing principle. It remains the best account of the workings of the communal organizations of American Jewry. In *Jewish Power* (1996), J. J. Goldberg celebrates American Jewish entry into the center of society and details the emergence of AIPAC, the Israel lobby, as a political powerhouse. Jonathan Woocher's *Sacred Survival* (1986) perceives such organizational support—particularly of Israel—as a vital component of what he terms the new "civil religion" of American Jews. While his notion of a secularized religion has been controversial, Woocher's arguments raise vital questions about the future of American Jews.

Woocher's book is but one of the many speculating upon the future of American Jewry. Charles Silberman's *A Certain People: American Jews and Their Lives Today* (1985) is an extremely optimistic account of American Jews' contemporary condition and future prospects. Based upon hundreds of interviews, Silberman's work documents Jewish social and material success and predicts spiritual and demographic renewal. Arthur Hertzberg's *The Jews in America: Four Centuries of an Uneasy Encounter* (1989) presents the familiar pattern of Jewish material success and spiritual erosion. Although criticized for some historical inaccuracies, the book is provocative and stimulating, particularly in its pessimistic conclusions about the future of American Jews. Jack Wertheimer perceives not assimilation but internal division within and among Judaism's major streams as the principal threat to American Jewry. *A People Divided* (1997), his excellent survey of contemporary Jewry, reveals growing disunity and intolerance.

A prescription for the maladies of American Jewry is offered by Leonard Fein in *Where Are We: The Inner Life of American Jews* (1988). Fein maintains that the path to Jewish renewal is to be found in political liberalism and social action. By contrast, Ruth Wisse, in *If I Am Not for Myself . . . The Liberal Betrayal of the Jews* (1992), provides an articulate polemic against the notion that political liberalism is a part of Jewish identity or even good for the Jews. On the contrary, it could lead to Israel's destruction.

Index